Finding Wildflowers in the Washington-Baltimore Area

Finding Wildflowers

in the Washington-Baltimore Area

By *CRISTOL FLEMING,*
MARION BLOIS LOBSTEIN,
and *BARBARA TUFTY*

with a foreword by Stanwyn G. Shetler

The Johns Hopkins University Press · Baltimore and London

For Jon, George, and Hal

It is our sincere hope that this book will be used to enjoy plants in their natural settings. Our readers are urged to help preserve wildflowers by only looking at or photographing them—never removing, picking, or disturbing them. If you go off the trail to take a closer look at a flower, watch where you put your feet, knees, and hands. If you set up your photographic equipment, be careful not to damage any plants.

Drawings by Nicky Staunton
Maps by Jo Moore

This book has been brought to publication with the generous assistance of the Audubon Naturalist Society of the Central Atlantic States, Inc. and the Laurence Hall Fowler Fund.

The Johns Hopkins University Press
2715 North Charles Street
Baltimore, Maryland 21218-4319
The Johns Hopkins Press Ltd., London

Library of Congress Cataloging-in-Publication Data will be found at the end of this book.
A catalog record for this book is available from the British Library.

ISBN 0-8018-4994-2
ISBN 0-8018-4995-0 (pbk)

Contents

THE SPECIES 229

Foreword

There are probably millions of people in North America who enjoy studying the native flora and go afield each year to look for botanical "hot spots" and unusual plant species. For plants, as for birds, there are many good identification guides, covering most parts of the continent. We who live in the populous Washington-Baltimore area are able to select from several excellent popular guides and technical manuals for identifying the plants of our region.

Until now, however, we have not had a general guide to finding plants in our area. With this pacesetting book, the authors have opened up a whole world of fascinating natural places to people who live in or visit our region. Indeed, it is a book that, in my experience, stands by itself. I cannot recall seeing a book quite like it for any other area of North America.

Over the more than 30 years that I have lived and botanized in the Washington-Baltimore region, I have come to know its great natural wealth—its enormous diversity of easily accessible habitats and species. A day's drive can take one from the Atlantic seashore or Chesapeake Bay country through the Piedmont to the Appalachian Mountains. During these years I have seen an almost explosive growth in the public's interest in the region's biological diversity and natural resources. But I also have witnessed an alarming fragmentation and loss of habitats. However, many parks, preserves, and other parcels of nature still remain, thanks to wise efforts over the years by federal and local officials as well as concerned private citizens.

This network of natural areas preserves much of the rich array of plant species found in the region. The authors introduce us to 122 of these areas, providing for each place careful instructions for finding it and a sampler of the flora to be found there, particularly the unusual species. Coverage in many cases includes the summer and fall wildflowers as well as the better known spring flowers. Cris Fleming, a field botanist and teacher, has written the accounts of the individual areas and has done a particularly thorough job of tracking down the hard-to-identify fall-flowering asters and goldenrods. This makes the guide especially valuable to those who carry their wildflower searches to an advanced level.

The authoritative checklist of species, prepared by Marion Lobstein, a college professor and botanist, is arranged by plant family and provides the user with a systematic way of recording the species seen and relating them to the most widely used manuals and popular guides for the region. Barbara Tufty, an experienced nature writer and editor, presents us with an excellent overview of the natural environment of our region in the introductory section.

Finding Wildflowers in the Washington-Baltimore Area is clearly and logically organized. By giving the scientific and common names for all species discussed, the authors have made the information accessible to both professional and amateur botanists. This book should become an indispensable resource for anyone interested in the study, appreciation, and conservation of plants growing naturally in our area. It is a "must" for botanists, wildflower enthusiasts, teachers and students in botany and other natural history courses, foresters, conservationists, field ecologists, natural heritage workers, park naturalists, and recreational hikers who wish to enrich their experiences in nature.

This book distills years of painstaking field research. From it we learn that many wonderful natural areas still remain in our region, and the authors help us to find and learn about them. The authors have issued an enticing invitation to come outside with them and enjoy the treasures of our region. One wants to start at the beginning and methodically visit every place. Whether you are a serious plant "lister" or simply one who wants to get the most out of hiking, this book is for you.

STANWYN G. SHETLER
Curator of Botany
National Museum of Natural History
The Smithsonian Institution

Preface and Acknowledgments

The three authors of this book have come together through their mutual interest in wildflowers and wildflower places.

Barbara Tufty is a natural science writer and the conservation editor for the Audubon Naturalist Society. Cris Fleming is a teacher of plant identification courses for the U.S. Department of Agriculture Graduate School and a field trip leader for the Audubon Naturalist Society and The Smithsonian Associates. Marion Blois Lobstein is associate professor of biology, Northern Virginia Community College-Manassas Campus, and a field trip leader for The Smithsonian Associates.

This book is the result of many years of talking, planning, organizing, studying, visiting sites, writing, checking with others, and then reorganizing and rewriting. The three authors have worked together, meeting often to go over even the smallest details, and each author also has been responsible for a certain part of the book.

Barbara Tufty is the author of the first three chapters, "The Settings," covering the geology, climate, and habitats of the Washington-Baltimore area. Cris Fleming researched and wrote chapters four through ten, "The Places," describing wildflower places and how to reach them. Marion Blois Lobstein prepared the final two chapters, "The Species," providing useful information on hundreds of wildflower species.

The authors would like to thank the following people whose skills helped create this book. Jo Moore produced the maps and Nicky Staunton drew the illustrations. Hal Horwitz provided the cover photograph and George Lobstein designed the blooming calendar. Eleanor deChadenedes carefully reviewed the entire manuscript and Rose Meier helped prepare the manuscript copy.

There are many people who have helped in many ways, including showing us places where we had never been, sharing knowledge, and reading our manuscripts. It is fair to say that this project could not have been completed without the assistance of these people, and we give grateful thanks to all of them.

We wish to express our special appreciation to the following: Stanwyn Shetler and Gary Fleming, for reading and commenting on the entire manuscript; Jim O'Connor, who served as mentor for the geology section; and Donna Ware, Stuart Ware, and Mark Garland, who advised on the climate and habitats parts.

For checking over the state-rare species, we wish to thank Chris Ludwig, botanist with the Virginia Division of Natural Heritage, and Gene Cooley, botanist with the Maryland Natural Heritage Program. For advice on taxonomy, we thank Stanwyn Shetler and Dan Nicolson, both of the Department of Botany of the Smithsonian Institution, and Peter Mazzeo, botanist at the National Arboretum.

Special thanks to Allen Belden, who helped explore many places and recorded the directions and mileage to several sites.

Many people shared information on their favorite wildflower places. Some went even further and shared their lists, their field notes, and their files. Some even took us to their special sites. We appreciate the extra assistance of the following: Bob and Jo Solem, for showing us Howard County sites and sharing their lists of wildflowers of these sites; Dave Pyle, for taking us to places in Baltimore County and Carroll County; Steve Hogan, for showing us other sites in Baltimore County; Denise Gibbs, for taking us special places in Montgomery County; Ed Martin, for lending his card file of species found along the C&O Canal; Helen Johnston, for sending her extensive records of wildflowers found at Great Falls Tavern; and Lynette Scaffidi, for sharing her lists of species found at Wheaton Regional Park.

Many other people showed us around particular places or checked over our manuscript. For their interest and assistance, we thank the following: Clara Ailes, Olin Allen, Tom Ambrose, David Askegaard, Rodney Bartgis, Allen Belden, Pam Beltz, Kathy Bilton, Susan Bloomfield, Dan Boone, Judy Bromley, Cole Burrell, Melinda Byrd, Bob Chance, Roger Cole, Sherna Comerford, Marcia Cooper, Jenny Coranzo, Paul Engman, Louise Everett, Jane Fallon, Joan Feely, Gary Fleming, Clyde Gamber, Carolyn Gamble, Tina Hall, Elaine Haug, Amy Henry, Nancy Herwig, Steven Hill, Steve

Hootman, Joe Howard, Ben Hren, Barbara Larabee, Sam Lyon, Sandy Lyon, Barbara Mauller, Joan Meder, Bill Melson, Jim Merriman, Ken Nicholls, Yvette Ogle, Sarah Phillips, Theo Ranneft, Chris Sacchi, Bernie Samm, Dan Sealy, Steve Sekscienski, Rob Simpson, Brenda Skarpol, Jocelyn Sladen, Al Studholme, Jim Subach, Chris Swarth, Mark Swick, Marta Sylvester, Claudia Thompson-Deahl, Jean Tierney, John Walsh, Jack Wennerstrom, Richard Wiegand, and Dwight Williams.

We deeply appreciate the financial support of the Board of Directors of the Audubon Naturalist Society of the Central Atlantic States.

We give thanks to Ted Rivinus, who conceived the idea for this book, and to Larry Morse, who read the proposal.

We are grateful for the patience and persistence of our editors at the Johns Hopkins University Press: Robert J. Brugger, Richard O'Grady, Jeanne Pinault, Stephen Siegforth, and George Thompson.

Introduction

This book is a guide to places where wildflowers can be found in the Washington-Baltimore area, ranging from the western shores of the Chesapeake Bay to the Appalachian Mountains. It is not a guide to identifying wildflowers—many good field guides on wildflowers already do that.

The book is divided into three parts. The first part, "The Settings," gives background information on the geology, climate, and habitats of the Washington-Baltimore area. In Chapter 1, Geology, the six physiographic regions of this area are described, from the low flat Coastal Plain, through the hilly and fertile Piedmont, to the mountain regions of the Blue Ridge, the Great Valley, the Ridge and Valley, and the Allegheny Plateau—all part of the Appalachian Mountain system.

Chapter 2 reviews the area's climate—the seasonal weather on the Coastal Plain, in the Piedmont, and in the mountains, as well as various microclimates that occur throughout. A brief account is given of the climatic changes occurring at the time of the last glaciation and subsequent warming trends.

Habitats of this area, described in Chapter 3, include wetlands, woodlands, rocky habitats, and open spaces, including roadsides and other disturbed sites. Dynamic factors such as temperature, sunlight, moisture, soil, altitude, and organisms help determine the kinds of plant communities that grow in different habitats.

The second part, "The Places," the heart of the book, gives detailed information on specific locations in the Washington-Baltimore area where wildflowers can be found in national, state, regional, and local parks, as well as some privately owned sites and preserves. Chapters 4 through 10 describe more than 120 places in an area extending about a hundred miles around

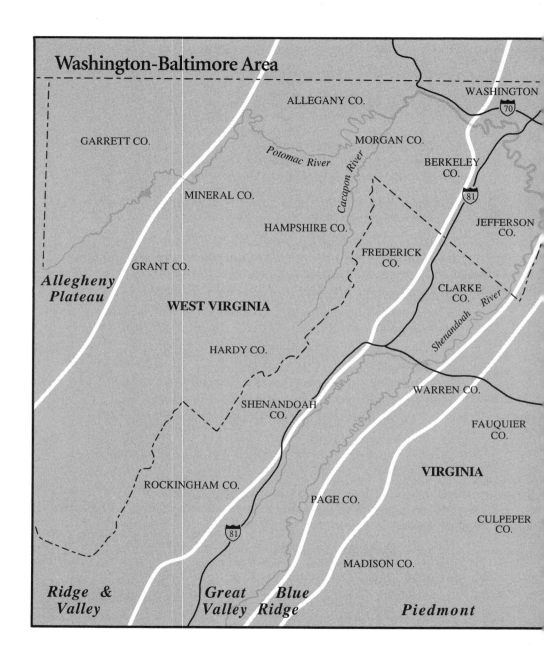

Washington-Baltimore Area

ALLEGANY CO.

GARRETT CO.

WASHINGTON

70

MORGAN CO.

Potomac River

BERKELEY
CO.

Cacapon River

81

MINERAL CO.

JEFFERSON
CO.

HAMPSHIRE CO.

FREDERICK
CO.

GRANT CO.

CLARKE
CO.

Allegheny
Plateau

WEST VIRGINIA

Shenandoah River

HARDY CO.

WARREN CO.

SHENANDOAH
CO.

FAUQUIER
CO.

VIRGINIA

ROCKINGHAM CO.

PAGE CO.

CULPEPER
CO.

81

Ridge &
Valley

Great
Valley

Blue
Ridge

MADISON CO.

Piedmont

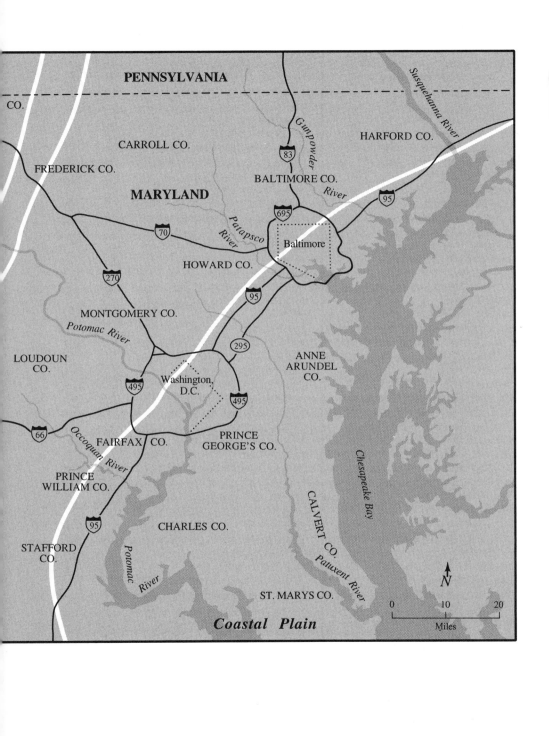

PENNSYLVANIA

CO.

CARROLL CO.

FREDERICK CO.

MARYLAND

HARFORD CO.

Susquehanna River

Gunpowder

River

83

BALTIMORE CO.

95

70

695

Patapsco River

Baltimore

HOWARD CO.

95

270

MONTGOMERY CO.

295

Potomac River

ANNE
ARUNDEL
CO.

LOUDOUN
CO.

495

Washington,
D.C.

95

495

66

Occoquan River

FAIRFAX CO.

PRINCE
GEORGE'S CO.

PRINCE
WILLIAM CO.

95

STAFFORD
CO.

CHARLES CO.

CALVERT
CO.

Patuxent River

Chesapeake Bay

Potomac

River

ST. MARYS CO.

Coastal Plain

N

0   10   20

Miles

Washington and Baltimore, mostly in Maryland and Virginia and including a few places in Pennsylvania and West Virginia. The organization of this part follows as closely as possible state and county boundaries, as well as the larger, more natural physiographic regions. Maps of the different regions are included, along with directions to specific locations.

The final part, "The Species," lists more than 730 wildflower species found in the area. Chapter 11 covers monocotyledons and Chapter 12, dicotyledons. Each species is then listed alphabetically by family and by scientific name, then by the common name, blooming dates, distribution, and typical habitats within the area covered by this book. Information is also given as to whether a species is native or introduced to the United States, and whether it is abundant, common, uncommon, rare, or very rare in our area.

The authors have focused on the more showy native and naturalized plants of the woods, fields, and wetlands and on easily accessible places in the metropolitan area. To list all wildflowers that grow in the Washington-Baltimore area and all the places where they can be found would make this book at least twice as long.

Scientific nomenclature used in this book for the most part follows Fernald, *Gray's Manual of Botany,* eighth edition, which is also the authority for popular field guides such as Peterson and McKenny, *A Field Guide to Wildflowers of the Northeastern and North-central North America,* and Newcomb, *Newcomb's Wildflower Guide.* For some species, the scientific names given in these references are no longer accepted by many botanists. In such cases, the scientific names follow the second edition of Gleason and Cronquist, *Manual of Vascular Plants of Northeastern United States and Adjacent Canada.*

Appendix A gives the scientific names used in this book that differ from those in *Gray's Manual.* Appendix B offers a blooming calendar for 180 common and showy species of wildflowers. Appendix C gives names and addresses of selected regional organizations concerned with wildflower conservation and of park administrative offices in the Washington-Baltimore area. The bibliography lists books useful for reference and information. The index includes both the scientific and common names of each species and the wildflower places described in the book.

The authors are active conservationists who encourage preservation of native plants and their habitats. Rare species and sensitive locations have been carefully checked with the Maryland Natural Heritage Program and the Virginia Division of Natural Heritage, as well as the Maryland, Virginia, and West Virginia Chapters of The Nature Conservancy. For purposes of conservation, we have not included many of the area's rarest plants. When we do mention a rare species, we give only a general idea of its location.

Whether this book is used to find a particular wildflower, to enrich an outing to a natural area, or to learn about the local flora, we hope that area residents and visiting naturalists will enjoy it.

THE SETTINGS

The mid-Atlantic area around Washington and Baltimore encompasses six major physiographic provinces. The Coastal Plain extends from the sands of the Atlantic Ocean across the Delmarva Peninsula and Chesapeake Bay and up to the rocky fall line, where the gently rolling Piedmont region begins. Farther westward rise the provinces of the Blue Ridge, Great Valley, Ridge and Valley, and Allegheny Plateau—all part of the geological system of the Appalachian Mountains.

These different regions stretching from the mountains to the sea contain small but significant variations in climate and harbor a rich medley of habitats that range from wetlands to woodlands, open spaces, and rock outcrops. All of these factors contribute to the remarkably diverse array of wildflowers throughout the area.

1

Geology

More than 200 million years ago, the ancient Appalachian mountains dominated the region, standing perhaps as high as today's Himalayas, with slopes extending for hundreds of miles. These mountains were formed near the end of the Paleozoic era, about 250 million years ago, when the huge continents of Europe and Africa collided with North America, pushing up the mountains and folding over billions of tons of rock, much of it old sea floors. By 65 million years ago the giant land mass Pangaea had split apart, and the modern Atlantic Ocean had formed. Even now, the continents of North America and Eurasia continue to separate and the ocean to widen.

For millions of years the lofty ancient mountains were worn down by snow, ice, wind, and rain, disintegrating and decomposing into stony rubble and debris which were carried eastward by streams and rainwater across the Piedmont province and deposited to form the Coastal Plain.

COASTAL PLAIN

The Coastal Plain, technically known as the Atlantic Coastal Plain, begins at the eastern edge of the continental shelf beneath the Atlantic Ocean, some hundreds of miles east of the shoreline. As the continent emerges from the sea, barrier islands form the first line of land, protecting the tidal wetlands and the mainland behind them from pounding waves and wind. Windswept dunes and fine sandy beaches are interspersed with tidal flats, salt marshes, and estuaries where saline waters sweep in and out with the tides. The relatively flat Delmarva peninsula of the lower Coastal Plain stretches westward to the Chesapeake Bay. The upper Coastal Plain rises from the western shores of the Bay and reaches to the Piedmont.

The Coastal Plain is the youngest of our geological regions. It was formed during the past 100 million years from weathered material carried eastward from the eroding highlands by rivers such as the Susquehanna, Potomac, Rappahannock, and James. When these rivers reached the flatter terrain near the ocean, their velocity slowed and their loads of gravel, sand, silt, and clay settled to form the Coastal Plain. For tens of thousands of years, warm tropical seas oscillated back and forth across the mid-Atlantic area, adding remains of marine organisms to the sediment and reworking the old debris eroded from the mountains.

During the past two million years, huge ice sheets advanced and retreated perhaps four times across the northern part of the North American continent. Although the ice sheets pressed no farther south than north-central Pennsylvania, they influenced the development of the Atlantic Coastal Plain. Enormous quantities of water were locked up in the ice sheets, lowering the sea level and periodically exposing the continental shelf. Then, about 15,000 years ago, as the climate warmed, the glaciers began thawing; during the next 5,000 years they gradually retreated north. Water from their melting slopes caused the seas to rise, flooding the lower part of the Susquehanna River Valley and forming the Chesapeake Bay.

The Coastal Plain province rises gradually toward the west to an elevation of about 500 feet above sea level at the fall zone, where it merges with the Piedmont. The area where the two provinces meet, often called the fall zone, is about 14 miles wide in places. The eastern edge of this fall zone, called the fall line, follows the edge of the hard Piedmont rocks, where rivers and streams flowing to the sea fall onto the soft sediments of the Coastal Plain.

The fall line has been weathered and eroded and is not easily seen, except in some places where an obvious change in elevation is apparent. This drop in elevation can be observed on Theodore Roosevelt Island in the Potomac River near Washington, and in the Prince William Forest Park near Triangle, Virginia. Although Great Falls on the Potomac River is above the actual fall line, it offers a spectacular view as the river plunges downward about 60 feet over exposed Piedmont rocks toward the Coastal Plain. Near Baltimore, the fall line can be observed at Gunpowder Falls in the Gunpowder Falls State Park. Highways US-1 and I-95 run close to the fall line from the Delaware River to the North Carolina border, and the major cities of Philadelphia, Baltimore, Washington, and Richmond are located along the fall zone, which is the upstream limit of ocean-going boats on our mid-Atlantic rivers.

PIEDMONT

The Piedmont province, also called the Piedmont Plateau (from two French words meaning "foot" of the "mountain"), is a gently rolling hilly region, with many valleys, streams, creeks, and rivers. From the fall line at the western edge of the Coastal Plain, the Piedmont province stretches some 30 to 50 miles westward and extends about 840 miles from New York to Alabama. Today, its eroded top rises almost 800 feet above sea level and abuts the Blue Ridge province to the west.

The geology of the Piedmont is complex, for throughout hundreds of millions of years the ancient bedrock has been changed by heat and pressure of numerous geological events. As continents collided, the old ocean floors were shoved up, heated, folded over many times, and pushed westward, one on top of another, like slabs of ice shoved by the wind and water along the edges of a frozen river. When these folds and slabs of ancient ocean bottom cooled, they solidified into metamorphosed rock, primarily gneiss, schist, and quartzite, which are interspersed in local areas with metamorphic igneous rocks such as soapstone and serpentinite. Molten magma repeatedly pushed between the folds and fractures, then cooled, hardened, and crystallized into the granite and basalt rocks we see today.

A seam of metamorphosed serpentinite runs through the Piedmont province from New York through Pennsylvania and Maryland into Virginia. Outcrops from this serpentinite band create habitats of thin, nutrient-poor, and magnesium-laden soil called serpentine barrens.

Toward the west, the Piedmont soils include 500-million-year-old sedimentary rock deposits of limestone and dolostone. A younger fault-produced rift called the Mesozoic or Triassic basin contains unconnected basins filled with ancient lake and river deposits. These basins have local names—for example, the Danville, Culpeper/Potomac, and Gettysburg basins. Fine sandstone and siltstone bluffs, such as Ball's Bluff, occur in this area. The maroon sandstones and shales of this region have often been used in brownstone architecture from Boston to Richmond.

BLUE RIDGE

The western edge of the Piedmont joins the Blue Ridge province, named for the soft bluish haze that often obscures the tops of the ridges in summer. This narrow zone of ancient erosion-resistant granite, gneiss, quartzite, greenstone, slate, and phyllite runs in a northeast-southwest direction for more than 600 miles from Pennsylvania to Georgia.

The easternmost ridge of this province begins as a single low crest in southern Pennsylvania, then expands to an irregular chain of hills, ridges, and highlands some eight to ten miles wide. The complex geologic fold of the Blue Ridge in our area includes the Catoctin and Bull Run mountains to the east; and South Mountain, Elk Ridge, Loudoun Heights, and the high ridges of the Shenandoah National Park to the west. Between these ridges lies the eroded valley underlain with hard, resistant grayish gneisses. The youngest rocks are metamorphosed quartzites and purple phyllites formed from sedimentary rocks such as sandstones and mudstones.

The mountains of this province are rugged and high. Hawksbill and Stony Man mountains in the Shenandoah National Park, for example, are higher than 4,000 feet. Here the acidic to neutral soils are generally heavy and loamy, and often rocky.

Many small streams drain down the steep sides of the Blue Ridge, flowing east and west, carving out short canyons as they erode the terrain. On the eastern side, the mountain streams cascade into the Piedmont area, spilling into tributaries of the Potomac and Rappahannock rivers that run into the Chesapeake Bay and on into the Atlantic Ocean. On the western side of the ridge, streams tumble into the Shenandoah River, which flows northward into the Potomac River, creating a gap in the Blue Ridge at Harpers Ferry.

GREAT VALLEY

On the western side of the Blue Ridge province lies a broad pastoral valley known by different names in different regions—Great Valley, Great Carbonate Valley, Limestone Valley, Hagerstown Valley, Shenandoah Valley, or Valley of Virginia. This corridor, from 15 to 26 miles wide, runs from New York to Alabama and marks the eastern edge of the Ridge and Valley province.

About 500 million years ago, this region was inundated by warm, shallow seas abounding with marine invertebrates. As these creatures died, their calcium-rich remains sank and formed miles-deep layers of sediment that hardened into easily soluble limestone and dolomite. With continuing geological activities, the thick layers of the ocean floor were heaved up again and again, folded, and tilted. During the Cenozoic era, beginning 65 million years ago, weak acidic groundwater and rain percolated through cracks in these folds, dissolving the limestone of the ancient ocean floor and forming sinkholes, caverns, caves, and other limestone formations called karst topography.

The terrain of this gently rolling valley is dominated in Virginia by the Shenandoah River meandering northward and in Maryland by limestone bluffs along the Potomac River. The relatively flat terrain and the loamy, nutrient-rich calcareous soil have long attracted settlers and farmers to the Great Valley.

RIDGE AND VALLEY

The long parallel series of ridges and valleys to the west of the Great Valley emerged when the colliding continents shoved the old ocean floor into ridges and valleys, like folds of a heavy rug when pushed from the side. The more weather-resistant shale, siltstone, and sandstone ridges, formed from ancient muddy silt and sand, stand some 1,800 to 2,900 feet above sea level. In the Ridge and Valley province, sometimes called the Valley and Ridge province, the stony soils are thin and dry, leached by rains. Some ridges of Oriskany sandstone contain high amounts of pure silica sand. In this region, shale barrens—unusual habitats with many rare plants—can be found on some steep, south-facing, shale slopes.

In the low valleys, the softer sedimentary shale containing marine fossils is easily eroded and broken into deposits of fertile soil. Ancient remnants from the lush forests that once grew there have formed deposits of bituminous coal in Maryland and Virginia and anthracite coal in Pennsylvania.

ALLEGHENY PLATEAU

This is the westernmost province in the Appalachian Mountain system. Bordered on the east by the Ridge and Valley province, the Allegheny Plateau rises more than 3,000 feet and then slopes gradually to the west and merges into the flatter regions of the midwest. The Plateau is the continent's eastern drainage divide, with streams and rivers running east toward the Chesapeake Bay and into the Atlantic Ocean or west toward the Ohio and Mississippi rivers and on into the Gulf of Mexico.

The province is composed of high plateaus, gentle forested slopes, and high narrow valleys. Highly acidic soil and extensive peat deposits in some areas create open heaths, large peatlands, bogs, and swamps. The horizontal strata include bituminous coal deposits interspersed with layers of sandstone and shale.

2

Climate

The climate of the mid-Atlantic area varies considerably from the ocean to the mountains because of the complex interactions of temperature, humidity, precipitation, altitude, and wind. This climatic variation contributes to the diversity of habitats and plant communities.

Overall, the mid-Atlantic area has a relatively humid and temperate climate. Seasonal temperatures may range from well below 0°F. in the mountains in winter to more than 100°F. on the Piedmont and Coastal Plain in summer. Precipitation throughout the area generally totals 40 to 50 inches annually and is distributed quite evenly throughout the year.

On the Coastal Plain, the waters of the Chesapeake Bay and Atlantic Ocean help create a moderate and relatively moist climate, with humidity often climbing to 95 percent and above in late summer. Spring on the Coastal Plain and Piedmont may arrive as early as late February and is very pleasant, particularly from mid-March through May. In summer, the prevailing westerly winds usually bring clear weather, while easterly winds from the Atlantic can bring storms; southwesterly winds from the Gulf of Mexico bring tropical temperatures and sultry humidity. When the Bermuda high-pressure system stalls off the Atlantic Coast, hot humid weather with temperatures rising over 95°F. may stagnate over the region. Sudden showers and intense thunderstorms often sweep across the area in summer, but droughts may occur in some years. The warmth, high humidity, and sunny days during the long growing season produce abundant dense green vegetation in the woods and wetlands.

Autumn months on the Coastal Plain and Piedmont are pleasant, with many crisp, sunlit days when the humidity drops and the cloudless sky is a brilliant blue. Leaves of maples, dogwoods, black gum, sassafras, and other deciduous trees turn bright shades of red and gold. In late summer and fall, hurricanes may sweep up the coast and drop large amounts of rainfall over the area. These storms can be beneficial in breaking the summer droughts, but they are often destructive, too, bringing heavy rains and flooding rivers. The first frost arrives in late September on the Piedmont and in October at lower elevations. Winters on the Piedmont are mild and wet, with average temperatures ranging from just below freezing to 45°F. or higher. Snowfalls may accumulate up to a foot or more, but the snow often lasts only a few days before turning to slush and melting away.

In the mountains to the west, the climate is quite different from that on the Coastal Plain and the Piedmont. At higher elevations, temperatures are cooler. A rise in elevation of 1,000 feet is accompanied by an average drop in temperature of about 3.5°F.; thus temperatures in the mountain regions rising over 3,000 feet average 10°F. cooler than in the lowlands of the Piedmont and Coastal Plain. Temperatures at high elevations in the mid-Atlantic Appalachians are similar to those at low elevations in northern New England. In spring, the leafing-out of trees and flowering of plants progress up the mountain slopes at an average rate of a hundred feet a day. Thus, spring arrives in the high mountains one or two weeks later than in the lowlands.

Summers in the highlands are pleasant, with warm, sunny days and cool nights. Thunderstorms rumble through the mountains, depositing more rainfall on the western slopes than on those to the east. At high elevations, in a reverse of the spring pattern, the brilliant autumn coloration starts early and moves slowly down the mountain slopes. During the mountain winters, temperatures average in the low 30s and may fall as low as minus 30°F. Heavy snowstorms are common in some areas, and snow may cover the ground for weeks, sometimes for most of the winter.

Microclimates occur in all regions, the result of small local differences in topography, temperature, or moisture. Factors influencing the formation of a microclimate include the orientation and steepness of a slope, the way the soil retains or sheds water, and the presence of rocks and boulders. For instance, a south-facing slope catches the more direct sun rays and creates a warm dry spot, whereas a north-facing slope may remain in cool, moist shadows. During the day, temperatures around a pile of boulders may heat up 10° to 15° higher than the surrounding terrain as the rocks absorb and radiate heat. In contrast, the microclimate beneath a rock ledge could be more humid and several degrees cooler than that of a nearby sunlit field.

Plants themselves create a microclimate by tempering or changing conditions in a local spot. For instance, shrubs may form hedgerows that bear the brunt of winds and offer protection to plants behind them. Trees shade and protect an area from the direct rays of the sun and cool the surrounding air with moisture evaporating from the leaves.

Over the eons, changing climates in our area have brought varying habitats. For hundreds of thousands of years during the Pleistocene epoch, the climate changed dramatically as glaciers advanced and retreated over much of the Northern Hemisphere. Although the ponderous ice masses came only as far south as north-central Pennsylvania, their cooling influence penetrated into what is now our mid-Atlantic area. During the last glacial advance, called the Wisconsin Glaciation, northern plants migrated south in front of the advancing ice, and conifers dominated our forests. When the glaciers began retreating some 15,000 years ago, temperatures slowly rose as the ice melted. The cool-weather boreal plants slowly migrated north, returning to New England and Canada. However, some species, such as bunchberry (*Cornus canadensis*) and twinflower (*Linnaea borealis*), remained behind in the cool high mountains of the mid-Atlantic area—isolated relicts of the glacial age.

As the region warmed in the wake of the retreating glaciers, tree species of temperate climates—oaks, hickories, and tuliptree—gradually moved back into the area and replaced the conifers as the dominant forest species.

About 8,000 years ago, a warm, dry period occurred in our area. During this time some plants from the midwestern prairies migrated eastward into the mid-Atlantic region. Then, as the climate became more humid in eastern North America, most of these plants disappeared from our area, although some species such as hoary puccoon (*Lithospermum canescens*) still persist in hot, dry habitats.

3

Habitats

Habitats are places where plants and animals live. Each habitat is the sum total of environmental conditions in that place. The amount of sunlight or moisture, type of soil, and range of temperatures determine what species of plants can grow there and, in turn, what other organisms may be associated with them, including mammals, birds, amphibians, arthropods, earthworms, fungi, and soil microorganisms. The word *habitat* comes from the Latin word *habitare*, "to inhabit" or "to dwell."

Availability of water is one of the primary conditions determining the plant species that grow in a particular habitat. The amount of water depends on rainfall, groundwater level, type of soil, and ground cover, which affects the extent to which precipitation is retained and allowed to percolate into the soil. Springs, streams, or rivers may provide a constant water supply. Local topographic terrain affects drainage and is another important factor in the supply of water to plant habitats. The plant species of poorly drained areas or of low-lying wetlands are quite different from those of well-drained slopes of hills and mountains.

Soils also help determine what species grow in a particular habitat. Soils are composed of weathered rock particles, organic matter (humus), trapped air, and water. The particles range from fine-grained clay to silt to coarse sand. Different combinations of minerals and organic matter make different types of soils with varying capacities to retain water and air and to make those materials available to plants. For instance, water drains rapidly through sandy soil, while moisture is retained in rich organic soils.

Availability of oxygen in the soil is another determinant of the species that grow in a habitat. Species that grow in oxygen-poor, water-logged soils are quite different from those that thrive in loose, loamy soil.

Soils can be acidic, neutral, or alkaline, depending on the type and concentration of chemicals and minerals they contain. Calcareous soils, such as those formed from limestone, are nutrient-rich and neutral to alkaline, providing fine habitat for wildflowers such as shooting star (*Dodecatheon meadia*) and twinleaf (*Jeffersonia diphylla*). Acidic soils, derived from rocks such as sandstone and granite, are lower in available nutrients and provide habitats for members of the heath family such as trailing arbutus (*Epigaea repens*) and pinxter flower (*Rhododendron periclymenoides*).

The yearly temperature range also plays a significant part in determining what species grow where. Some plants such as yellow clintonia (*Clintonia borealis*) cannot tolerate a hot climate; others cannot withstand an extended exposure to cold temperatures during the growing season. Seeds of many of our wildflowers such as bloodroot (*Sanguinaria canadensis*), sessile trillium (*Trillium sessile*), and wild ginger (*Asarum canadense*) require a cold period before they will sprout.

Variations in average temperature at different elevations are other factors affecting the habitat. As one climbs higher up a mountain, one encounters cooler temperatures. In our area, a rise of each 1,000 feet up a mountain is equal to a move north of about 250 miles. Thus many plant species that can be found in the higher latitudes of New England and Canada—for example, nodding trillium (*Trillium cernuum*), starflower (*Trientalis borealis*), and common wood-sorrel (*Oxalis montana*)—also grow in the cool habitats of the higher elevations of the mountains in western Virginia, western Maryland, and West Virginia.

Amount of exposure to sunlight is another critical habitat factor. Species growing in an open field in full sunlight are different from those in a shaded woodland. Black-eyed Susan (*Rudbeckia hirta*) and butterflyweed (*Asclepias tuberosa*) are adapted to hot, dry, sunny places, while blue-stemmed goldenrod (*Solidago caesia*) and heart-leaved aster (*Aster cordifolius*) prefer the shady woods. Species growing on a shady north-facing slope may be quite different from those on a sunny south-facing slope.

Some species adapt with seeming ease to many different habitats and environments. For instance, spring beauty (*Claytonia virginica*) can be found on moist floodplains as well as on well-drained wooded slopes. Other species have specific habitats, such as the thread-leaved sundew (*Drosera filiformis*), which is found only in Coastal Plain bogs.

Many diverse habitats occur in the Washington-Baltimore area. One common way to categorize these habitats is to place them into four major types: 1) wetlands such as marshes, swamps, bogs, streambanks and riverbanks, floodplains, edges of ponds and lakes, springs, seeps, seepage swamps, ditches, and swales; 2) woodlands, both deciduous and coniferous, including upland woods, bottomland woods, edges of woods, and thickets; 3) open lands such as fields, meadows, rights-of-way, disturbed sites, and lawns; and 4) rocky areas such as cliffs, rocky bluffs, rock outcrops, and barrens.

Habitats to the west—in the ridges, valleys, and mountains of western Virginia, western Maryland, and West Virginia—lie outside the general area of this book and are only briefly mentioned here, as are the ocean dunes and beaches at the eastern edge of Maryland and Virginia. The following descriptions of various habitats refer specifically to those found in the Washington-Baltimore area.

WETLANDS

Wetlands are areas where the soil is saturated at least several weeks each year. Wetlands usually occur on low ground where water drains poorly or where streams or springs constantly replenish the moisture in the soil. The types of soil and specific plant species are essential criteria in defining wetlands.

Wetlands may be permanently or temporarily wet; they may be flooded twice daily by incoming tides or seasonally by heavy rains. They may be small or large, deep or shallow. Wetlands may be freshwater, brackish, or saltwater. Freshwater nontidal wetlands are fed by rivers, rain, springs, or underground aquifers. Freshwater tidal wetlands occur along upper tidal portions of streams and rivers where incoming ocean tides invade freshwater tributaries and push a body of fresh water upstream. Saltwater and brackish wetlands on the Coastal Plain are affected by the daily tides of the Chesapeake Bay and the Atlantic Ocean.

Marshes

Marshes contain few if any woody plants. Open to the sun and sky, their wet soils are mucky with organic matter. Marshes range from inland freshwater marshes to those at the edges of the sea, where they are inundated by salty tides. Many herbaceous plants of the marshes are members of the grass, sedge, and rush families.

Freshwater nontidal marshes are found along ponds and rivers not subject to tidal fluctuations, where the salinity of the water is less than 0.5 parts per thousand. Fresh water is present either permanently (all year round) or seasonally. Spatterdock (*Nuphar advena*), broad-leaved cattail (*Typha latifolia*), and pickerelweed (*Pontederia cordata*) are typical wildflowers of these inland marshes. Examples of freshwater nontidal marshes can be found at Hughes Hollow in Montgomery County, Maryland; Flag Ponds in Calvert County, Maryland; and Huntley Meadows near Alexandria, Virginia.

Freshwater tidal marshes are found along streams and rivers at the upper part of an estuary where they are affected by daily tides. Freshwater tidal marshes contain species such as sweetflag (*Acorus calamus*), arrow arum (*Peltandra virginica*), and swamp rose mallow (*Hibiscus moscheutos*). Wild rice (*Zizania aquatica*) can be found in freshwater tidal marshes, but only in a few locations. Maryland's tidal marshes include Jug Bay on the Patuxent River, Black Marsh in Baltimore County, and Otter Point Creek in Harford County; Dyke Marsh is in Virginia on the Potomac River.

Brackish marshes are tidal marshes where fresh water is mixed with salt water and the salinity is between 0.5 and 30 parts per thousand. These marshes are found along the middle and lower parts of estuarine rivers and creeks. Many rushes and sedges grow in this habitat, as well as big cordgrass (*Spartina cynosuroides*) and narrow-leaved cattail (*Typha angustifolia*).

Salt marshes are found throughout the Coastal Plain near the ocean, where they are strongly affected by the daily tides and the twice-monthly higher tides. Here the water has a salinity of 30 or more parts per thousand. In the low-lying marshes flooded regularly by tides, extensive open meadows of salt-marsh cordgrass (*Spartina alterniflora*) sway in the wind. In the higher marshes that are reached only irregularly by high tides, stands of salt-meadow hay (*Spartina patens*) are interspersed with spikegrass (*Distichlis spicata*) and sea lavender (*Limonium carolinianum*).

Swamps

Swamps are wooded freshwater wetlands characterized by trees and shrubs that can tolerate standing water or waterlogged soils. Although swamps may become dry for part of the year, the typical swamp vegetation is present all year. In this habitat trees such as red maple, green ash, tupelo, and sycamore are commonly found. Swamp shrubs include silky dogwood (*Cornus amomum*), buttonbush (*Cephalanthus occidentalis*), and arrowwood (*Viburnum dentatum*). Relatively few herbaceous species grow in this moist, shaded environment, but colonies of lizard's-tail (*Saururus cernuus*) and skunk cabbage (*Symplocarpus foetidus*) can be found.

Bogs

Bogs are wetlands where drainage is poor and the soil is acidic and low in oxygen and nutrients. Sphagnum mosses are characteristic plants of this habitat, and sedges and heaths may be prominent. As the sphagnum mosses die and slowly decay beneath the water, they decompose incompletely into peat.

Bogs in our area are located in two geologic regions—the Coastal Plain and the Allegheny Plateau. Coastal Plain bogs have formed in small depressions on gentle slopes in association with headwaters of slowly moving streams. Most bogs of the Washington-Baltimore area have been drained or filled in. Suitland Bog in Prince George's County, Maryland, an example of a Coastal Plain bog, is the only remaining bog of the more than thirty bogs that once existed in the immediate Washington area.

Cold mountain bogs, also called boreal bogs, are acidic wetlands found in high elevations with cool temperatures. The mountain bog called Cranesville Swamp in Garrett County, Maryland, on the Allegheny Plateau was formed about 18,000 years ago, at the time when the glaciers reached their southern limit. Here the American larch reaches one of its southernmost point in the United States.

Typical plants of both the Coastal Plain and mountain bogs are maleberry (*Lyonia ligustrina*), sheep laurel (*Kalmia angustifolia*), the delicate rose pogonia (*Pogonia ophioglossoides*), and carnivorous plants such as northern pitcher-plant (*Sarracenia purpurea*) and round-leaved sundew (*Drosera rotundifolia*).

Streambanks

Streambanks are moist edges of long narrow watercourses, sometimes steep and often shaded with woody vegetation. Typical wildflowers that grow here include tall meadowrue (*Thalictrum pubescens*) and false pimpernel (*Lindernia dubia*).

Riverbanks

Riverbanks are found along the shores of rivers. They often have muddy soil and, in some places, river-scoured rocks. Because a river is wider than a stream, the banks are more open to sunlight. In this habitat, look for halberd-leaved rose mallow (*Hibiscus laevis*) and American germander (*Teucrium canadense*).

Floodplains

Floodplains occur along rivers and streams that seasonally spill over with heavy rains, depositing rich alluvial soils. In this habitat one can find trees that have adapted to changing levels of soil moisture and can tolerate their roots being submerged in water for long periods of time. Typical floodplain trees include sycamore, silver maple, slippery elm, river birch, and green ash.

Wildflowers that grow near a flood-prone river are adapted to rapidly changing conditions of periodic flooding. In early spring, carpets of Virginia bluebells (*Mertensia virginica*) and wild blue phlox (*Phlox divaricata*) spread over rich floodplain soils along streams and rivers.

Sometimes seeds or vegetative parts of plants are carried downstream in floods from regions farther upstream and take root in the alluvial soil along rivers. That's why you might sometimes find plants that are rare in an area. For instance, white trout-lily (*Erythronium albidum*) is rare around Washington but can be found along the shores of the Potomac River.

Floodplains occur in the C&O Canal National Historical Park along the Maryland side of the Potomac River, in the Hereford area of Gunpowder Falls State Park in Baltimore County, Maryland, and in Bull Run Regional Park and Riverbend Park in Fairfax County, Virginia.

Edges of Ponds and Lakes

Edges of ponds and lakes are the wet borders around inland bodies of water. When the edges of man-made lakes have been allowed to revert to natural vegetation, they are graced with flowering plants such as swamp milkweed (*Asclepias incarnata*), square-stemmed monkey-flower (*Mimulus ringens*), and cardinal flower (*Lobelia cardinalis*). There are no natural lakes in the Washington-Baltimore area, but several man-made ponds and lakes can be found in parks of various counties. For instance, in Maryland two lakes occur in Rock Creek Regional Park in Montgomery County, and Phoenix Pond is located in Baltimore County.

Springs

Springs are outlets for cool fresh water bubbling from underground sources. Found throughout the area, they offer cool oases where watercress (*Nasturtium officinale*) may grow in the running water.

Seeps

Seeps are small water-logged areas fed by springs or headwaters of streams. Characteristic plants found in these wet places include Pennsylvania bittercress (*Cardamine pensylvanica*), golden saxifrage (*Chrysosplenium americanum*), and swamp buttercup (*Ranunculus septentrionalis*).

Seepage Swamps

Seepage swamps are extensive networks of seeps and shallow braided streams on gently sloping wooded terrain. Wildflowers that grow in this habitat include false hellebore (*Veratrum viride*), marsh blue violet (*Viola cucullata*), and swamp saxifrage (*Saxifraga pensylvanica*). Seepage swamps can be found along the Big Meadows Swamp Trail in the Shenandoah National Park and at the Thompson Wildlife Management Area, both in the Blue Ridge of Virginia.

Ditches

Ditches are small narrow trenches that are quite moist at certain seasons of the year and are usually found along roadsides or fields. They are often man-made for purposes of drainage or irrigation. Broad-leaved cattail (*Typha latifolia*) and hollow Joe-Pye-weed (*Eupatorium fistulosum*) can be found in these habitats.

Swales

Swales are low-lying depressed stretches of land that often remain damp and marshy with standing water. New York ironweed (*Vernonia noveboracensis*), seedbox (*Ludwigia alternifolia*), spotted jewelweed (*Impatiens capensis*), and other wetland species often grow in swales.

WOODLANDS

The mid-Atlantic region was once part of a great deciduous forest, mostly of hardwoods such as oaks, hickories, beech, and chestnut, that stretched almost continuously from the Coastal Plain to the tall grass prairies of the midwest.

Over the centuries, the trees have been cut for timber and to make way for pastures, hay fields, crops, and other farming activities. In recent decades, housing developments, highways, and malls have paved over much of what once were forests as population has increased along the eastern seaboard. Today the large virgin forests are gone, and the second-growth woods and forests are composed of tuliptree, beech, oaks, and hickories.

In cleared open places that were once forests, you can find evidence of the slow return of woody vegetation in the first phase of the process called succession. Sun-loving eastern red cedar and Virginia pine are often the first trees to appear in an abandoned field, gradually shading out grasses and other herbaceous plants. Seeds of deciduous trees, carried by wind or birds, are deposited in the fields and develop over time into trees that shade out the cedars. Eventually, the pines also gradually die out, and oaks, hickories, tuliptree, and beech become dominant. Understory trees such as flowering dogwood (*Cornus florida*), redbud (*Cercis canadensis*), and common shadbush (*Amelanchier arborea*) bring color to the woods in spring. In early spring, before the leaves unfold and shut out the sunlight from the ground, many forest floors are brightened with ephemeral wildflowers such as bloodroot (*Sanguinaria canadensis*), Dutchman's breeches (*Dicentra cucullaria*), and cut-leaved toothwort (*Dentaria laciniata*).

Wooded habitats can be divided into four types, depending on the terrain, elevation, and the amount of moisture in the soil: upland woods, bottomland woods, edges of woods, and thickets.

Upland Woods

Upland woods occur on hilly terrains, where the soil is often well drained or dry because rainwater drains quickly down the hillsides. Most soils here are nutrient-poor. The driest upland woods are often found on southwest- and west-facing slopes and on ridges. Oaks and hickories are dominant in these habitats. Rattlesnake-weed (*Hieracium venosum*), bastard toadflax (*Comandra umbellata*), and plantain-leaved pussytoes (*Antennaria plantaginifolia*) grow in these dry upland woods. In the more acidic dry soils, usually under pines, pink lady's-slipper (*Cypripedium acaule*) may be present.

Soils of moist upland woods often retain moderate levels of moisture. Wild ginger (*Asarum canadense*) prefers these woods, as do Jack-in-the-pulpit (*Arisaema triphyllum*) and sessile trillium (*Trillium sessile*). These upland habitats often face north and can be found above stream valleys such as Scott's Run Nature Preserve in Fairfax County, Virginia, and Cabin John Stream Valley Park in Montgomery County, Maryland.

Bottomland Woods

Bottomland woods occur in low-lying areas where the land is flat and moist. They are often found on floodplains along streams or rivers. Dwarf ginseng (*Panax trifolius*) and trout-lily (*Erythronium americanum*) bloom in bottomland woods. These wooded habitats can be found at Roosevelt Island near Washington, D.C., Fraser Preserve in Fairfax County, Virginia, and Oregon Ridge–Ivy Hill in Baltimore County, Maryland.

Edges of Woods

Edges of woods are the borders between shaded forests or woods and the more sunny open habitats of fields and meadows. Here you can find various deciduous tree species competing with conifers such as eastern red cedar and Virginia pine for available sunlight. Herbaceous plants found here include Indian tobacco (*Lobelia inflata*) and downy false-foxglove (*Aureolaria virginica*).

Thickets

Thickets are tangles of vegetation including small saplings and brambles such as blackberries and multiflora rose (*Rosa multiflora*). Some vines that grow in thickets are sandvine (*Ampelamus albidus*) and yellow passion flower (*Passiflora lutea*).

OPEN LANDS

Open lands are fields, meadows, and other stretches of land with few or no trees. Some were once forested lands that have been cleared and farmed and are still being modified by human intervention such as mowing, grazing, or burning. Other open spaces are naturally free from woody vegetation because of poor soil or underlying rocks.

Fields

Fields are open lands that have been cleared of trees and are in constant use for cultivation and pasture. Summer wildflowers found in open fields include Deptford pink (*Dianthus armeria*), Venus's looking-glass (*Triodanis perfoliata*), and ox-eye daisy (*Chrysanthemum leucanthemum*).

Early colonists who cut down the forests to cultivate the land planted many seeds they brought from their European homeland—vegetables, herbs, and garden flowers. Inevitably, some seeds escaped from the tended gardens, and the more hardy ones such as true forget-me-not (*Myosotis scorpioides*) and orange poppy (*Papaver dubium*) spread throughout the countryside. Other seeds arrived uninvited. Seeds of common European wildflowers of roadsides and wasteplaces made the voyage across the ocean tucked inadvertently in pants pockets, cuffs, or other belongings. Some wildflowers such as Queen Anne's lace (*Daucus carota*), chicory (*Cichorium intybus*), and spotted knapweed (*Centaurea maculosa*) quickly took over the dry roadsides and fields of the new land.

Meadows

Meadows are open places that are free from encroaching woody vegetation, either because they have been deliberately burned or mowed, or because they have naturally dry or thin soil. Sometimes, too, a high water table may prevent woody plants from growing. Many eastern meadows are only temporarily halted in an early stage of succession, unlike prairie meadows to the west, where scarce rainfall is a constant limiting factor for growth of woody plants.

Depending on the relative amount of moisture in the soil, meadows may be defined as dry, moist, or wet.

Dry meadows are well-drained, open habitats on a slightly sloping terrain where the soils are usually thin. Here you can find black-eyed Susan (*Rudbeckia hirta*), tall goldenrod (*Solidago canadensis*), lyre-leaved sage (*Salvia lyrata*), hyssop-leaved boneset (*Eupatorium hyssopifolium*), and sweet everlasting (*Gnaphalium obtusifolium*). Another wildflower that grows in this habitat is wild bergamot (*Monarda fistulosa*), a native of dry meadows farther west. Dry meadows can be found in Virginia at Ellanor C. Lawrence Park in Fairfax County and in Maryland at Seneca Creek State Park in Montgomery County, Hollofield Area in Howard County, and the Hashawha Environmental Appreciation Center in Carroll County.

Moist meadows are low, open sites with wildflowers such as Virginia meadow beauty (*Rhexia virginica*) and common hedge-nettle (*Stachys tenuifolia*) in midsummer. Tickseed-sunflower (*Bidens polylepis*) and swamp milkweed (*Asclepias incarnata*) also grow in moist meadows. As autumn approaches, New England aster (*Aster novae-angliae*) and lance-leaved goldenrod (*Solidago graminifolia*) begin to flower. Moist meadows can be found along streams and under power lines.

Wet meadows occur where the water table is high. Here certain wild-flowers grow in the wet soil—closed gentian (*Gentiana clausa*), swamp milkweed (*Asclepias incarnata*), and New York ironweed (*Vernonia nove-boracensis*). Wet meadows are at their showiest in late summer at Maryland's Little Bennett Regional Park in Montgomery County and Virginia's James Long Park in western Prince William County.

Rights-of-Way

Rights-of-way are elongated tracts of land designated for transportation purposes or utility lines. They are often maintained free of shrubs and trees by mowing, cutting, or applying herbicides. Roadsides, old train track sidings, and the long stretches of land under powerlines and over gas pipelines form habitats for species such as butter-and-eggs (*Linaria vulgaris*) and common evening-primrose (*Oenothera biennis*). Sunny strips of meadows may also occur under powerlines or over pipelines.

In disturbed sites such as vacant lots or places torn up by bulldozers, common mullein (*Verbascum thapsus*) is quick to take root, as is yellow sweet clover (*Melilotus officinalis*).

Lawns

Grassy lawns surrounding houses in urban or suburban areas vary in their quality as habitats, depending on the soils and on how often the grass is mowed, watered, and weeded. In early spring, gill-over-the-ground (*Glechoma hederacea*) and purple dead-nettle (*Lamium purpureum*) appear in lawns. Later, white clover (*Trifolium repens*) blooms, as well as bulbous buttercup (*Ranunculus bulbosus*) and shepherd's purse (*Capsella bursa-pastoris*). In the summer, lady's thumb (*Polygonum persicaria*) and Asiatic dayflower (*Commelina communis*) poke up in yards and gardens and along edges of less tended walks or fences.

ROCKY AREAS

Many plants have adapted to the thin, poor soils of rocky areas. These habitats are often steeply sloping and dry because the rainwater runs off so swiftly. Occasionally, however, seeps from underground springs saturate the ground. Many of the species that cling to dry rocky cliffs have special adaptations to find or conserve water: long roots that extend to a source of moisture, or very shallow root systems that make maximum use of what little moisture or soil is available. Thick leaves and hairy stems also protect plants in dry environments by reducing loss of water by evaporation.

Cliffs

Cliffs are high steep faces of rock. Some are bare, and others may retain small amounts of soil lodged in crevices and ledges. Wild columbine (*Aquilegia canadensis*), moss phlox (*Phlox subulata*), and prickly pear (*Opuntia humifusa*) grow in this habitat.

Rocky Bluffs

Rocky bluffs are high rocky walls that have been carved by the erosive force of flowing rivers. Lyre-leaved rockcress (*Arabis lyrata*) and wild pink (*Silene caroliniana*) live in this habitat. Riverbank goldenrod (*Solidago racemosa*) can be found on rocky bluffs of the Potomac River gorge near Great Falls. Look for rocky bluffs on both the Maryland and Virginia sides of the Potomac River at Great Falls, at Red Rock Wilderness Overlook Regional Park in Loudoun County, Virginia, and in the Hollofield Area of Patapsco Valley State Park in Howard County, Maryland.

Limestone bluffs, such as those at Mountain Lock and Snyders Landing in Maryland's Washington County and Shenk's Ferry in Pennsylvania, have rich alkaline soils where ferns thrive and wildflowers grow in profusion. Species growing in calcareous environments include twinleaf (*Jeffersonia diphylla*), shooting star (*Dodecatheon meadia*), and dwarf larkspur (*Delphinium tricorne*).

Rock Outcrops

Rock outcrops can occur in the midst of other habitats. These small areas of exposed bare rock have little or no soil, but species such as wild stonecrop (*Sedum ternatum*), early saxifrage (*Saxifraga virginiensis*), and alumroot (*Heuchera americana*) find toeholds in small cracks in the rocks and manage to take root in the thin soil.

Barrens

Barrens are open rocky places with dry nutrient-poor soil.

Serpentine barrens contain serpentinite, a metamorphosed igneous rock that crumbles into thin soils lacking the important plant nutrients of phosphorus, nitrogen, and calcium. These soils have high concentrations of heavy metals such as magnesium, nickel, and chromium, which are toxic to some plants and retard growth in others. A few plants have adapted remarkably well to these harsh conditions—trees such as post oak and black-jack oak, and wildflowers such as whorled milkweed (*Asclepias verticillata*), fameflower (*Talinum teretifolium*), and slender knotweed (*Polygonum tenue*). Prairie grasses such as Indian grass (*Sorghastrum nutans*) and big bluestem (*Andropogon gerardi*) can also be found in this habitat. The eastern serpentine barrens occur along seams of serpentinite rock running in an irregular swath through Pennsylvania and Maryland. Two barrens in our area are Soldiers Delight in Baltimore County and Nottingham Barrens near Nottingham, Pennsylvania.

Shale barrens are very hot, dry habitats found on some south-facing shale slopes. This exposed environment, with poor thin soil, is hardly conducive to plant growth. Surprisingly, some plants have adapted to these difficult conditions, including Kate's Mountain clover (*Trifolium virginicum*), mountain pimpernel (*Taenidia montana*), pussytoes ragwort (*Senecio antennariifolius*), and shale-barren evening-primrose (*Oenothera argillicola*). In our area, shale barrens are found in Fort Valley in the Massanutten mountains west of Front Royal, Virginia, and in Green Ridge State Forest in Allegany County, Maryland.

THE PLACES

The Washington-Baltimore area has many places where a wide variety of wildflowers can be found at different seasons of the year. Many of these places are on public parkland or, if privately owned, are open to the public. Some sites are open only at certain times or by special permission from the owner.

Most of the 122 wildflower places described in this book are within 100 miles of Washington and Baltimore. A few places beyond that range, such as the sites in western Maryland, are included because they have unusual habitats and species for our area. Each site has been visited by the author of this section at least once and many have been explored over several years. Fellow field botanists, park naturalists, and other wildflower enthusiasts generously shared information about their favorite places.

The places to find wildflowers are organized first by state, then by physiographic region (Piedmont, Coastal Plain, mountains), and then by county. Within each county, the places are arranged along the major highway routes radiating out from the urban areas. For each site described, the following information is given: general location, habitats found there, monthly highlights of flowers blooming in different habitats, management of the place, and directions to the specific site.

One final caveat: plants change and places change. From year to year, some species bloom at different times. Some wildflowers may even completely disappear from a site. A few places described in this book could be closed due to park budget constraints. Other places may have been destroyed by road or building construction. It is a good idea to call before you visit a site to find out what days and hours the site is open and if any fee is charged.

4

Maryland Piedmont

Washington, D.C., and Montgomery County

WASHINGTON: WITHIN THE CITY

Washington, called "city in the woods" by the Audubon Naturalist Society in 1953, is richly endowed with parks and natural places. Despite a burgeoning population and the intense development of surrounding areas, many green places still exist within the city.

Like many other cities of the eastern United States, Washington is located on the fall line between the Piedmont and the Coastal Plain. The broad Potomac River flows through both regions along the city's western edge.

Washington is surrounded by Maryland's Montgomery and Prince George's counties to the north and east, and Virginia's Arlington and Fairfax counties to the west.

Major roads leading to natural areas in the city include the Clara Barton Parkway and MacArthur Boulevard near the river, the George Washington Memorial Parkway in Virginia, Rock Creek Parkway and Beach Drive through Rock Creek Park, and New York Avenue (US-50) to the east. The Capital Beltway (I-495) encircles the city, passing through its Maryland and Virginia suburbs.

Roosevelt Island

Theodore Roosevelt Island is an 88-acre park in the Potomac River directly across from the Kennedy Center. Although a major highway bridge bisects the island and airplanes roar overhead, the park is a peaceful oasis in the heart of the busy city.

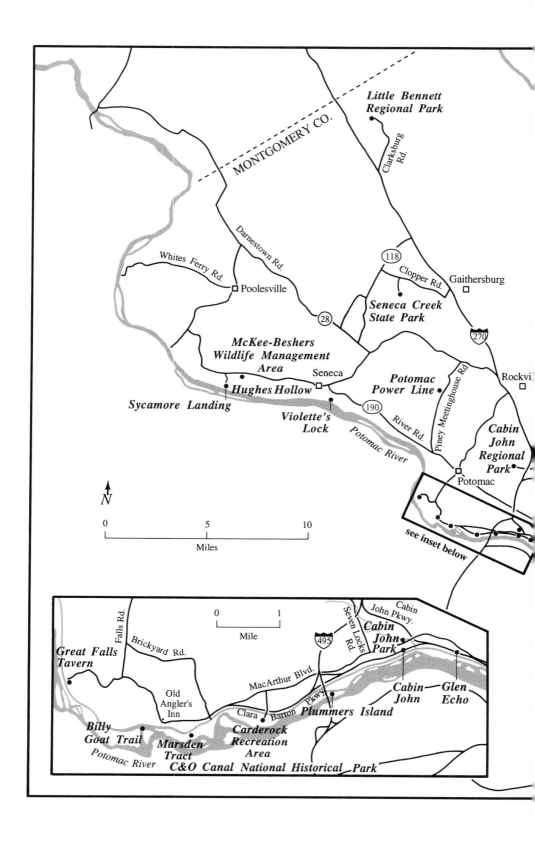

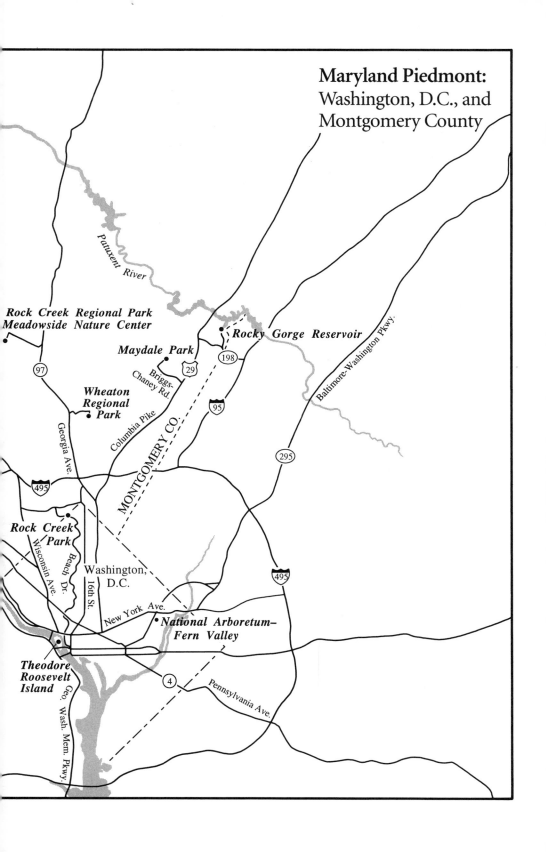

Maryland Piedmont:
Washington, D.C., and
Montgomery County

Patuxent River

Rock Creek Regional Park
Meadowside Nature Center

Maydale Park

Rocky Gorge Reservoir

(198)

(29)

(97)

Briggs-
Chaney Rd.

Wheaton
Regional
Park

Columbia Pike

(95)

MONTGOMERY CO.

Baltimore-Washington Pkwy.

Georgia Ave.

(295)

(495)

Rock Creek
Park

Beach Dr.

Wisconsin Ave.

16th St.

Washington,
D.C.

(495)

New York Ave.

National Arboretum–
Fern Valley

Theodore
Roosevelt
Island

Geo. Wash. Mem. Pkwy.

(4)

Pennsylvania Ave.

Roosevelt Island contains several natural habitats, including a tidal freshwater marsh, shrub swamp, and bottomland woods. Three trails wander the length of the island and a short bridge crosses the marsh. Just north of the marsh, the fall line is obvious as a sudden dip in the trail.

Trees on the island include typical bottomland species such as sycamore, green ash, silver maple, and red maple. Bald-cypress, a tree of southern swamps, has been planted in the swamp here. Among the wetland shrubs are silky dogwood (*Cornus amomum*) and buttonbush (*Cephalanthus occidentalis*).

In April, the moist woods bloom with trout-lily (*Erythronium americanum*), spring beauty (*Claytonia virginica*), lesser celandine (*Ranunculus ficaria*), cut-leaved toothwort (*Dentaria laciniata*), and golden ragwort (*Senecio aureus*). In early May, look for smooth Solomon's-seal (*Polygonatum biflorum*) and false Solomon's-seal (*Smilacina racemosa*).

During May, the wetlands flower with sweetflag (*Acorus calamus*), arrow arum (*Peltandra virginica*), and yellow iris (*Iris pseudacorus*). Later-blooming marsh plants include broad-leaved arrowhead (*Sagittaria latifolia*), spatterdock (*Nuphar advena*), pickerelweed (*Pontederia cordata*), swamp rose mallow (*Hibiscus moscheutos*), halberd-leaved tearthumb (*Polygonum arifolium*), and arrow-leaved tearthumb (*Polygonum sagittatum*).

In summer, the open areas have field flowers such as Deptford pink (*Dianthus armeria*), white sweet clover (*Melilotus alba*), field chamomile (*Anthemis arvensis*), and ox-eye daisy (*Chrysanthemum leucanthemum*).

The marsh reaches its height of color in September with the blooming of white turtlehead (*Chelone glabra*), yellow sneezeweed (*Helenium autumnale*), New York ironweed (*Vernonia noveboracensis*), and hollow Joe-Pye-weed (*Eupatorium fistulosum*).

Theodore Roosevelt Island is managed by the National Park Service as part of the George Washington Memorial Parkway. A comfort station is located along the trail to the marsh.

Directions: Roosevelt Island is accessible only from the northbound lanes of the George Washington Memorial Parkway in Virginia. From downtown Washington, cross the river on the Roosevelt Bridge or Memorial Bridge to the northbound parkway. The Roosevelt Island parking area is the first exit on the right. A footbridge leads across the river to the island.

Rock Creek Park — Boundary Bridge

Washington's Rock Creek Park is the largest urban natural park in the country. Containing almost 1,800 acres, the park follows the watershed of Rock Creek from the District of Columbia–Maryland line through northwest Washington to the Potomac River.

The Boundary Bridge area is located at the northern end of Rock Creek Park near the District line. For a place only six miles from the White House, this area is remarkably rich in early spring wildflowers. The mature forest contains several different habitats: bottomlands along Rock Creek, a small swamp, and rocky upland woods. Horse trails and walking trails meander through the area, but you can see the most wildflowers by crossing the bridge and following the main trail to the left.

Late March to late April are the times to walk here, for the flowers pass quickly, and Japanese honeysuckle, poison ivy, and English ivy soon take over the woodlands.

Skunk cabbage (*Symplocarpus foetidus*), the earliest plant to flower, is abundant in the swampy area between the creek and the main trail. In some years, the purple-spotted hoods can be found poking through the ice in January or February. By late March, spring beauty (*Claytonia virginica*) and lesser celandine (*Ranunculus ficaria*) carpet the forest floor, bloodroot (*Sanguinaria canadensis*) brightens the upland woods, and round-lobed hepatica (*Hepatica americana*) flowers high up on the rocks.

Mid-April brings a fine display of Virginia bluebells (*Mertensia virginica*) in the moist soil along the creek. Trout-lily (*Erythronium americanum*) and smooth yellow violet (*Viola pensylvanica*) provide a golden contrast to the bluebells, and there is a small population of Dutchman's breeches (*Dicentra cucullaria*). Unfortunately, the introduced lesser celandine has been crowding out these native wildflowers in the bottomlands.

Wild ginger (*Asarum canadense*), star chickweed (*Stellaria pubera*), rue-anemone (*Anemonella thalictroides*), and cut-leaved toothwort (*Dentaria laciniata*) flower on the hillsides, while early saxifrage (*Saxifraga virginiensis*) and alumroot (*Heuchera americana*) bloom on the rocks. A few plants of lemon-scented yellow trillium (*Trillium luteum*) are found along the trail. This species, native to the southern Appalachians, may have spread into the woods from nearby gardens.

By late April, Jack-in-the-pulpit (*Arisaema triphyllum*), perfoliate bellwort (*Uvularia perfoliata*), smooth Solomon's-seal (*Polygonatum biflorum*), Mayapple (*Podophyllum peltatum*), sweet cicely (*Osmorhiza claytoni*), and golden ragwort (*Senecio aureus*) bloom along the main trail. In a moist ravine just off the trail, the large golden flowers of celandine poppy (*Stylophorum diphyllum*) are interspersed with wild blue phlox (*Phlox divaricata*) and pale violet (*Viola striata*). The poppy, native to midwestern states, is rare in our area and may have naturalized from local gardens.

The Boundary Bridge area in Rock Creek Park is managed by the National Park Service. Information is available at the Rock Creek Nature Center, 5200 Glover Road, Washington, DC 20015; telephone (202)426-6829.

Directions: From 16th Street or Connecticut Avenue, take East-West Highway (MD-410) to Beach Drive. Go south on Beach Drive for one mile. When you see the sign for Rock Creek Park, turn left into a small parking lot. The Boundary Bridge area can be reached from downtown Washington via Beach Drive on weekdays, but this section of the road is closed to cars on weekends.

National Arboretum — Fern Valley

The National Arboretum is a 440-acre botanical garden located in northeast Washington. The arboretum is famous for its display of flowering azaleas and dogwoods and its fine collection of bonsai and specialty gardens. A less well-known attraction of the arboretum is Fern Valley, a natural wooded area planted with shrubs, ferns, and wildflowers native to the eastern United States. Next to the woods is a meadow planted with native and naturalized species of this habitat.

In Fern Valley, you can see plants native to different eastern regions such as the southern Appalachian Mountains, mid-Atlantic Piedmont, and New England forests. Fern Valley is a fine place to learn to recognize different species because they are labeled and easily observed.

In April and May, several plants indigenous to the southern Appalachians are in flower, including yellow trillium (*Trillium luteum*), galax (*Galax aphylla*), shortia (*Shortia galacifolia*), creeping phlox (*Phlox stolonifera*), foamflower (*Tiarella cordifolia*), and Virginia heartleaf (*Asarum virginicum*).

Spring flowers of the Piedmont region include sessile trillium (*Trillium sessile*), wild ginger (*Asarum canadense*), wild columbine (*Aquilegia cana-*

densis), rue-anemone (*Anemonella thalictroides*), wild geranium (*Geranium maculatum*), Virginia bluebells (*Mertensia virginica*), wild blue phlox (*Phlox divaricata*), and chrysogonum (*Chrysogonum virginianum*).

The northern forest is represented by large-flowered trillium (*Trillium grandiflorum*), erect trillium (*Trillium erectum*), nodding trillium (*Trillium cernuum*), Canada Mayflower (*Maianthemum canadense*), marsh marigold (*Caltha palustris*), sharp-lobed hepatica (*Hepatica acutiloba*), white bane-berry (*Actaea alba*), and miterwort (*Mitella diphylla*).

During June, the woodland flowers fade but the nearby meadow comes into its own with butterflyweed (*Asclepias tuberosa*), narrow-leaved moun-tain-mint (*Pycnanthemum tenuifolium*), wild bergamot (*Monarda fistu-losa*), white beardtongue (*Penstemon digitalis*), ox-eye daisy (*Chrysanthe-mum leucanthemum*), and black-eyed Susan (*Rudbeckia hirta*). In July and August, wet areas of the meadow bloom with swamp milkweed (*Asclepias incarnata*), cardinal flower (*Lobelia cardinalis*), New York ironweed (*Ver-nonia noveboracensis*), and purple-stemmed aster (*Aster puniceus*).

Many other plants have been introduced to both the wooded valley and the open meadow. Fern Valley is interesting at any time of year.

The National Arboretum is operated by the U.S. Department of Agri-culture and is located at 3501 New York Avenue, NE, Washington, DC 20002; telephone (202)475-4815.

Directions: From New York Avenue (US-50), go south on Bladensburg Road for a few blocks and turn left on R Street to the Arboretum entrance. Bear right and follow the signs for the Fern Valley parking area.

MONTGOMERY COUNTY: THE POTOMAC RIVER VALLEY

Maryland's Montgomery County lies just northwest of Washington. From the Potomac River on the west to its border with Prince George's County on the east, the county epitomizes the rolling terrain of the Pied-mont region. The areas along the river have nutrient-rich alluvial soil, a wide variety of habitats, and a very diverse flora.

In the Piedmont region, the Maryland shore of the Potomac is lower and more eroded than the Virginia shore, but many habitats and species are common to both sides of the river. Several plants rare in both states are found along the Potomac River in this region, including white trout-lily

(*Erythronium albidum*), blue false indigo (*Baptisia australis*), Coville's phacelia (*Phacelia ranunculacea*), few-flowered valerian (*Valeriana pauciflora*), and river bank goldenrod (*Solidago racemosa*).

Montgomery County's shore of the Potomac River is easily accessible to walkers and naturalists by way of the C&O Canal towpath. In lower Montgomery County, the towpath usually is approached from MacArthur Boulevard or the Clara Barton Parkway; north of Great Falls, it is reached from River Road.

C&O Canal National Historical Park

The C&O Canal National Historical Park stretches for 185 miles along the Maryland shore of the Potomac River. From Georgetown in Washington, D.C., to Cumberland in western Maryland, the canal and its towpath provide public access to the river and a nearly level walkway through rich deciduous woods. Established in 1971, the park preserves both history and nature.

The water-filled section of the canal from Georgetown to Seneca is used by fishermen, paddlers, and ice skaters, while the towpath is used by hikers, runners, and bikers. The rich woods along the river are favorite haunts of botanists, birders, and other naturalists.

This long, narrow park has many diverse habitats such as alluvial floodplains, moist woodlands, and high rocky bluffs. The Potomac River gorge, between Little Falls and Great Falls, has an exceptionally large variety of habitats. Many plants rare in Maryland occur in this part of the park, including racemed milkwort (*Polygala polygama*), false gromwell (*Onosmodium virginianum*), rock skullcap (*Scutellaria saxatilis*), tall coreopsis (*Coreopsis tripteris*), and western sunflower (*Helianthus occidentalis*).

In Montgomery County, the canal traverses the Piedmont region of the Potomac River Valley. Many of the best wildflower areas along the river are part of the C&O Canal National Historical Park, including Glen Echo, Cabin John, Carderock, Marsden Tract, Billy Goat Trail, Great Falls Tavern, and Violette's Lock. For areas farther west on the C&O Canal, see Chapter 7, Maryland Mountains.

The C&O Canal National Historical Park is managed by the National Park Service. The Great Falls Tavern Visitor Center serves as the headquarters for the park between Georgetown and Edward's Ferry. It is located at

11710 MacArthur Boulevard, Potomac, MD 20854; telephone (301)299-3613. Informative pamphlets, maps, and books may be obtained at the visitor center.

Glen Echo, Cabin John, and Plummers Island

The section of the C&O Canal National Historical Park between Glen Echo and Seven Locks runs parallel to the Clara Barton Parkway inside the Capital Beltway. Areas between the Potomac River and the towpath, such as Glen Echo, Cabin John, and Plummers Island, are well worth exploring. The bottomland woods along the river have fine wildflower displays in early spring.

In early April to mid-April, you can find trout-lily (*Erythronium americanum*), spring beauty (*Claytonia virginica*), cut-leaved toothwort (*Dentaria laciniata*), Dutchman's breeches (*Dicentra cucullaria*), common blue violet (*Viola papilionacea*), wild blue phlox (*Phlox divaricata*), and golden ragwort (*Senecio aureus*). White trout-lily (*Erythronium albidum*), a midwestern species not often seen in our area, also is found along the floodplain here.

In low-lying places near the river, there are masses of Virginia bluebells (*Mertensia virginica*), as well as sessile trillium (*Trillium sessile*) and Jack-in-the-pulpit (*Arisaema triphyllum*).

Near the lockhouse at Lock 11 is a narrow trail leading through the woods to Plummers Island, a 15-acre island donated to the park by the Washington Biologists' Field Club. The island is usually inaccessible from the river shore, but in times of low water, you may be able to pick your way across the rocks to this well-studied place. If you make it over to the island, be sure to hike up to the cabin on the high bluffs for a wonderful view of the Potomac River and the Virginia Palisades.

Plummers Island has many of the same early spring wildflowers as other places along the river in this region, including some less common ones such as harbinger-of-spring (*Erigenia bulbosa*), twinleaf (*Jeffersonia diphylla*), golden Alexanders (*Zizia aurea*), and Coville's phacelia (*Phacelia ranunculacea*).

In midsummer, look in wet places near the canal and river for arrow arum (*Peltandra virginica*), lizard's-tail (*Saururus cernuus*), tall meadowrue (*Thalictrum pubescens*), swamp milkweed (*Asclepias incarnata*), square-stemmed monkey-flower (*Mimulus ringens*), water willow (*Justicia americana*), and cardinal flower (*Lobelia cardinalis*). Late summer flowers in this area include mad-dog skullcap (*Scutellaria lateriflora*), great lobelia (*Lobelia siphilitica*), New York ironweed (*Vernonia noveboracensis*), thin-leaved sunflower (*Helianthus decapetalus*), and green-headed coneflower (*Rudbeckia laciniata*).

The National Park Service manages this stretch of the C&O Canal National Historical Park through the park office at Great Falls Tavern. For more information, contact the C&O Canal National Historical Park, 11710 MacArthur Boulevard, Potomac, MD 20854; telephone (301)299-3613.

Directions: From the westbound Clara Barton Parkway, you must turn around at Carderock to access the eastbound lane of the parkway. Park at Lock 10 and walk upriver for Plummers Island; park at Lock 8 and walk downriver for Cabin John; and park at Lock 7 for Glen Echo.

Carderock Recreation Area

Carderock Recreation Area, part of the C&O Canal National Historical Park, is located on the Potomac River just outside the Capital Beltway. There are extensive playing fields and picnic grounds, and the area is heavily used for recreational purposes. Natural features include rocky bluffs, moist hillsides, and a narrow band of bottomland woods.

Like other areas along the river, Carderock gives its best wildflower display in mid-April to late April. Masses of wild blue phlox (*Phlox divaricata*) and golden ragwort (*Senecio aureus*) flower on the hillsides, along with wild ginger (*Asarum canadense*), spring beauty (*Claytonia virginica*), cut-leaved toothwort (*Dentaria laciniata*), yellow corydalis (*Corydalis flavula*), Dutchman's breeches (*Dicentra cucullaria*), squirrel corn (*Dicentra canadensis*), smooth yellow violet (*Viola pensylvanica*), and Virginia bluebells (*Mertensia virginica*).

On the rock outcrops are star chickweed (*Stellaria pubera*), smooth rockcress (*Arabis laevigata*), wild stonecrop (*Sedum ternatum*), and early saxifrage (*Saxifraga virginiensis*).

The blooming continues in early May with the flowering of smooth Solomon's-seal (*Polygonatum biflorum*), false Solomon's-seal (*Smilacina racemosa*), early meadowrue (*Thalictrum dioicum*), bulbous buttercup (*Ranunculus bulbosus*), Mayapple (*Podophyllum peltatum*), and wild geranium (*Geranium maculatum*). In the dry woods at the top of the bluffs grow bastard toadflax (*Comandra umbellata*), field chickweed (*Cerastium arvense*), bluets (*Houstonia caerulea*), plantain-leaved pussytoes (*Antennaria plantaginifolia*), and rattlesnake-weed (*Hieracium venosum*).

In mid-May, look for lyre-leaved sage (*Salvia lyrata*) in dry open areas and lyre-leaved rockcress (*Arabis lyrata*) on the exposed rocks above the river. A high rock outcrop shelters a colony of Miami mist (*Phacelia purshii*), and the woods are filled with Virginia waterleaf (*Hydrophyllum virginianum*).

Carderock Recreation Area is managed by the National Park Service through the park office at Great Falls Tavern. For more information, contact the C&O National Historical Park, 11710 MacArthur Boulevard, Potomac, MD 20854; telephone (301)299-3613.

Directions: From the Capital Beltway (I-495), take the Clara Barton Parkway west for almost one mile. Exit at the sign for Carderock and turn left into the recreation area. There are three large parking lots, and all have interlocking trails that are useful for wildflower exploration. The last lot to the right also provides access to the Marsden Tract via the towpath.

Marsden Tract

Marsden Tract, on the C&O Canal just upriver from Carderock, is a wonderful wildflower area with many diverse habitats such as old fields, moist woodlands, dry open uplands, rock outcrops, and bluffs along the river. The presence of calcareous-habitat plants such as twinleaf (*Jeffersonia diphylla*) and green violet (*Hybanthus concolor*) indicates that the soil is less acidic than usual in the Piedmont region.

Marsden is a good place to visit at the end of March to look for early bloomers such as spring beauty (*Claytonia virginica*), round-lobed hepatica (*Hepatica americana*), twinleaf, and harbinger-of-spring (*Erigenia bulbosa*).

Early April brings an explosion of wildflowers, including trout-lily (*Erythronium americanum*), sessile trillium (*Trillium sessile*), star chickweed (*Stellaria pubera*), rue-anemone (*Anemonella thalictroides*), bloodroot (*Sanguinaria canadensis*), yellow corydalis (*Corydalis flavula*), Dutchman's breeches (*Dicentra cucullaria*), cut-leaved toothwort (*Dentaria laciniata*), slender toothwort (*Dentaria heterophylla*), and early saxifrage (*Saxifraga virginiensis*). The small Coville's phacelia (*Phacelia ranunculacea*), a midwestern species found along the Potomac River in our area, occurs at Marsden and a few other nearby areas.

Hepatica americana —
Round-lobed hepatica
(height: 4″–6″)

In mid-April, many of these flowers continue to bloom and are joined by golden Alexanders (*Zizia aurea*), Virginia bluebells (*Mertensia virginica*), wild blue phlox (*Phlox divaricata*), and golden ragwort (*Senecio aureus*).

Return to Marsden in early May to check rock outcrops for the unusual green violet and search in swampy places for green dragon (*Arisaema dracontium*), a close relative of Jack-in-the-pulpit (*Arisaema triphyllum*). Other uncommon plants at Marsden include veiny pea (*Lathyrus venosus*) and hairy beardtongue (*Penstemon hirsutus*) on the open bluffs, Miami mist (*Phacelia purshii*) in the moist woods, and few-flowered valerian (*Valeriana pauciflora*) on the floodplain.

In mid-May, the grassy field at the picnic area is filled with the colorful blossoms of bulbous buttercup (*Ranunculus bulbosus*), Carolina cranesbill (*Geranium carolinianum*), and lyre-leaved sage (*Salvia lyrata*). In the dry woods near the campground are field chickweed (*Cerastium arvense*), three-lobed violet (*Viola triloba*), and hairy skullcap (*Scutellaria elliptica*).

Marsden Tract is part of the C&O Canal National Historical Park and is managed by the National Park Service. Because it has no recreational facilities or parking lots, Marsden Tract draws fewer visitors than other areas in this part of the park. For more information, contact the park office at 11710 MacArthur Boulevard, Potomac, MD 20854; telephone (301)299-3613.

Directions: From the Capital Beltway (I-495), take the Clara Barton Parkway west. Where the parkway ends, turn left on MacArthur Boulevard. Go about one-half mile, pass Brickyard Road on the right, and turn around to park along the south side of MacArthur Boulevard. Cross the canal on the wooden bridge, turn either left or right on the towpath, and take a blue-blazed trail down toward the river. As a parking alternative, you can park at the last lot at Carderock and walk upriver on the towpath for about one-half mile to the wooden bridge.

Billy Goat Trail

The Billy Goat Trail is located on high rocky bluffs along the Potomac River just below Great Falls. The two-mile trail climbs along the bluffs and ravines of Bear Island and offers magnificent views of Mather Gorge and the Virginia Palisades.

Billy Goat Trail is aptly named, for it involves considerable scrambling over rocks, climbing up large boulders, and occasional rock-hopping. In times of heavy rain or flooding, low areas of the trail may be wet and muddy. This rugged riverside trail connects with the C&O Canal towpath at each end.

The many different habitats include rocky bluffs, high wooded terraces, moist hillsides, deep ravines, small ponds, alluvial floodplains, and river-scoured rocks. This variety of habitats supports a rich diversity of flowering plants all year.

In late March and early April, the flower show begins on Billy Goat Trail. If the days have been warm and sunny, spring beauty (*Claytonia virginica*), twinleaf (*Jeffersonia diphylla*), bloodroot (*Sanguinaria canadensis*), cut-leaved toothwort (*Dentaria laciniata*), slender toothwort (*Dentaria heterophylla*), and harbinger-of-spring (*Erigenia bulbosa*) may all be in bloom.

The lower end of Billy Goat Trail, near the Widewater section of the canal, is a particularly good area for wildflowers. In mid-April, the ravines harbor sessile trillium (*Trillium sessile*), trout-lily (*Erythronium americanum*), wild ginger (*Asarum canadense*), Dutchman's breeches (*Dicentra cucullaria*), squirrel corn (*Dicentra canadensis*), and the rare Coville's phacelia (*Phacelia ranunculacea*).

In late April, a rocky cove at the first stream crossing is filled with field chickweed (*Cerastium arvense*), swamp buttercup (*Ranunculus septentrionalis*), wild geranium (*Geranium maculatum*), pale violet (*Viola striata*), and golden Alexanders (*Zizia aurea*). Small-flowered phacelia (*Phacelia dubia*) blooms at the top of the bluff.

Along the river, the sandy floodplains and even the moist hillsides are carpeted with Virginia bluebells (*Mertensia virginica*) and wild blue phlox (*Phlox divaricata*).

On the dry upland terraces, you can find bastard toadflax (*Comandra umbellata*), wild pink (*Silene caroliniana*), ovate-leaved violet (*Viola fimbriatula*), violet wood-sorrel (*Oxalis violacea*), bluets (*Houstonia caerulea*), and plantain-leaved pussytoes (*Antennaria plantaginifolia*). Wild columbine (*Aquilegia canadensis*) and alumroot (*Heuchera americana*) grow on the rocky bluffs, and moss phlox (*Phlox subulata*) flowers on the bare rocks along the riverbank.

Rock outcrops in the woods are habitat for lyre-leaved rockcress (*Arabis lyrata*) and spreading rockcress (*Arabis patens*), while the rich woodland soil harbors perfoliate bellwort (*Uvularia perfoliata*) and wood anemone (*Anemone quinquefolia*).

In early May, look on the moist hillsides for Miami mist (*Phacelia purshii*) and chrysogonum (*Chrysogonum virginianum*). Wild stonecrop (*Sedum ternatum*) blooms on the bare rocks, and lyre-leaved sage (*Salvia lyrata*) and rattlesnake-weed (*Hieracium venosum*) flower on the dry terraces.

June bloomers in the terrace forest include state-rare species such as rock skullcap (*Scutellaria saxatilis*) and false gromwell (*Onosmodium virginianum*). Out on the rocks of Bear Island are other rare species including blue false indigo (*Baptisia australis*) and racemed milkwort (*Polygala polygama*), as well as more common plants such as leatherflower (*Clematis viorna*) and goat's-rue (*Tephrosia virginiana*).

In July and August, look in marshy areas along the canal for halberd-leaved rose mallow (*Hibiscus laevis*), swamp rose mallow (*Hibiscus moscheutos*), swamp milkweed (*Asclepias incarnata*), and square-stemmed monkey-flower (*Mimulus ringens*). September flowers along the towpath include thin-leaved sunflower (*Helianthus decapetalus*), blue-stemmed goldenrod (*Solidago caesia*), and silverrod (*Solidago bicolor*).

Even in October, you can find plants flowering along the Billy Goat Trail. White wood aster (*Aster divaricatus*), paniculed aster (*Aster lanceolatus*), heart-leaved aster (*Aster cordifolius*), and wavy-leaved aster (*Aster undulatus*) still bloom in the woods. On the rocky bluffs near the river, late purple aster (*Aster patens*) and riverbank goldenrod (*Solidago racemosa*) are in flower. The rare riverbank goldenrod is found in rock crevices on both the Maryland and Virginia shores near Great Falls.

Billy Goat Trail is part of the C&O Canal National Historical Park. The area is managed by the National Park Service, although the trail itself is maintained by the Potomac Appalachian Trail Club. For information, contact the park office at Great Falls Tavern, 11701 MacArthur Boulevard, Potomac, MD 20854; telephone (301)299-3613.

Directions: From the Capital Beltway (I-495), take the Clara Barton Parkway west. Where the parkway ends, turn left on MacArthur Boulevard and go one mile to the dirt parking lot opposite Old Angler's Inn. Walk upriver on the towpath to the blue-blazed trail on the left, the lower end of Billy Goat Trail. The upper end of the trail can be reached by walking downriver one-half mile from Great Falls Tavern.

Great Falls Tavern

From the Maryland shore, the Great Falls of the Potomac River appear as a series of rapids, cascades, and chutes. With such scenic beauty, the area around the Great Falls Tavern on the C&O Canal is popular with the general public as well as hikers, bikers, botanists, and birders.

The towpath along the canal is the main trail in the area but many other trails branch off the towpath toward the river. Behind the visitor center, a trail meanders up through the wooded hillside of the Gold Mine Tract. The very rocky Billy Goat Trail joins the towpath one-half mile below the visitor center. The bridges and walkways to Olmstead Island, destroyed by Hurricane Agnes in 1972, were rebuilt and reopened in 1992. Attractive signs along the walkways point out unusual habitats and rare plants such as blue false indigo (*Baptisia australis*) and riverbank goldenrod (*Solidago racemosa*).

At Great Falls, the many diverse habitats include open rocky bluffs, high wooded terraces, grassy glades, alluvial floodplains, small wetlands around the woodland ponds, and even tiny marshes in the rock potholes. Habitats unusual in the east are found on the islands and include dry oak-pine savannas reminiscent of midwestern prairies and bedrock floodplains with little alluvial soil. According to the Maryland Natural Heritage Program, the Maryland side of Great Falls has outstanding examples of these unusual habitats and is one of the most diverse areas under National Park Service management in the mid-Atlantic states.

Spring flowering begins early at Great Falls. In late March the tiny harbinger-of-spring (*Erigenia bulbosa*) can be found along the floodplain above the falls. This small early bloomer occurs mainly along Potomac River bottomlands in our area. Other early flowers such as spring beauty (*Claytonia virginica*), round-lobed hepatica (*Hepatica americana*), blood-root (*Sanguinaria canadensis*), and trailing arbutus (*Epigaea repens*) are scattered in the upland woods.

In late April and early May, the rocky hillsides turn rosy with wild pink (*Silene caroliniana*) and moss phlox (*Phlox subulata*) beneath the pinxter flower (*Rhododendron periclymenoides*). Flowers in the uplands include bastard toadflax (*Comandra umbellata*), rue-anemone (*Anemonella thalictroides*), early saxifrage (*Saxifraga virginiensis*), birdfoot violet (*Viola pedata*), bluets (*Houstonia caerulea*), and rattlesnake-weed (*Hieracium venosum*).

During May, the rocky woods near the rapids harbor spiderwort (*Tradescantia virginiana*), smooth Solomon's-seal (*Polygonatum biflorum*), false Solomon's-seal (*Smilacina racemosa*), field chickweed (*Cerastium arvense*), golden Alexanders (*Zizia aurea*), and wild blue phlox (*Phlox divaricata*). On the high terrace overlooking the river grow wild geranium (*Geranium maculatum*), violet wood-sorrel (*Oxalis violacea*), lyre-leaved sage (*Salvia lyrata*), round-leaved ragwort (*Senecio obovatus*), chrysogonum (*Chrysogonum virginianum*), and robin's plantain (*Erigeron pulchellus*).

Look in low seepy areas for Jack-in-the-pulpit (*Arisaema triphyllum*) and its uncommon cousin, green dragon (*Arisaema dracontium*), and search the open rocks for lyre-leaved rockcress (*Arabis lyrata*), alumroot (*Heuchera americana*), and wild stonecrop (*Sedum ternatum*).

In June, the rocky bluffs still bloom with leatherflower (*Clematis viorna*), goat's-rue (*Tephrosia virginiana*), hairy skullcap (*Scutellaria elliptica*), large-leaved houstonia (*Houstonia purpurea*), and Venus's looking-glass (*Triodanis perfoliata*). The big northern iris called larger blue flag (*Iris versicolor*) flowers in a woodland pond near the towpath, and tasselrue (*Trautvetteria caroliniensis*), a southern Appalachian species, blooms in a cool seep high above the river. In late June, look in the rocky woods for the first of the sunflowers, woodland sunflower (*Helianthus divaricatus*).

In July and August, square-stemmed monkey-flower (*Mimulus ringens*), white turtlehead (*Chelone glabra*), and cardinal flower (*Lobelia cardinalis*) bloom in marshy areas around the ponds. Out on the open rocks of the islands, look for tall coreopsis (*Coreopsis tripteris*) and western sunflower (*Helianthus occidentalis*), a midwestern species that is rare in our area.

September brings asters and goldenrods such as heart-leaved aster (*Aster cordifolius*), white wood aster (*Aster divaricatus*), calico aster (*Aster lateriflorus*), early goldenrod (*Solidago juncea*), rough-stemmed goldenrod (*Solidago rugosa*), and lance-leaved goldenrod (*Solidago graminifolia*). October bloomers include late purple aster (*Aster patens*), stiff aster (*Aster linariifolius*), aromatic aster (*Aster oblongifolius*), zigzag goldenrod (*Solidago flexicaulis*), silverrod (*Solidago bicolor*), and riverbank goldenrod (*Solidago racemosa*), a rare species which in our area is found only on the rocky bluffs of the Potomac River gorge.

Great Falls Tavern is part of the C&O Canal National Historical Park and is administered by the National Park Service. The Great Falls Tavern serves as headquarters for all of the park between Georgetown and Edward's Ferry. It is located at 11710 MacArthur Boulevard, Potomac, MD 20854; telephone (301)299-3613.

A visitor center and museum in the historical tavern are open all year. There is plentiful parking but the area is often very crowded, particularly on mild spring weekends. Wildflower walks are held year-round and records kept by volunteer leaders show the changes in wildflower populations over many years.

Directions: From the Capital Beltway (I-495), take the Clara Barton Parkway west until it ends at MacArthur Boulevard. Turn left on MacArthur and continue for about three miles until the road ends at the Great Falls Tavern.

Violette's Lock

Violette's Lock is on the C&O Canal about one mile downriver from the Seneca area. Although the wide section of the Potomac River at Seneca is a center for recreational boating, the Violette's Lock area has been left natural and undeveloped. Turn left on the towpath, and look for the narrow trail to the river.

In late March, the diminutive harbinger-of-spring (*Erigenia bulbosa*) flowers in low moist areas in the woods, along with spring beauty (*Claytonia virginica*) and cut-leaved toothwort (*Dentaria laciniata*).

April wildflowers along the towpath here include wild ginger (*Asarum canadense*), Dutchman's breeches (*Dicentra cucullaria*), squirrel corn (*Di-

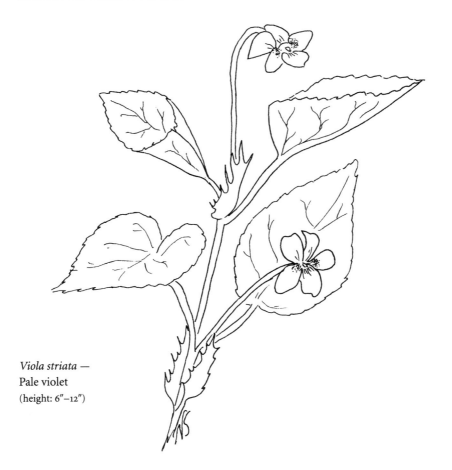

Viola striata —
Pale violet
(height: 6″–12″)

centra canadensis), common blue violet (*Viola papilionacea*), and pale violet (*Viola striata*). There is a large colony of sessile trillium (*Trillium sessile*), mostly maroon but some of the green form. And Violette's Lock is one of the locations along the Potomac River where white trout-lily (*Erythronium albidum*) can be found, as well as the more familiar trout-lily (*Erythronium americanum*).

By early May, the bottomlands along the river are carpeted with wild blue phlox (*Phlox divaricata*) and golden ragwort (*Senecio aureus*). In mid-May, the lovely Miami mist (*Phacelia purshii*) flowers in the woods while Kenilworth ivy (*Cymbalaria muralis*) and celandine (*Chelidonium majus*) bloom on the walls of the lock.

Late July is another good time to visit Violette's Lock. Turning right on the towpath, look along the canal for tall meadowrue (*Thalictrum pubescens*), fringed loosestrife (*Lysimachia ciliata*), pale jewelweed (*Impatiens pallida*), basil balm (*Monarda clinopodia*), pale-leaved sunflower (*Helianthus strumosus*), and sweet Joe-Pye-weed (*Eupatorium purpureum*). Broad-leaved arrowhead (*Sagittaria latifolia*), small water-plantain (*Alisma subcordatum*), and halberd-leaved rose mallow (*Hibiscus laevis*) bloom right in the canal bed.

On the mud flats and rocks beside the river and in shallow areas of the river itself grow water stargrass (*Heteranthera dubia*) and water willow (*Justicia americana*). On the muddy riverbank are mad-dog skullcap (*Scutellaria lateriflora*) and fog-fruit (*Lippia lanceolata*).

Like other areas along the C&O Canal, the Violette's Lock area is managed by the National Park Service. For more information, contact the Great Falls Tavern, 11710 MacArthur Boulevard, Potomac, MD 20854; telephone (301)299-3613.

Directions: Take River Road (MD-190) from Potomac for eight miles and turn left on Violette's Lock Road. The alternative spelling, Violet's Lock, indicates the lock may have been named for the profusion of violets around it, but the more common theory is that it was named for a lockkeeper, Mrs. Alfred L. Violette.

McKee-Beshers Wildlife Management Area

The 2,000-acre McKee-Beshers Wildlife Management Area adjoins the C&O Canal west of Seneca. The old farmlands and forests are managed primarily for gamebird hunting, but the diversity of habitats makes the area excellent for birding, botanizing, and general nature study. Different habitats are found at different sites, such as bottomland forest at Sycamore Landing, open fields and wetlands at Hughes Hollow, and rocky hillsides along River Road at the west end of the management area.

Sycamore Landing abuts the C&O Canal with easy access to the towpath and the Potomac River. In mid-April, the floodplain between the canal and the river has a fine show of early spring wildflowers. As the canal is not filled with water beyond Seneca, the vegetation in this area literally spills into the old canal bed.

From the end of Sycamore Landing Road, a right turn on the towpath will bring you to a blue haze of Virginia bluebells (*Mertensia virginica*) interspersed with trout-lily (*Erythronium americanum*), the rarer white trout-lily (*Erythronium albidum*), sessile trillium (*Trillium sessile*), spring beauty (*Claytonia virginica*), Dutchman's breeches (*Dicentra cucullaria*), and squirrel corn (*Dicentra canadensis*). An unusual meadowrue here has deep red pistillate flowers. Originally thought to be a separate species, Steele's meadowrue, it is now considered a lowland form of leatherleaf meadowrue (*Thalictrum coriaceum*).

Driving west on River Road from Sycamore Landing Road, the road narrows and the wooded hillside on the right becomes steep and rocky. In early May, the moist areas along the road have several uncommon plants, including green dragon (*Arisaema dracontium*), dwarf larkspur (*Delphinium tricorne*), spring avens (*Geum vernum*), and Miami mist (*Phacelia purshii*). About one-half mile from Sycamore Landing Road, look on the right for a high rock outcrop. These red siltstone rocks have a grand display of wild columbine (*Aquilegia canadensis*), wild pink (*Silene caroliniana*), thyme-leaved sandwort (*Arenaria serpyllifolia*), lyre-leaved rockcress (*Arabis lyrata*), yellow pimpernel (*Taenidia integerrima*), and round-leaved ragwort (*Senecio obovatus*).

One of the few places in Montgomery County where open fields are maintained, Hughes Hollow is a good place to find sun-loving summer wildflowers. Other habitats to explore include two large ponds that have become nontidal marshes, swamp-like forested wetlands, and bottomland woods along the canal. Hughes Hollow is accessed from Hughes Road just east of Sycamore Landing Road.

From mid-July to mid-August, the fields and ponds at Hughes Hollow are filled with colorful summer flowers. Over 50 species can be found in bloom on a single day. Flowers of the open fields include rose pink (*Sabatia angularis*), common evening-primrose (*Oenothera biennis*), white vervain (*Verbena urticifolia*), American germander (*Teucrium canandense*), Indian tobacco (*Lobelia inflata*), teasel (*Dipsacus sylvestris*), black-eyed Susan (*Rudbeckia hirta*), and wingstem (*Verbesina alternifolia*).

Among the wetland plants in bloom in late summer are broad-leaved arrowhead (*Sagittaria latifolia*), pickerelweed (*Pontederia cordata*), lizard's-tail (*Saururus cernuus*), spatterdock (*Nuphar advena*), swamp rose mallow (*Hibiscus moscheutos*), halberd-leaved rose mallow (*Hibiscus laevis*), swamp milkweed (*Asclepias incarnata*), buttonbush (*Cephalanthus occidentalis*), and cardinal flower (*Lobelia cardinalis*).

A short drive to the siltstone outcrop on River Road reveals summer flowers of a completely different habitat. Several plants uncommon in the Maryland Piedmont are found here, including butterfly pea (*Clitoria*

Hibiscus moscheutos —
Swamp rose mallow
(height: 3′–6′)

mariana), prostrate tick-trefoil (*Desmodium rotundifolium*), tall bellflower (*Campanula americana*) and broad-leaved ironweed (*Vernonia glauca*).

The McKee-Beshers Wildlife Management Area is managed by the Maryland Department of Natural Resources, Wildlife Division. Although hunters use the area, usually the sound of gunshots is far away, and there is no conflict between the different uses. For more information, contact the Maryland Department of Natural Resources, Wildlife Division, Tawes State Office Building, 580 Taylor Avenue, Annapolis, MD 21401; telephone (410)974-3195 or the regional office in Seneca at (301)258-7308.

Directions: Take River Road (MD-190) through Potomac, turn left where River Road changes to MD-112 and continue to Seneca. Go past

Seneca for about three and one-half miles and turn left on Hughes Road for Hughes Hollow. Sycamore Landing Road is one-half mile past Hughes Road and is also a left turn from River Road. The road winds through the wildlife reserve before reaching the parking area at the canal. The rocky cliffs along River Road are found about one-half mile beyond Sycamore Landing Road. Parking is very limited in this section.

CENTRAL AND EASTERN MONTGOMERY COUNTY

Montgomery County is a highly developed suburban county. The down-county areas around Bethesda and Silver Spring have long been bedroom communities for Washington, and in recent years, even the up-county towns of Rockville and Gaithersburg have undergone intensive residential and commercial development.

However, Montgomery County has several large parks and many stream valleys designated as natural areas. The bottomland woods near the streams display many of the same wildflowers that are seen along the Potomac River on the western edge of the county. Other habitats in the central and eastern parts of the county include upland woods, dry meadows, wet meadows, and nontidal wetlands.

Three major highways lead from down-county to up-county; moving from west to east they are I-270, MD-97 (Georgia Avenue), and US-29 (Colesville Road–Columbia Pike).

Cabin John Stream Valley Park

The Cabin John Stream Valley Park protects the stream valley of Cabin John Creek through suburban Bethesda. The Cabin John Creek Trail begins at Cabin John Park near the creek's confluence with the Potomac River and follows the creek upstream to Cabin John Regional Park. A walk here could be combined with a trip to the Glen Echo and Cabin John sections of the C&O Canal.

The lower area of the stream valley has a fine showing of spring wildflowers similar to displays along other tributaries of the Potomac River in this region. In late April, the hillsides along the creek are filled with wild ginger (*Asarum canadense*), spring beauty (*Claytonia virginica*), round-lobed hepatica (*Hepatica americana*), rue-anemone (*Anemonella thalictroides*), Dutchman's breeches (*Dicentra cucullaria*), cut-leaved toothwort

(*Dentaria laciniata*), early saxifrage (*Saxifraga virginiensis*), wild blue phlox (*Phlox divaricata*), and golden ragwort (*Senecio aureus*).

The deep ravine of this stream valley also shelters several species that are less common in the Maryland Piedmont, such as wood anemone (*Anemone quinquefolia*), miterwort (*Mitella diphylla*), dwarf ginseng (*Panax trifolius*), Coville's phacelia (*Phacelia ranunculacea*), and the only known population of shooting star (*Dodecatheon meadia*) in Montgomery County. The presence of these flowers, plus a stand of eastern hemlock trees, as well as ostrich fern and broad beech fern, indicates a slightly cooler microclimate along this lower part of Cabin John Creek. This small habitat difference supports these plants that are more common north and west of the Piedmont region.

Cabin John Stream Valley Park is managed by the Maryland National Capital Park and Planning Commission. You can begin the Cabin John Creek Trail at Cabin John Park on MacArthur Boulevard in Cabin John. A small playground and tennis courts mark the park. For more information, contact the Maryland National Capital Park and Planning Commission, Montgomery County Department of Parks, 9500 Brunett Avenue, Silver Spring, MD 20901; telephone (301)495-2525.

Directions: Take MacArthur Boulevard west to the west end of the old stone Cabin John Bridge. Cabin John Park is on the right at the end of the bridge. The trail begins down the hill from the parking lot. The C&O Canal towpath can be reached by crossing MacArthur Boulevard and walking under the parkways.

Cabin John Regional Park

The 500-acre Cabin John Regional Park in northern Bethesda is maintained primarily for recreational uses but does have some nice natural trails through woodlands and open fields. Locust Grove Nature Center is located in the southern section of this park. The Cabin John Creek Trail winds along the creek for over four miles and connects this large park with the small Cabin John Park on MacArthur Boulevard in Cabin John.

From the nature center, the Meadow Trail winds through dry oak woods down to a wet meadow and a little wetland near the creek. Summer wildflowers found in the wet meadow include seedbox (*Ludwigia alternifolia*), square-stemmed monkey-flower (*Mimulus ringens*), wild mint (*Mentha arvensis*), mad-dog skullcap (*Scutellaria lateriflora*), boneset (*Eupatorium perfoliatum*), and a large stand of New York ironweed (*Vernonia noveboracensis*). Look in the tiny marsh for broad-leaved arrowhead (*Sagittaria latifolia*).

Some late summer bloomers in the woods are panicled tick-trefoil (*Desmodium paniculatum*), blue-stemmed goldenrod (*Solidago caesia*), early goldenrod (*Solidago juncea*), white wood aster (*Aster divaricatus*), calico aster (*Aster lateriflorus*), and lion's-foot (*Prenanthes serpentaria*).

In September and early October, many composites still flower along roadsides, in open fields, and under power lines. Where the power line runs through Cabin John Regional Park, several late-blooming species can be found, including a large colony of New England aster (*Aster novae-angliae*), as well as white heath aster (*Aster pilosus*), panicled aster (*Aster lanceolatus*), Maryland golden-aster (*Chrysopsis mariana*), sweet everlasting (*Gnaphalium obtusifolium*), hyssop-leaved boneset (*Eupatorium hyssopifolium*), tall boneset (*Eupatorium altissimum*), lance-leaved goldenrod (*Solidago graminifolia*), rough-stemmed goldenrod (*Solidago rugosa*), tall goldenrod (*Solidago canadensis*), and tickseed-sunflower (*Bidens polylepis*).

Cabin John Regional Park is managed by the Maryland National Capital Park and Planning Commission. For more information, contact the Locust Grove Nature Center, 7777 Democracy Boulevard, Bethesda, MD 20817; telephone (301)299-1990.

Directions: From the Capital Beltway (I-495), take Old Georgetown Road north for about one-half mile and turn left on Democracy Boulevard. The Locust Grove Nature Center is located on Democracy Boulevard just west of Montgomery Mall. Other areas in the park can be accessed from Westlake Drive or the main park entrance on Tuckerman Lane.

Potomac Power Line

Power lines provide man-made meadows in the eastern United States. Because the woody vegetation is suppressed by mowing and herbicides, the sun-loving wildflowers of summer and fall favor this habitat. The power line near the village of Potomac runs parallel to and about two miles north of River Road, and traverses a band of serpentinite. Although the typical serpentine vegetation is not found here, the hot, dry habitat does support some species found in serpentine barrens, such as slender gerardia (*Agalinis tenuifolia*) and gray goldenrod (*Solidago nemoralis*).

The power line meadow begins blooming in late May with yellow stargrass (*Hypoxis hirsuta*), waxy meadowrue (*Thalictrum revolutum*), bowman's-root (*Porteranthus trifoliatus*), bluets (*Houstonia caerulea*), large-leaved houstonia (*Houstonia purpurea*), balsam ragwort (*Senecio pauperculis*), rattlesnake-weed (*Hieracium venosum*), and field hawkweed (*Hieracium caespitosum*).

Late June flowers include purple milkweed (*Asclepias purpurascens*), hyssop skullcap (*Scutellaria integrifolia*), hairy skullcap (*Scutellaria elliptica*), downy false-foxglove (*Aureolaria virginica*), and whorled coreopsis (*Coreopsis verticillata*).

In late July, look for rose pink (*Sabatia angularis*), pink wild bean (*Strophostyles umbellata*), narrow-leaved mountain-mint (*Pycnanthemum tenuifolium*), cornel-leaved aster (*Aster infirmus*), and woodland sunflower (*Helianthus divaricatus*).

Mid-September is the height of flowering time for this meadow habitat. The hillsides are covered with flowers of the composite family, including tickseed-sunflower (*Bidens polylepis*), smooth aster (*Aster laevis*), calico aster (*Aster lateriflorus*), white heath aster (*Aster pilosus*), wavy-leaved aster (*Aster undulatus*), tall goldenrod (*Solidago canadensis*), lance-leaved goldenrod (*Solidago graminifolia*), rough-stemmed goldenrod (*Solidago rugosa*), silverrod (*Solidago bicolor*), and gray goldenrod.

Other interesting plants of this dry, open habitat include nodding ladies'-tresses (*Spiranthes cernua*), wild yellow flax (*Linum virginianum*), purple milkwort (*Polygala sanguinea*), blue curls (*Trichostema dichotomum*), dittany (*Cunila origanoides*), American pennyroyal (*Hedeoma pulegioides*), and slender gerardia.

The power line runs over both public and private property. If you explore along the power line, be aware of "no trespassing" signs in some places.

Directions: From the village of Potomac, take River Road (MD-190) north for almost two miles to Piney Meeting House Road. Turn right and go for two and one-half miles. Park along the road. Both the uphill and downhill areas are interesting.

Rock Creek Regional Park

Rock Creek Regional Park is located in central Montgomery County northeast of Rockville. The park contains 2,700 acres of protected stream valley stretching from the headwaters of Rock Creek to the District line, where it joins Washington's Rock Creek Park. In most places, the parkland follows a narrow strip on either side of the creek and often is inaccessible to walkers, but a 300-acre area has been preserved for nature study near Meadowside Nature Center and the adjacent Lake Frank.

The area around the nature center and the Smith Environmental Education Center contains several miles of well-marked trails. Varied habitats in this area of the park include open meadows, woodlands, several ponds, small wetlands, and the lakeshore. Although many wildflowers occur naturally, the park flora has been expanded by judicious planting of native species.

In late April, the trails from the nature center down to the creek pass through hillsides filled with spring beauty (*Claytonia virginica*), star chickweed (*Stellaria pubera*), rue-anemone (*Anemonella thalictroides*), round-lobed hepatica (*Hepatica americana*), cut-leaved toothwort (*Dentaria laciniata*), early saxifrage (*Saxifraga virginiensis*), and dwarf ginseng (*Panax trifolius*).

May flowers along these trails include perfoliate bellwort (*Uvularia perfoliata*), showy orchis (*Orchis spectabilis*), wild columbine (*Aquilegia canadensis*), wild geranium (*Geranium maculatum*), and pennywort (*Obolaria virginica*). Golden club (*Orontium aquaticum*) and false hellebore (*Veratrum viride*) grow in a swampy area across Muncaster Mill Road. Several trillium species, including large-flowered trillium (*Trillium grandiflorum*) and yellow trillium (*Trillium luteum*), also occur in this part of the park. These showy trilliums, not native to the Piedmont region, must have been planted here in the past and have naturalized on the hill.

Early June is a good time to visit the Meadowside area, as the sun-loving plants begin to flower in the meadows. You can see native species such as butterflyweed (*Asclepias tuberosa*), large-leaved houstonia (*Houstonia purpurea*), Venus's looking-glass (*Triodanis perfoliata*), and balsam ragwort (*Senecio pauperculis*). Lance-leaved coreopsis (*Coreopsis lanceolata*), a midwestern species, was planted here and has thrived in the dry meadows. Also blooming in the open meadows are familiar European imports such as bulbous buttercup (*Ranunculus bulbosus*), Deptford pink (*Dianthus armeria*), yellow sweet clover (*Melilotus officinalis*), Queen Anne's lace (*Daucus carota*), rough-fruited cinquefoil (*Potentilla recta*), yarrow (*Achillea millefolium*), and ox-eye daisy (*Chrysanthemum leucanthemum*).

Around the edges of the pond and lake are several species of wetland plants. Arrow arum (*Peltandra virginica*), larger blue flag (*Iris versicolor*), and true forget-me-not (*Myosotis scorpioides*) flower in June. Swamp milkweed (*Asclepias incarnata*), square-stemmed monkey-flower (*Mimulus ringens*), and cardinal flower (*Lobelia cardinalis*) bloom in late July. In early fall come great lobelia (*Lobelia siphilitica*), New York ironweed (*Vernonia noveboracensis*), New England aster (*Aster novae-angliae*), and tickseed-sunflower (*Bidens polylepis*).

Even in October, the fields at the Meadowside area are colorful with tall goldenrod (*Solidago canadensis*), rough-stemmed goldenrod (*Solidago rugosa*), lance-leaved goldenrod (*Solidago graminifolia*), calico aster (*Aster lateriflorus*), panicled aster (*Aster lanceolatus*), purple-stemmed aster (*Aster puniceus*), and hollow Joe-Pye-weed (*Eupatorium fistulosum*).

Rock Creek Regional Park is managed by the Maryland National Capital Park and Planning Commission. Meadowside Nature Center is located at 5100 Meadowside Lane, Rockville, MD 20853; telephone (301)924-4141. The trails are always open and several loop walks are possible. Ask at the nature center for checklists of flowers blooming in different seasons.

Directions: From the Capital Beltway (I-495), take Georgia Avenue (MD-97) north for about seven miles. Turn left on Norbeck Road, then take an immediate right on Muncaster Mill Road. Go about one and one-half miles and turn left on Meadowside Lane. The parking area for the nature center is at the end of the road.

Seneca Creek State Park

Seneca Creek State Park contains about 4,500 acres in central Montgomery County. Established to protect the watershed of Seneca Creek, the park follows the creek for 12 miles from Gaithersburg to the Potomac River at Seneca. At its lower end, it adjoins the McKee-Beshers Wildlife Management Area on River Road, but there is no easy access between the two areas.

Much of the park is devoted to recreational uses, including extensive picnic facilities as well as boating and fishing on the 90-acre Lake Clopper. However, natural areas also abound and the park habitats include open fields, wetlands, moist woodlands, and rock outcrops.

On the rocky trail above Black Rock Mill, trailing arbutus (*Epigaea repens*) blooms in early April and wild columbine (*Aquilegia canadensis*) flowers in early May. Several orchids, including large whorled pogonia (*Isotria verticillata*) and round-leaved orchid (*Habenaria orbiculata*), grow in the woods near the mill. June bloomers in the woods include spotted wintergreen (*Chimaphila maculata*) and partridgeberry (*Mitchella repens*).

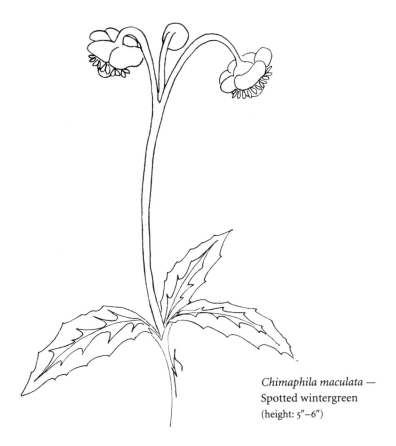

Chimaphila maculata —
Spotted wintergreen
(height: 5″–6″)

September brings a wave of colorful flowers to the wetlands and open fields along Seneca Creek. A small marsh near Black Rock Mill is filled with arrow-leaved tearthumb (*Polygonum sagittatum*), climbing false buckwheat (*Polygonum scandens*), and purple-stemmed aster (*Aster puniceus*). In the nearby woods are wavy-leaved aster (*Aster undulatus*) and blue-stemmed goldenrod (*Solidago caesia*).

The dry, open fields around Clopper Lake are habitat for clammy cuphea (*Cuphea viscosissima*), blue curls (*Trichostema dichotomum*), tall goldenrod (*Solidago canadensis*), lance-leaved goldenrod (*Solidago gramini-folia*), rough-stemmed goldenrod (*Solidago rugosa*), sweet everlasting (*Gnaphalium obtusifolium*), and Maryland golden-aster (*Chrysopsis mariana*).

Seneca Creek State Park is managed by the Maryland Department of Natural Resources, State Forest and Park Service. It is located at 11950 Clopper Road, Gaithersburg, MD 20760; telephone (301)924-2127.

Directions: From I-270, take Quince Orchard Road (MD-124) west, turn right on Clopper Road (MD-117) to the park entrance. This takes you to the lake, picnic areas, and visitor center. For the Black Rock Mill area, continue west on Clopper Road, turn left on Darnestown-Germantown Road (MD-118), and right on Black Rock Road. Continue for about one and one-half miles to the creek crossing and the old mill. Black Rock Road is also accessible from Darnestown Road (MD-28) west of Rockville.

Little Bennett Regional Park

Little Bennett Regional Park, in northern Montgomery County near Clarksburg, contains over 3,600 acres of old farmlands and several pristine streams. It is the county's most rural and least developed park. Although a golf course is planned at the park, at present the only "improvement" is a pleasant campground.

The Little Bennett Creek Valley formerly contained many farms, several mills, and even a one-room schoolhouse. As people left the community, the land returned to a more natural condition, producing habitats such as old fields, oak-pine woodlands, rocky hillsides, wet meadows, and freshwater wetlands along the main stream and its tributaries. Little Bennett is pleasant at any time of year, but like other places with extensive open fields and meadows, the most diverse floral display is in late summer and early fall.

In early May, the woods along Little Bennett Creek bloom with star chickweed (*Stellaria pubera*), rue-anemone (*Anemonella thalictroides*), and spring cress (*Cardamine rhomboidea*). The rocky hillsides along the Kingsley Trail support wild pink (*Silene caroliniana*), wild columbine (*Aquilegia canadensis*), birdfoot violet (*Viola pedata*), three-lobed violet (*Viola triloba*), violet wood-sorrel (*Oxalis violacea*), and long-leaved houstonia (*Houstonia longifolia*). On the Big Oak Trail above the nature center, look for pink lady's-slipper (*Cypripedium acaule*) and the basal rosettes of downy rattlesnake-plantain (*Goodyera pubescens*).

In July and August come flowers of the wet meadows, including Turk's-cap lily (*Lilium superbum*), swamp milkweed (*Asclepias incarnata*), square-stemmed monkey-flower (*Mimulus ringens*), American germander (*Teucrium canadense*), cardinal flower (*Lobelia cardinalis*), and ox-eye (*Heliopsis helianthoides*).

Late September and early October bring the flowering of fringe-tip closed gentian (*Gentiana andrewsii*), perhaps the only population of this rare species in our area. At Little Bennett, this robust gentian grows in wet meadows along the stream. Other fall-blooming species in the meadows include virgin's bower (*Clematis virginiana*), dwarf St. Johnswort (*Hypericum mutilum*), clammy cuphea (*Cuphea viscosissima*), purple-leaved willowherb (*Epilobium coloratum*), purple-stemmed aster (*Aster puniceus*), panicled aster (*Aster lanceolatus*), tall goldenrod (*Solidago canadensis*), lance-leaved goldenrod (*Solidago graminifolia*), and New York ironweed (*Vernonia noveboracensis*).

Little Bennett Regional Park, managed by the Maryland National Capital Park and Planning Commission, is located at 23701 Frederick Road, Clarksburg, MD 20871; telephone (301)972-6581.

Directions: From I-270, take the Clarksburg exit (MD-121 east). At the intersection of Clarksburg Road and Frederick Road (MD-355), turn left on Frederick Road to reach the campground or continue straight on Clarksburg Road to Hyattstown Mill Road. Turn left to explore the wet meadows or right for the Kingsley Trail.

Wheaton Regional Park

Wheaton Regional Park, a 500-acre green oasis in the highly developed Wheaton area, is known primarily for recreational facilities. However, the area around Brookside Nature Center has several trails through the woods, a small pond, and a meandering stream that leads to Northwest Branch.

The trails wander up and down hills, through dry oak woodlands, and across several man-made meadows. Despite the surrounding urbanization and the heavy use of the park, there is a good diversity of wildflowers throughout the growing season.

In mid-April, the moist woods bloom with trout-lily (*Erythronium americanum*), spring beauty (*Claytonia virginica*), star chickweed (*Stellaria pubera*), rue-anemone (*Anemonella thalictroides*), spring cress (*Cardamine rhomboidea*), cut-leaved toothwort (*Dentaria laciniata*), sweet white violet (*Viola blanda*), and golden ragwort (*Senecio aureus*). Virginia bluebells (*Mertensia virginica*) and celandine poppy (*Stylophorum diphyllum*) have been planted and have naturalized along the brook.

May flowers of the dry woods include several orchids. There is a large colony of pink lady's-slipper (*Cypripedium acaule*) and many clumps of showy orchis (*Orchis spectabilis*), as well as lily-leaved twayblade (*Liparis lilifolia*), puttyroot (*Aplectrum hyemale*), and, along nearby Sligo Creek,

Cypripedium acaule —
Pink lady's-slipper
(height: 6″–15″)

large whorled pogonia (*Isotria verticillata*). Later-flowering orchids seen in leaf are cranefly orchid (*Tipularia discolor*) and downy rattlesnake-plantain (*Goodyera pubescens*). Perfoliate bellwort (*Uvularia perfoliata*), Indian cucumber-root (*Medeola virginiana*), wild geranium (*Geranium maculatum*), and dwarf ginseng (*Panax trifolius*) are other flowers found in May.

June flowers of the woodlands include the waxy white Indian pipe (*Monotropa uniflora*), spotted wintergreen (*Chimaphila maculata*), and partridgeberry (*Mitchella repens*). In the open meadows, June brings fringed loosestrife (*Lysimachia ciliata*), large-leaved houstonia (*Houstonia purpurea*), Venus's looking-glass (*Triodanis perfoliata*), and ox-eye daisy (*Chrysanthemum leucanthemum*).

In late July and August, other meadow species bloom, including rose pink (*Sabatia angularis*), spotted St. Johnswort (*Hypericum punctatum*), butterflyweed (*Asclepias tuberosa*), and early goldenrod (*Solidago juncea*). Wetland plants in flower are tall meadowrue (*Thalictrum pubescens*), swamp milkweed (*Asclepias incarnata*), winged monkey-flower (*Mimulus alatus*), cardinal flower (*Lobelia cardinalis*), and New York ironweed (*Vernonia noveboracensis*).

Even in September and October, you can find plants in bloom at Wheaton Regional Park. Late-flowering species include groundnut (*Apios americana*), horse-balm (*Collinsonia canadensis*), blue-stemmed goldenrod (*Solidago caesia*), and New England aster (*Aster novae-angliae*).

Wheaton Regional Park is managed by the Maryland National Capital Park and Planning Commission. Brookside Nature Center is located at 1400 Glenallan Avenue, Wheaton, MD 20902; telephone (301)949-9071.

Directions: From the Capital Beltway (I-495), go north on Georgia Avenue (MD-97) for about one mile past Wheaton, turn right on Randolph Road (MD-183), and then right on Glenallan Road. The Nature Center entrance is at the end of the road just past Brookside Gardens.

Maydale Park

Maydale Park is a little gem of natural diversity tucked away in eastern Montgomery County near Burtonsville. Only 20 acres of parkland, it contains open meadows, an old orchard, hedgerows, deciduous woodlands, two ponds, a fine marsh, and an unpolluted stream called Paint Branch.

In late April, the woodlands at Maydale Park contain wildflowers such as Jack-in-the-pulpit (*Arisaema triphyllum*), smooth Solomon's-seal (*Polygonatum biflorum), Indian cucumber-root (*Medeola virginiana*), sessile bellwort (*Uvularia sessilifolia*), and rue-anemone (*Anemonella thalictroides*). The area is best known for a large population of dwarf ginseng (*Panax trifolius*) carpeting the forest floor.

In late July and August, the wetlands come into flower with the blooming of pickerelweed (*Pontederia cordata*), lizard's-tail (*Saururus cernuus*), spatterdock (*Nuphar advena*), swamp milkweed (*Asclepias incarnata*), and square-stemmed monkey-flower (*Mimulus ringens*).

Flowering continues in the open fields and edges of the ponds even through late September and October. Late-blooming species include great lobelia (*Lobelia siphilitica*), swamp beggar-ticks (*Bidens connata*), tickseed-sunflower (*Bidens polylepis*), bushy aster (*Aster dumosus*), purple-stemmed aster (*Aster puniceus*), tall goldenrod (*Solidago canadensis*), rough-stemmed goldenrod (*Solidago rugosa*), and New York ironweed (*Vernonia noveboracensis*).

Maydale Park, located at 1726 Briggs-Chaney Road in Silver Spring, is managed by the Maryland National Capital Park and Planning Commission. For more information, contact Brookside Nature Center, 1400 Glenallan Avenue, Wheaton, MD, 20902: telephone (301)949-9071.

Directions: From the Capital Beltway (I-495), go north on Colesville Road/Columbia Pike (MD-29) for about six miles, turn left on Briggs-Chaney Road for two miles, right on Claude Lane, and left on Maydale Road.

Rocky Gorge Reservoir

The Rocky Gorge Reservoir near Burtonsville is part of the Patuxent River Watershed Park that follows the Piedmont portion of the Patuxent River between Montgomery and Howard counties.

Woodland trails along the tributary streams offer pleasant walking in April and May. Early spring flowers found in these woods include spring beauty (*Claytonia virginica*), rue-anemone (*Anemonella thalictroides*), and round-lobed hepatica (*Hepatica americana*). Upland wildflowers blooming in early May are perfoliate bellwort (*Uvularia perfoliata*), pink lady's-slipper (*Cypripedium acaule*), showy orchis (*Orchis spectabilis*), and one-flowered cancer-root (*Orobanche uniflora*).

May also brings false Solomon's-seal (*Smilacina racemosa*), primrose-leaved violet (*Viola primulifolia*), violet wood-sorrel (*Oxalis violacea*), and long-leaved houstonia (*Houstonia longifolia*). The shiny leaves of round-leaved pyrola (*Pyrola rotundifolia*) are seen in May and the flowers appear in June.

Rocky Gorge Reservoir is managed by the Washington Suburban Sanitary Commission. Portions of this reservoir, the Tridelphia Reservoir, and their watersheds are open to the public for boating, fishing, hiking, horseback riding, and picnicking.

Directions: From Colesville Road-Columbia Pike (US-29) in Burtonsville, take Spencerville-Sandy Spring Road (MD-198) east for about one mile. Turn left on Riding Stable Road, and left on Aitcheson Lane to its end, where there is a small parking area.

5

Maryland Piedmont
Baltimore and Nearby Counties

HOWARD AND CARROLL COUNTIES

Howard County lies between Montgomery County and Baltimore County. With small towns, large farms, and several historical sites, the county retained its rural character for many years. However, the planned community of Columbia and many housing developments have changed the landscape of Howard County.

Howard County shares the Patuxent River with Montgomery County to its south and the Patapsco River with Baltimore County to its north. The Patapsco Valley State Park provides the best botanizing areas in the county, with several different areas along the river. Most areas are accessible from I-95, I-70, or the Baltimore Beltway (I-695).

Howard County has a slightly cooler climate than nearby Montgomery County, and several mountain species have been found here, including erect trillium (*Trillium erectum*), nodding trillium (*Trillium cernuum*), goldenseal (*Hydrastis canadensis*), miterwort (*Mitella diphylla*), and dog violet (*Viola conspersa*).

Carroll County lies north of Howard County and west of Baltimore County. The countryside is mainly agricultural, with small towns and scattered homes, except for intensive development around the central town of Westminster. MD-26 leads from Baltimore and MD-97 leads from Washington to Carroll County.

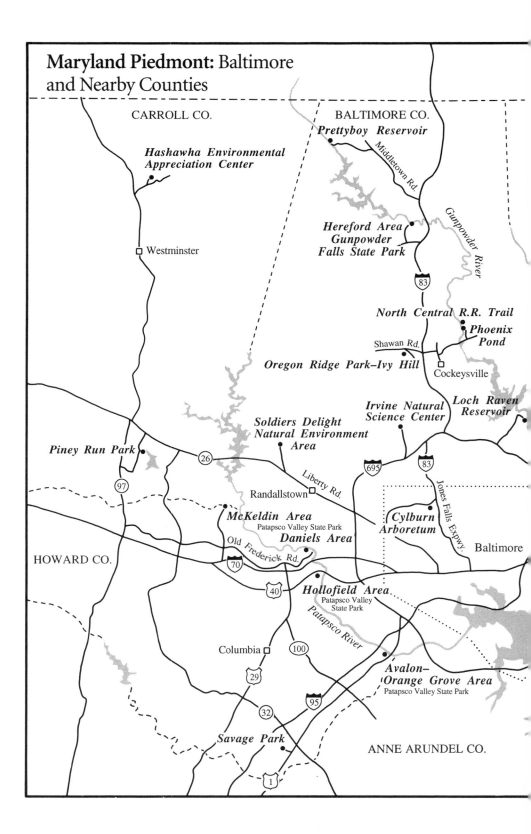

Maryland Piedmont: Baltimore and Nearby Counties

CARROLL CO.

BALTIMORE CO.

Prettyboy Reservoir

Middletown Rd.

Hashawha Environmental Appreciation Center

Gunpowder River

Hereford Area Gunpowder Falls State Park

83

□ Westminster

North Central R.R. Trail

Phoenix Pond

Shawan Rd.

Oregon Ridge Park–Ivy Hill

□ Cockeysville

Loch Raven Reservoir

Irvine Natural Science Center

Soldiers Delight Natural Environment Area

Piney Run Park

26

695

83

Liberty Rd.

97

Randallstown □

Jones Falls Expwy.

McKeldin Area
Patapsco Valley State Park

Cylburn Arboretum

Daniels Area

Old Frederick Rd.

HOWARD CO.

70

Baltimore

40

Hollofield Area
Patapsco Valley State Park

Patapsco River

Columbia □

100

Avalon– Orange Grove Area
Patapsco Valley State Park

29

32

95

Savage Park

ANNE ARUNDEL CO.

1

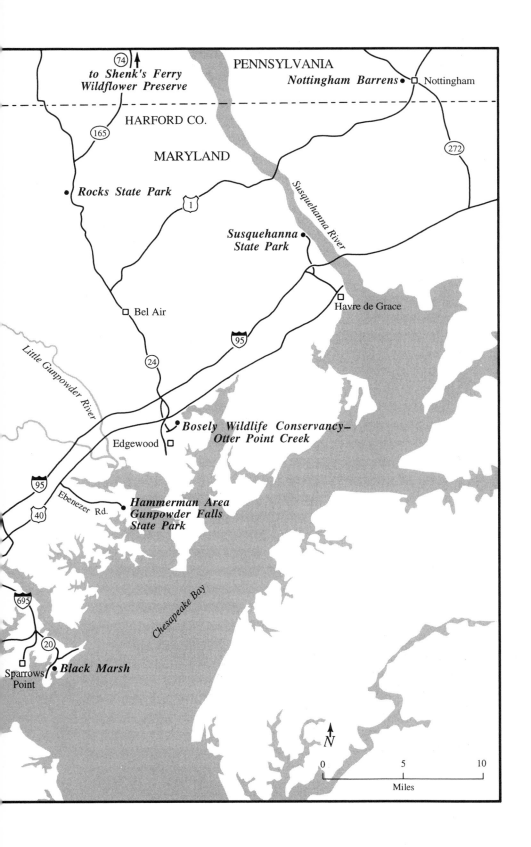

Savage Park

Savage Park is located in the old mill town of Savage, about halfway between Washington and Baltimore. The Savage Mill Historic Trail and the River Trail, both along the Little Patuxent River, contain rich bottomlands, rocky hillsides, and upland forests.

Savage Park is an excellent place to find early spring wildflowers. Among the woodland plants blooming in mid-April are spring beauty (*Claytonia virginica*), star chickweed (*Stellaria pubera*), rue-anemone (*Anemonella thalictroides*), bloodroot (*Sanguinaria canadensis*), yellow corydalis (*Corydalis flavula*), spring cress (*Cardamine rhomboidea*), smooth rockcress (*Arabis laevigata*), early saxifrage (*Saxifraga virginiensis*), bluets (*Houstonia caerulea*) and golden ragwort (*Senecio aureus*).

Mid-May brings the flowering of smooth Solomon's-seal (*Polygonatum biflorum*), false Solomon's-seal (*Smilacina racemosa*), Indian cucumber-root (*Medeola virginiana*), perfoliate bellwort (*Uvularia perfoliata*), yellow stargrass (*Hypoxis hirsuta*), showy orchis (*Orchis spectabilis*), pennywort (*Obolaria virginica*), and one-flowered cancer-root (*Orobanche uniflora*). The floodplain is carpeted with false mermaid (*Floerkea proserpinacoides*).

In the open fields, you can find bulbous buttercup (*Ranunculus bulbosus*), dame's rocket (*Hesperis matronalis*), wild geranium (*Geranium maculatum*), golden Alexanders (*Zizia aurea*), and lyre-leaved sage (*Salvia lyrata*).

Located near the fall line that divides the Piedmont region from the Coastal Plain, Savage Park has an interesting combination of plants from both regions. Several species found here are more common to the north or west, including wood anemone (*Anemone quinquefolia*), wild sarsaparilla (*Aralia nudicaulis*), bowman's-root (*Porteranthus trifoliatus*), goatsbeard (*Aruncus dioicus*), and wild comfrey (*Cynoglossum virginianum*). Plants more typical of places to the south or east are cat's-ear (*Hypochoeris radicata*) and Mayweed (*Anthemis cotula*).

Savage Park is managed by the Howard County Department of Recreation and Parks and is located near the Savage Mill marketplace at Foundry Street and US-1, Savage, MD 20763; telephone (410)792-2820.

Directions: From I-95, take MD-32 east for one and one-half miles. Turn south on US-1, turn right at Howard/Baltimore Street (first light), go one mile and turn right on Fair Street into the park. The River Trail begins beyond the tennis courts. For the Savage Mill Historic Trail, park at the mill and cross the Bollman Truss Bridge.

Patapsco Valley State Park

The Patapsco River runs between Howard County and Baltimore County a few miles west and south of Baltimore. Patapsco Valley State Park, comprising about 13,000 acres along both sides of the river, extends from Elkridge in the east to Sykesville in the west.

The park is rich in historical interest, with sites of former industries such as iron works, textile mills, and railroad lines. Many fine wildflower places are found along the river, including the following areas moving west from Elkridge: Avalon-Orange Grove Area, Hollofield Area, Daniels Area, and McKeldin Area.

Several plants that are uncommon in Maryland occur in Patapsco Valley State Park, such as nodding trillium (*Trillium cernuum*), waxy meadowrue (*Thalictrum revolutum*), whorled milkweed (*Asclepias verticillata*), showy skullcap (*Scutellaria serrata*), balsam ragwort (*Senecio pauperculus*), and cornel-leaved aster (*Aster infirmus*).

Patapsco Valley State Park is managed by the Maryland Department of Natural Resources, State Forest and Park Service. The park office is at 1100 Hilton Avenue, Baltimore, MD 21228; telephone (410)747-6602.

Avalon-Orange Grove Area

The Avalon-Orange Grove Area of Patapsco Valley State Park is near Elkridge, a few miles south of the Baltimore Beltway. The habitats include mature deciduous woodlands, a small coniferous forest, and moist hillsides along cascading streams. Although located at the eastern edge of the Piedmont region, a combination of geology, soil type, slope direction, and microclimates has produced an environment that supports several mountain species.

Most noticeable of the mountain plants are the eastern hemlocks along the Cascade Trail. Other species more commonly found in the mountains are erect trillium (*Trillium erectum*), false hellebore (*Veratrum viride*), blue cohosh (*Caulophyllum thalictroides*), miterwort (*Mitella diphylla*), wild sarsaparilla (*Aralia nudicaulis*), and goatsbeard (*Aruncus dioicus*).

In mid-April, the upland woods have a fine display of early-flowering species such as wild ginger (*Asarum canadense*), spring beauty (*Claytonia virginica*), round-lobed hepatica (*Hepatica americana*), rue-anemone (*Anemonella thalictroides*), bloodroot (*Sanguinaria canadensis*), Dutchman's breeches (*Dicentra cucullaria*), slender toothwort (*Dentaria hetero-phylla*), and trailing arbutus (*Epigaea repens*).

In early May, walk along the old River Road to see star chickweed (*Stellaria pubera*), sweet white violet (*Viola blanda*), and bluets (*Houstonia caerulea*) beneath the pinxter flower (*Rhododendron periclymenoides*). Goatsbeard, miterwort, and blue cohosh are also found in the woods above River Road. In the upland woods, particularly along the Cascade Trail, look for Jack-in-the-pulpit (*Arisaema triphyllum*), false Solomon's-seal (*Smilacina racemosa*), Indian cucumber-root (*Medeola virginiana*), wild geranium (*Geranium maculatum*), and Virginia waterleaf (*Hydrophyllum virginianum*).

In June, look in swampy places for false hellebore as well as tall meadowrue (*Thalictrum pubescens*). In the drier woods, search for one-flowered cancer-root (*Orobanche uniflora*) and showy skullcap (*Scutellaria serrata*).

Wildflowers of late summer and fall include American germander (*Teucrium canadense*), Maryland figwort (*Scrophularia marilandica*), beechdrops (*Epifagus virginiana*), cornel-leaved aster (*Aster infirmus*), heartleaved aster (*Aster cordifolius*), New England aster (*Aster novae-angliae*), and zigzag goldenrod (*Solidago flexicaulis*).

The Avalon-Orange Grove Area of Patapsco Valley State Park is managed by the Maryland Department of Natural Resources, State Forest and Park Service. The park office is located at 1100 Hilton Avenue, Baltimore, MD 21228; telephone (410)747-6602.

Directions: From I-95, go east on MD-100 for one mile, turn left on US-1 and continue for almost six miles through the town of Elkridge. Cross the Patapsco River and turn left on South Street and left again into the park. From the Baltimore Beltway (I-695), take US-1 south for three miles, turn right on South Street and follow the above directions.

Hollofield Area

Heading upriver from the Avalon Area, the Hollofield Area of Patapsco Valley State Park is located west of the Baltimore Beltway. The picnic and camping areas are on a high bluff overlooking the Patapsco River far below. The dry ridgetop woods and steep slopes have a very different environment for plants from the rich bottomland and upland woods of the Avalon Area.

April wildflowers are not as abundant in this dry habitat as at other riverside areas, but by early May there are many plants in flower, including wild pink (*Silene caroliniana*), field chickweed (*Cerastium arvense*), rue-

Hypoxis hirsuta —
Yellow stargrass
(height: 3″–6″)

anemone (*Anemonella thalictroides*), hispid buttercup (*Ranunculus hispidus*), lyre-leaved rockcress (*Arabis lyrata*), three-lobed violet (*Viola triloba*), pennywort (*Obolaria virginica*), and bluets (*Houstonia caerulea*).

In mid-June, the bluffs below the scenic overlook bloom with goat's-rue (*Tephrosia virginiana*), hairy skullcap (*Scutellaria elliptica*), and balsam ragwort (*Senecio pauperculus*). In the meadow under the power line grow Canada lily (*Lilium canadense*), yellow stargrass (*Hypoxis hirsuta*), waxy meadowrue (*Thalictrum revolutum*), spiked lobelia (*Lobelia spicata*), ox-eye daisy (*Chrysanthemum leucanthemum*) and black-eyed Susan (*Rudbeckia hirta*). Along the roadside you may see black cohosh (*Cimicifuga racemosa*), white beardtongue (*Penstemon digitalis*), and Venus's looking-glass (*Triodanis perfoliata*).

In July and August, other plants of dry open habitats can be found, including pencil flower (*Stylosanthes biflora*), wild yellow flax (*Linum virginianum*), whorled milkweed (*Asclepias verticillata*), green milkweed (*Asclepias viridiflora*), American pennyroyal (*Hedeoma pulegioides*), narrow-leaved mountain-mint (*Pycnanthemum tenuifolium*), downy false-foxglove (*Aureolaria virginica*), and whorled rosinweed (*Silphium trifoliatum*).

The Hollofield Area of Patapsco Valley State Park is managed by the Maryland Department of Natural Resources, State Forest and Park Service. There are picnic and camping areas, rest rooms, and an office. For more information, contact the park office at 1100 Hilton Avenue, Baltimore, MD 21228; telephone (410)747-6602.

Directions: From the Baltimore Beltway (I-695), take US-40 west for four miles, cross the Patapsco River, and turn left at the sign for the park. From Columbia Pike (MD-29), go north to US-40, go east on US-40 for two miles, and turn right at the sign.

Daniels Area

The Daniels Area of Patapsco Valley State Park is only two miles upriver from the Hollofield Area, but there are no connecting trails or roads. Set in a quiet rural area and undeveloped for recreational uses, the Daniels Area has rich bottomlands and steep rocky uplands.

A wide trail goes along the river, and there are several miles of trails on the hillsides. In mid-April, the moist uplands have a fine display of early spring wildflowers including wild ginger (*Asarum canadense*), round-lobed hepatica (*Hepatica americana*), rue-anemone (*Anemonella thalictroides*), bloodroot (*Sanguinaria canadensis*), Dutchman's breeches (*Dicentra cucullaria*), yellow corydalis (*Corydalis flavula*), slender toothwort (*Dentaria heterophylla*), and sweet white violet (*Viola blanda*). On the rocks grow several clumps of wild columbine (*Aquilegia canadensis*), as well as early saxifrage (*Saxifraga virginiensis*) and trailing arbutus (*Epigaea repens*).

The north-facing hillside, endowed with rich, moist soil and a cool microclimate, has several species more common in the mountain regions. Early May flowers on these bluffs include nodding trillium (*Trillium cernuum*), showy orchis (*Orchis spectabilis*), miterwort (*Mitella diphylla*), woolly blue violet (*Viola sororia*), wild sarsaparilla (*Aralia nudicaulis*), and Greek valerian (*Polemonium reptans*).

In late summer, look along the river for black cohosh (*Cimicifuga racemosa*), fringed loosestrife (*Lysimachia ciliata*), horse-balm (*Collinsonia canadensis*), square-stemmed monkey-flower (*Mimulus ringens*), great lobelia (*Lobelia siphilitica*), and yellow sneezeweed (*Helenium autumnale*).

The Daniels Area of Patapsco Valley State Park is managed by the Maryland Department of Natural Resources, State Forest and Park Service. There are no visitor facilities at Daniels and parking space is limited. For more information, contact the park office at 1100 Hilton Avenue, Baltimore, MD 21228; telephone (410)747-6602.

Directions: From the Baltimore Beltway (I-695), take I-70 west for six miles, go north on MD-29 for one-half mile and then east on Old Frederick Road. Go about one-half mile and turn left on Daniels Road. Continue for almost one mile to the parking area by the river. From the Washington area, take Columbia Pike (MD-29) north past I-70, go east on Old Frederick Road and follow the above directions.

McKeldin Area

The McKeldin Area of Patapsco Valley State Park is in the southeastern corner of Carroll County. The habitats include dry oak woods, moist hillsides, and bottomland woods near the river.

In mid-April, the Switchback Trail has many familiar spring flowers, including spring beauty (*Claytonia virginica*), round-lobed hepatica (*Hepatica americana*), rue-anemone (*Anemonella thalictroides*), yellow corydalis (*Corydalis flavula*), cut-leaved toothwort (*Dentaria laciniata*), spring cress (*Cardamine rhomboidea*), and smooth yellow violet (*Viola pensylvanica*).

On the drier hillsides grow star chickweed (*Stellaria pubera*), early saxifrage (*Saxifraga virginiensis*), ovate-leaved violet (*Viola fimbriatula*), trailing arbutus (*Epigaea repens*), bluets (*Houstonia caerulea*), plantain-leaved pussytoes (*Antennaria plantaginifolia*), and rattlesnake-weed (*Hieracium venosum*).

The McKeldin Area is developed for recreational uses, and there are several picnic pavilions and playgrounds in the park. For more information, contact Patapsco Valley State Park, 1100 Hilton Avenue, Baltimore, MD 21228; telephone (410)747-6602.

Directions: From the Baltimore Beltway (I-695), take I-70 west for nine miles. Go north on Marriottsville Road for three miles; the park is on the right. From Columbia Pike (MD-29), go north to I-70. Go west on I-70 for four miles and follow above directions.

Piney Run Park

Piney Run Park, in the rural countryside of southern Carroll County, has a 300-acre lake and 500 acres of woods and open space. Heavy recreational use of the park includes fishing, boating, tennis, hiking, and picnicking. An attractive nature center with hands-on exhibits is located in the park.

The dry oak woods support wildflowers typical of the Piedmont uplands. In late April, the trails near the nature center have smooth Solomon's-seal (*Polygonatum biflorum*), bulbous buttercup (*Ranunculus bulbosus*), Mayapple (*Podophyllum peltatum*), blue cohosh (*Caulophyllum thalictroides*), cut-leaved toothwort (*Dentaria laciniata*), wild geranium (*Geranium maculatum*), common blue violet (*Viola papilionacea*), and bluets (*Houstonia caerulea*).

Summer wildflowers of Piney Run Park include rough-fruited cinquefoil (*Potentilla recta*), yellow sweet clover (*Melilotus officinalis*), flowering spurge (*Euphorbia corollata*), common St. Johnswort (*Hypericum perforatum*), spotted wintergreen (*Chimaphila maculata*), ox-eye daisy (*Chrysanthemum leucanthemum*), black-eyed Susan (*Rudbeckia hirta*), and early goldenrod (*Solidago juncea*).

Piney Run Park is managed by the Carroll County Department of Recreation and Parks and is located at 30 Martz Road, Sykesville, MD 21784; telephone (410)795-3274.

Directions: Take MD-97 north from Montgomery and Howard counties, go about five miles past I-70, turn right on Obrecht Road for one mile, turn left on White Rock Road for almost two miles, turn right on Martz Road and follow it to the park. From the Baltimore Beltway (I-695), take MD-26 (Liberty Road) west, go two miles past the intersection with MD-32 (Sykesville Road) to White Rock Road, turn left and go about three miles to Martz Road.

Hashawha Environmental Appreciation Center

Hashawha Environmental Appreciation Center is located in northern Carroll County a few miles north of Westminster. The center offers environmental education programs to Carroll County students during the year and to the public in the summer. The nearby Bear Branch Nature Center supplements the programs of the Hashawha Center.

Hashawha sits high on a hill with a fine view of the rolling Piedmont terrain. The 300 acres used for programs are surrounded by 2,000 acres of protected parkland. Habitats vary from old farm fields, thickets, and dry oak-pine woods, to moist bottomland woods, swampy places beside the stream, and marshy areas around the pond. Several well-marked trails lead from the center into the woods and fields.

A late April walk along the dry hillsides may bring the sight of trailing arbutus (*Epigaea repens*) beneath the pinxter flower (*Rhododendron periclymenoides*). Other woodland plants in flower include star chickweed (*Stellaria pubera*), birdfoot violet (*Viola pedata*), northern blue violet (*Viola septentrionalis*), southern wood violet (*Viola hirsutula*), and rattlesnakeweed (*Hieracium venosum*).

The open fields bloom with wild strawberry (*Fragaria virginiana*), dwarf cinquefoil (*Potentilla canadensis*), ovate-leaved violet (*Viola fimbriatula*), and plantain-leaved pussytoes (*Antennaria plantaginifolia*).

Areas along the stream feature rich, moist soil and well-developed bottomland woods. Late April flowers here include spring beauty (*Claytonia virginica*), swamp buttercup (*Ranunculus septentrionalis*), spring cress (*Cardamine rhomboidea*), and common blue violet (*Viola papilionacea*). Also found in these moist woods are false hellebore (*Veratrum viride*), dog violet (*Viola conspersa*), Greek valerian (*Polemonium reptans*), and lousewort (*Pedicularis canadensis*), all mountain species that are uncommon in the Piedmont.

Near the old log cabin in the woods are celandine poppy (*Stylophorum diphyllum*) and peppermint (*Mentha piperita*); both species were surely planted here.

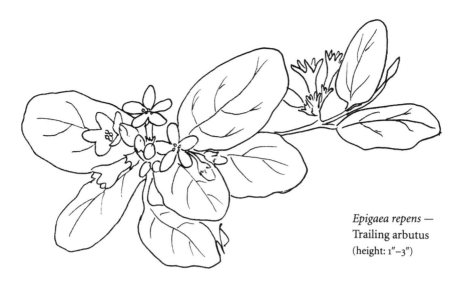

Epigaea repens —
Trailing arbutus
(height: 1″–3″)

Hashawha Environmental Appreciation Center and Bear Branch Nature Center are managed by the Carroll County Department of Recreation and Parks. Hashawha is located at 300 John Owings Road, Westminster, MD 21157; telephone (410)848-9040.

Directions: From the intersection of I-70 and MD-97 west of Baltimore, go north on MD-97 to Westminster. Continue on MD-97 through Westminster, go about four miles and turn right on John Owings Road. Go two miles to the Y in the road and bear left to Hashawha and Bear Branch.

BALTIMORE CITY AND BALTIMORE COUNTY

The city of Baltimore is a separate jurisdiction in Maryland. Like Washington, it lies on the fall line, the boundary between the Piedmont and the Coastal Plain. Baltimore is known more for its urban delights than its natural areas, but there are several pleasant parks within the city limits.

Baltimore County, which surrounds the city on all sides, has a great variety of natural landscapes ranging from beach communities on the Chesapeake Bay, through lush green farms in Hunt Valley, to rural villages in the north.

Gunpowder Falls State Park follows the watershed of the Gunpowder River from its source near Prettyboy Reservoir to its mouth on the Chesapeake Bay. Cool moist woodlands in the western section of the park are habitat for northern species such as Canada Mayflower (*Maianthemum canadense*) and wild sarsaparilla (*Aralia nudicaulis*). Probably the best-known botanical site in Baltimore County is Soldiers Delight, an unusually fine serpentine barren known for rare plants such as fringed gentian (*Gentiana crinita*) and fameflower (*Talinum teretifolium*).

The Baltimore Beltway (I-695) encircles the city of Baltimore and passes through Baltimore County. I-83 runs due north from the city toward Pennsylvania, and I-95 follows the fall line along the eastern edge of the county to Harford County and Delaware.

Soldiers Delight Natural Environment Area

Soldiers Delight is located near Randallstown in southwestern Baltimore County. It is said that the area acquired its unusual name from the fact that British soldiers liked to camp in the open grasslands. Whatever the source of the name, the place now delights naturalists, botanists, and ecologists more than soldiers.

The 2,000-acre natural environment area contains the largest serpentine barren in Maryland. Serpentine barrens run through the Piedmont province from Montgomery County, Maryland, to Philadelphia County, Pennsylvania, and support a flora quite unlike that of typical Piedmont deciduous forests.

The serpentine barrens habitat is stressful to most plants due to the high magnesium content of the underlying serpentine rock and the thin, dry, nutrient-poor soil. Some scrubby tree species grow here, such as Virginia pine, blackjack oak, and post oak, but the barrens are natural openings dominated by grasses and other herbaceous plants.

Species such as slender knotweed (*Polygonum tenue*), fameflower (*Talinum teretifolium*), and whorled milkweed (*Asclepias verticillata*) are adapted to very dry habitats and thus grow well on serpentine barrens. The hairy variety of field chickweed (*Cerastium arvense*) and serpentine aster (*Aster depauperatus*) are species found only on serpentine barrens.

Soldiers Delight contains several habitats other than the serpentine barrens, such as open fields under a power line, dry oak-pine woodlands, shallow streams, and small wetlands.

Flowers seen on the barrens in late April and early May include the hairy variety of field chickweed, as well as wild pink (*Silene caroliniana*), lyre-leaved rockcress (*Arabis lyrata*), birdfoot violet (*Viola pedata*), ovate-

Gentiana crinita —
Fringed gentian
(height: 1'–3')

leaved violet (*Viola fimbriatula*), moss phlox (*Phlox subulata*), bluets (*Houstonia caerulea*), and balsam ragwort (*Senecio pauperculus*).

The summer months bring flowers of dry habitats including slender ladies'-tresses (*Spiranthes gracilis*), slender knotweed, fameflower, whorled milkweed, green milkweed (*Asclepias viridiflora*), and spiked lobelia (*Lobelia spicata*).

A fine time to visit Soldiers Delight is in late September when fringed gentian (*Gentiana crinita*) is in bloom. Extreme care should be taken when observing the gentian, as Soldiers Delight is the only known site in Maryland for this beautiful species.

September-flowering plants on the barrens include prairie grasses such as big bluestem (*Andropogon gerardi*), little bluestem (*Andropogon scoparius*), and Indian grass (*Sorghastrum nutans*). Also brightening the barrens are wild yellow flax (*Linum virginianum*), pineweed (*Hypericum gentianoides*), slender gerardia (*Agalinis tenuifolia*), white heath aster (*Aster pilosus*), and gray goldenrod (*Solidago nemoralis*). In the open fields are rose pink (*Sabatia angularis*), fern-leaved false-foxglove (*Aureolaria pedicularia*), and spiked blazing-star (*Liatris spicata*), while near the stream are purple gerardia (*Agalinis purpurea*), New York ironweed (*Vernonia noveboracensis*), and New York aster (*Aster novi-belgii*).

At the southern edge of Soldiers Delight on Dolfield Road, a small wetland contains Canadian burnet (*Sanguisorba canadensis*), white turtlehead (*Chelone glabra*), great lobelia (*Lobelia siphilitica*), and swamp thistle (*Cirsium muticum*).

Soldiers Delight is managed by the Maryland Department of Natural Resources, State Forest and Park Service. A visitor center was built in 1990 to provide interpretive services for the site. It is located at 5100 Deer Park Road, Owings Mill, MD 21117; telephone (410)922-3044.

Soldiers Delight has been studied extensively by botanists and ecologists. Recently the Maryland Natural Heritage Program has been monitoring this unique Maryland site.

Directions: From the Baltimore Beltway (I-695), take Liberty Road (MD-26) west through Randallstown for about five miles. Turn right on Deer Park Road (at a big green water tower). Go two and one-third miles to the overlook and main parking lot on the left. The road to the visitor center (not always open) is before the main parking area. The small wetland is reached by returning south along Deer Park Road for one mile and turning left on Dolfield Road for one-half mile. Parking here is very limited.

Cylburn Arboretum

The Cylburn Arboretum, in the northwest section of the city of Baltimore, contains 176 acres of gardens, lawns, and rolling fields. An attractive wildflower trail, with many naturalized plants, is being developed in the wooded areas. The wildflower trail at Cylburn Arboretum, like Fern Valley at the National Arboretum in Washington, is a good place to learn wildflower identification since most species are labeled with name and place of origin. Although all flowers planted in the wildflower area are from the eastern United States, many are not native to the Baltimore area or even the Piedmont region.

In late April, along the circular trail, you can find Canada Mayflower (*Maianthemum canadense*), wild ginger (*Asarum canadense*), star chickweed (*Stellaria pubera*), rue-anemone (*Anemonella thalictroides*), wood anemone (*Anemone quinquefolia*), celandine poppy (*Stylophorum diphyllum*), miterwort (*Mitella diphylla*), foamflower (*Tiarella cordifolia*), wild blue phlox (*Phlox divaricata*), Virginia bluebells (*Mertensia virginica*), and golden ragwort (*Senecio aureus*).

There are several clumps of yellow lady's-slipper (*Cypripedium calceolus*) and fine stands of different species of trillium. Look for large-flowered trillium (*Trillium grandiflorum*), erect trillium (*Trillium erectum*), and nodding trillium (*Trillium cernuum*), all species of the mountains and New England; yellow trillium (*Trillium luteum*), native to the southern Appalachians; and sessile trillium (*Trillium sessile*), the only trillium common in the Piedmont region.

In a small area simulated as a limestone outcrop are walking fern and sharp-lobed hepatica (*Hepatica acutiloba*). Another area made into a mountain seep has ostrich fern and marsh marigold (*Caltha palustris*).

Cylburn Arboretum is managed by the City of Baltimore Department of Recreation and Parks and is located in Cylburn Park at 4915 Greenspring Avenue, Baltimore, MD 21209; telephone (410)367-2217. An herbarium, museum, and library are located in the old Cylburn Mansion.

Directions: From downtown Baltimore, take I-83 (Jones Falls Expressway) north to Northern Parkway. Turn left on the parkway, then left on Cylburn Avenue, left on Greenspring Avenue, and left again at the park entrance.

Irvine Natural Science Center

The Irvine Natural Science Center is located in southern Baltimore County just north of the Baltimore Beltway. The Irvine Center, an environmental education organization, uses the woodlands, meadows, streams, and pond of the 225-acre St. Timothy's School campus. Visitors are welcome to walk the trails but should remember that this is private property.

The well-maintained trails wander through dry oak woods and along a stream. Wild species are intermixed with ones that have been planted in a naturalized setting.

In mid-April, you can find spring beauty (*Claytonia virginica*), round-lobed hepatica (*Hepatica americana*), bloodroot (*Sanguinaria canadensis*), smooth yellow violet (*Viola pensylvanica*), common blue violet (*Viola papilionacea*), and trailing arbutus (*Epigaea repens*).

Late April brings Jack-in-the-pulpit (*Arisaema triphyllum*), smooth Solomon'-seal (*Polygonatum biflorum*), perfoliate bellwort (*Uvularia perfoliata*), and wild geranium (*Geranium maculatum*). Planted and naturalized in the woods are large-flowered trillium (*Trillium grandiflorum*), wild bleeding heart (*Dicentra eximia*), and Greek valerian (*Polemonium reptans*).

Irvine Natural Science Center has interesting exhibits oh local natural history. The center is located at St. Timothy's School, Greenspring Avenue, Stevenson, MD 21153; telephone (410)484-2413.

Directions: From the Baltimore Beltway (I-695), take Greenspring Avenue one mile north. St. Timothy's School Drive is on the left.

Oregon Ridge Park — Ivy Hill

Oregon Ridge Park, located north of Baltimore near Cockeysville, contains over 800 acres with different habitats, including old farm fields, open meadows, upland deciduous woods, and, at the Ivy Hill area, an eastern hemlock–white pine forest along Baisman Run. The northern section of the park is often crowded with visitors to the nature center and its surrounding woods, but the best wildflower areas are in the southern section near Ivy Hill.

The Ivy Hill Nature Trail winds down a steep hillside to the rich bottomlands along the stream. In late April, there are many wildflowers, including trout-lily (*Erythronium americanum*), sessile trillium (*Trillium sessile*), perfoliate bellwort (*Uvularia perfoliata*), wild ginger (*Asarum canadense*), rue-anemone (*Anemonella thalictroides*), cut-leaved toothwort (*Dentaria laciniata*), wild geranium (*Geranium maculatum*), sweet white violet (*Viola blanda*), wild blue phlox (*Phlox divaricata*), and dwarf ginseng (*Panax trifolius*).

In these Maryland Piedmont woods, it is surprising to come upon yellow trillium (*Trillium luteum*), crested iris (*Iris cristata*), Virginia heartleaf (*Asarum virginicum*), foamflower (*Tiarella cordifolia*), galax (*Galax aphylla*), shortia (*Shortia galacifolia*), and creeping phlox (*Phlox stolonifera*). All plants of the southern Appalachians, they must have been planted years ago and have naturalized so well that they seem to belong here.

Northern and mountain species found at Ivy Hill include Canada May-flower (*Maianthemum canadense*), large-flowered trillium (*Trillium grandiflorum*), nodding trillium (*Trillium cernuum*), wood anemone (*Anemone quinquefolia*), and dog violet (*Viola conspersa*).

Perhaps even the hemlocks and white pines were planted here, as this mixed deciduous-coniferous woods is unusual in the Piedmont region. With coniferous trees and mountain wildflowers, the Ivy Hill area does resemble an Appalachian mountain forest.

Upstream from the lovely pond at Ivy Hill grow a few wetland species flowering later in the year, such as golden club (*Orontium aquaticum*), false hellebore (*Veratrum viride*), yellow iris (*Iris pseudacorus*), and cardinal flower (*Lobelia cardinalis*).

In the upland woods of Oregon Ridge are several native orchids that bloom in May, including showy orchis (*Orchis spectabilis*), pink lady's-slipper (*Cypripedium acaule*), and yellow lady's-slipper (*Cypripedium calceolus*).

Oregon Ridge Park is managed by the Baltimore County Department of Recreation and Parks. It is located at 13555 Beaver Dam Road, Cockeysville, MD 21030; telephone (410)887-1815. The attractive nature center has many displays, trail maps, and other information about the natural history of the park.

Directions: From the Baltimore Beltway (I-695), take I-83 north for six miles, go west on Shawan Road, and turn left on Beaver Dam Road. The road to the nature center veers to the right. From the nature center, you can hike about one mile to Ivy Hill, or you may be able to get special permission to park at Ivy Hill.

Gunpowder Falls State Park

The Gunpowder River runs through northern Baltimore County in the Piedmont region and between Baltimore and Harford Counties as it flows through the Coastal Plain and enters the Chesapeake Bay. The Gunpowder Falls State Park protects almost 14,000 acres of watershed and provides recreational activities in several areas.

Habitats in the Piedmont region of the park include cool moist woods, dry oak woods, open fields, rock outcrops, and rich bottomlands along the tumbling river and its tributaries. Showy wildflowers found in the cool forests of this park include erect trillium (*Trillium erectum*), pink lady's-slipper (*Cypripedium acaule*), and wood anemone (*Anemone quinquefolia*).

Places in Gunpowder Falls State Park of special interest to naturalists include Loch Raven Reservoir, the North Central Railroad Trail, Phoenix Pond, and the Hereford area. Prettyboy Reservoir is located just west of the park. The Hammerman Area in the eastern section of the park is described in Chapter 6, Maryland Coastal Plain.

Gunpowder Falls State Park is managed by the Maryland Department of Natural Resources, State Forest and Park Service. For more information, contact the park office at P.O. Box 172, Glen Arm, MD 21057; telephone (410)592-2897.

Loch Raven Reservoir

Loch Raven Reservoir, formed by damming the Gunpowder River, lies just north of Baltimore. The bottomlands around the reservoir are famed for a large population of dwarf ginseng (*Panax trifolius*) as well as other common spring wildflowers. In mid-May, the uplands near the dam have Jack-in-the-pulpit (*Arisaema triphyllum*), clustered snakeroot (*Sanicula gregaria*), lyre-leaved sage (*Salvia lyrata*), large-leaved houstonia (*Houstonia purpurea*), and rattlesnake-weed (*Hieracium venosum*).

The area around Loch Raven Reservoir is part of Gunpowder Falls State Park. The park office address is P.O. Box 172, Glen Arm, MD 21057; telephone (410)592-2897.

Directions: From the Baltimore Beltway (I-695), take Providence Road north for almost three miles. Turn right on Loch Raven Road to the parking area by the dam. Other areas on the reservoir can be accessed from Dulaney Valley Road.

North Central Railroad Trail and Phoenix Pond

The North Central Railroad Trail, part of Gunpowder Falls State Park, is a popular hiking and biking trail running north from Cockeysville for twenty miles. Along the old railroad bed and under the power line are open fields with sun-loving wildflowers.

In late May, these fields bloom with bulbous buttercup (*Ranunculus bulbosus*), yellow sweet clover (*Melilotus officinalis*), common cinquefoil

Panax trifolius —
Dwarf ginseng
(height: 3″–8″)

(*Potentilla simplex*), viper's bugloss (*Echium vulgare*), lyre-leaved sage (*Salvia lyrata*), and common fleabane (*Erigeron philadelphicus*).

Just across the road from the North Central Railroad Trail at Phoenix is Phoenix Pond, owned by the city of Baltimore. The pond is filled with spatterdock (*Nuphar advena*), and the pond shores are brightened with swamp buttercup (*Ranunculus septentrionalis*) and true forget-me-not (*Myosotis scorpioides*).

In early April, the trail along the Gunpowder River north of the pond has trout-lily (*Erythronium americanum*) and bloodroot (*Sanguinaria canadensis*). In early May, the hillside above the pond has species typical of dry woodlands, including spiderwort (*Tradescantia virginiana*), early saxifrage (*Saxifraga virginiensis*), large-leaved houstonia (*Houstonia purpurea*), and field hawkweed (*Hieracium caespitosum*).

The North Central Railroad Trail and the trails around Phoenix Pond are part of Gunpowder Falls State Park. For more information, contact the park office at P.O. Box 172, Glen Arm, MD 21057; telephone (410)592-2897.

Directions: From the Baltimore Beltway (I-695), take I-83 north for six miles and go east on Shawan Road. Turn right on York Road, very quickly turn left on Paper Mill Road for three miles, and left on Phoenix Road for one mile. The parking area here will give you access to the railroad trail, the river trail, and Phoenix Pond.

Hereford Area

The Hereford Area of Gunpowder Falls State Park is near the village of Hereford in central Baltimore County. It has a pleasant trail along the river, a cool moist forest, and a fine display of late April wildflowers. The trail downriver goes through rocky woods filled with the white form of erect trillium (*Trillium erectum*) and wood anemone (*Anemone quinquefolia*), two species more common in the mountains than in the Piedmont.

The trail upriver goes along a floodplain covered with Canada May-flower (*Maianthemum canadense*), wild ginger (*Asarum canadense*), slender toothwort (*Dentaria heterophylla*), sweet white violet (*Viola blanda*), smooth yellow violet (*Viola pensylvanica*), and common blue violet (*Viola papilionacea*). Due to the cool microclimate here, early-blooming species such as bloodroot (*Sanguinaria canadensis*) and Dutchman's breeches (*Dicentra cucullaria*) may still be in flower in late April.

The upland woods have early saxifrage (*Saxifraga virginiensis*), dog violet (*Viola conspersa*), and bluets (*Houstonia caerulea*). A large boulder across from the parking area hosts a grand display of wild columbine (*Aquilegia canadensis*), rue-anemone (*Anemonella thalictroides*), and wild pink (*Silene caroliniana*).

The Hereford Area of Gunpowder Falls State Park is managed by the Maryland Department of Natural Resources, State Forest and Park Service. There are no visitor facilities at Hereford. The park office address is P.O. Box 172, Glen Arm, MD 21057; telephone (410)592-2897.

Directions: From the Baltimore Beltway (I-695), take I-83 north for about 14 miles, go west on Mt. Carmel Road (MD-137) for one mile, then north on Masemore Road for one and one-half miles. You will pass a stone house on a narrow curve and come to the parking area just before the river. Cross a little stream for the downriver trail or cross Masemore Road for the upriver trail.

Arisaema triphyllum —
Jack-in-the-pulpit
(height: 1'–3')

Prettyboy Reservoir

Prettyboy Reservoir, the water supply for Baltimore County, is located on the Gunpowder River in the northwestern corner of the county. The 800 acres around the reservoir resemble a forest in New England or the Blue Ridge Mountains, with stands of white pine and eastern hemlock shading the banks of rocky streams. Wildflowers of the north woods seem at home here, and it is not surprising to find Canada Mayflower (*Maianthemum canadense*) and wild sarsaparilla (*Aralia nudicaulis*) flowering in early May.

The moist, rich soil of the cool woods produces unusually large specimens of Jack-in-the-pulpit (*Arisaema triphyllum*), as well as smooth Solomon's-seal (*Polygonatum biflorum*), false Solomon's-seal (*Smilacina racemosa*), trout-lily (*Erythronium americanum*), and spring beauty (*Claytonia virginica*).

The drier hillsides support fine stands of pink lady's-slipper (*Cypripedium acaule*), rue-anemone (*Anemonella thalictroides*), birdfoot violet (*Viola pedata*), and bluets (*Houstonia caerulea*).

Open fields around the reservoir have a meadow-like appearance, with flowers such as stout blue-eyed grass (*Sisyrinchium angustifolium*), long-leaved stitchwort (*Stellaria longifolia*), wild strawberry (*Fragaria virginiana*), wild geranium (*Geranium maculatum*), corn salad (*Valerianella locusta*), and common fleabane (*Erigeron philadelphicus*).

Prettyboy Reservoir is located above Gunpowder Falls State Park. It is managed by the Baltimore County Water Department.

Directions: From the Baltimore Beltway (I-695), take I-83 north for about 19 miles, go west on Middletown Road to Middletown, turn left on Cotter–Clipper Mill road for four miles to Hoffmanville, and right on Gunpowder Road for less than one-half mile to the river crossing. Park on the right and walk downriver. There are several other trailheads along Beckleysville Road and Prettyboy Dam Road and many miles of hiking trails in the forests surrounding the reservoir.

HARFORD COUNTY

Harford County is bounded by Baltimore County on the west; Lancaster County, Pennsylvania on the north; the Susquehanna River on the east; and the Chesapeake Bay on the south. Bel Air, Havre de Grace, and Aberdeen are the largest towns of this rural county. The fall line divides Harford

County into two regions: the Piedmont in the northwest and the Coastal Plain in the southeast. Major highways through Harford County are I-95, US-1, and MD-24. Mileages given are from the west end of the Fort McHenry Tunnel in Baltimore.

Rocks State Park

Rocks State Park is located eight miles northwest of Bel Air in northern Harford County. The park contains over 600 acres in an area of impressive natural beauty. Massive boulders line the banks of tumbling Deer Creek. Ancient metamorphic rocks, resistant to erosion, stand high above the landscape and bear fanciful names such as "King and Queen Seats."

Rocks State Park was acquired to protect the rugged beauty and unique character of this area. Except for a few picnic areas, it has been left in its natural state for the enjoyment of hikers and other observers. Several trails wind through the rocky woods and along the streams.

In mid-May, the rich, cool woods above Deer Creek harbor flowering shrubs such as mountain laurel (*Kalmia latifolia*), fringetree (*Chionanthus virginicus*), and arrowwood (*Viburnum dentatum*). Wildflowers in bloom include smooth Solomon's-seal (*Polygonatum biflorum*), false Solomon's-seal (*Smilacina racemosa*), Indian cucumber-root (*Medeola virginiana*), wild geranium (*Geranium maculatum*), wild sarsaparilla (*Aralia nudicaulis*), and goutweed (*Aegopodium podagraria*), a garden escape. Wild ginger (*Asarum canadense*), bloodroot (*Sanguinaria canadensis*), and trailing arbutus (*Epigaea repens*) are earlier blooming species in these woods. The high ridgetops have species adapted to drier conditions, such as bluets (*Houstonia caerulea*) and rattlesnake-weed (*Hieracium venosum*).

The nature trail along Kellogg Branch winds through thickets of rose azalea (*Rhododendron prinophyllum*). The moist bottomland woods are carpeted with Canada Mayflower (*Maianthemum canadense*), sweet white violet (*Viola blanda*), marsh blue violet (*Viola cucullata*), true forget-me-not (*Myosotis scorpioides*), and golden ragwort (*Senecio aureus*).

Rocks State Park is managed by the Maryland Department of Natural Resources, State Forest and Park Service. The park office is located at 3318 Rocks Chrome Hill Road, Jarrettsville, MD 21084; telephone (410)557-7994.

Directions: Take I-95 north from Baltimore for about 24 miles. Then take MD-24 north through Bel Air for about 15 miles. Watch for the park signs on your left. To make a very full day of botanizing, you could combine

Rocks State Park with Susquehanna State Park in eastern Harford County or Shenk's Ferry across the river in Pennsylvania.

Susquehanna State Park

Susquehanna State Park is located along the Susquehanna River in eastern Harford County just north of Havre de Grace. Containing over 2,500 acres, the park parallels the lower Susquehanna River valley with its varying topography, rich forests, steep rocky cliffs, and interesting historical sites.

The east-facing slope along the river near the old Rock Run Grist Mill is reputed to have a large population of drooping trillium (*Trillium flexipes*), a midwestern trillium considered very rare in Maryland. However, many botanists believe that this stand is actually the white form of erect trillium (*Trillium erectum*). Comparison with the trilliums at Shenk's Ferry upriver on the Pennsylvania side of the Susquehanna tends to confirm this view.

Whichever the species, the thousands of white trilliums are quite spectacular on the rocky hillside in late April or early May. Other wildflowers in bloom among the trilliums include wild blue phlox (*Phlox divaricata*), star chickweed (*Stellaria pubera*), Dutchman's breeches (*Dicentra cucullaria*), blue cohosh (*Caulophyllum thalictroides*), downy yellow violet (*Viola pubescens*), and celandine (*Chelidonium majus*). The moist bottomland soil along Rock Run supports a fine colony of Virginia bluebells (*Mertensia virginica*).

Susquehanna State Park is managed by the Maryland Department of Natural Resources, State Forest and Park Service. For more information, contact the park office at 801 Stafford Road, Havre de Grace, MD 21078; telephone (301)939-0643.

Directions: Take I-95 north from Baltimore about 36 miles to Havre de Grace. Take MD-155 east, then turn left on Lapidum Road for two and one-half miles and bear left on Stafford Road along the river. Continue one mile to the old mill, where you can park and walk back to the major wildflower area.

PEEK INTO PENNSYLVANIA

Although most of Pennsylvania is beyond the range of this book, two areas in southeastern Pennsylvania are so interesting that it seemed a shame to leave them out. After all, plants do not recognize state lines, and these two areas have strong affinities with locations in northeastern Maryland. Nottingham Barrens, just over the state line, has a close association with Soldiers Delight and other serpentine areas in Maryland. And Shenk's Ferry Wildflower Preserve on the Susquehanna River is similar in many ways to Susquehanna State Park.

Nottingham Barrens

The Nottingham Barrens are part of the eastern serpentine belt that outcrops in the Piedmont region of Maryland and Pennsylvania. Located on the Maryland-Pennsylvania line near the town of Nottingham in Chester County, Pennsylvania, these serpentine barrens are sometimes called the State Line Barrens.

This line of serpentine outcrops extends over 1,000 acres from Nottingham, through the area called Goat Hill, and southwest to Rock Springs, Maryland. Much of this large serpentine barrens is privately owned, but at Nottingham County Park, over 400 acres have been designated as a natural and protected area.

The thin dry soil overlying serpentine rock produces a unique flora with few woody plants and open areas that resemble prairie grasslands. Only plants that are adapted to very dry, nutrient-poor soil can survive in serpentine barrens. Some serpentine species are midwestern plants accustomed to dry conditions, and some species are characteristic of eastern serpentine barrens. Many species occur both at Nottingham Barrens and at Soldiers Delight serpentine barrens west of Baltimore.

Mid-September is a good time to visit the serpentine barrens at Nottingham County Park. Although the main area of the park has picnic pavilions and other recreational facilities, the nature trail beyond the park office takes you right into the heart of the serpentine barrens natural area.

The dry, rocky hillside is covered with dry-habitat plants such as slender knotweed (*Polygonum tenue*), narrow-leaved mountain-mint (*Pycnanthemum tenuifolium*), and gray goldenrod (*Solidago nemoralis*). Also found on the barrens are beautiful midwestern grasses such as big bluestem (*Andropogon gerardi*), little bluestem (*Andropogon scoparius*), and Indian grass (*Sorghastrum nutans*). Two species unique to eastern serpentine barrens occur at Nottingham Barrens: the hairy variety of field chickweed (*Cerastium arvense*) and serpentine aster (*Aster depauperatus*), a dainty aster that is rare in our area. All but the serpentine aster also are found at Soldiers Delight.

Along the stream are bushy aster (*Aster dumosus*), wavy-leaved aster (*Aster undulatus*), round-leaved boneset (*Eupatorium rotundifolium*), and giant sunflower (*Helianthus giganteus*).

Several low wet places support stands of Canadian burnet (*Sanguisorba canadensis*), great lobelia (*Lobelia siphilitica*), and New York ironweed (*Vernonia noveboracensis*). This association of plants is very similar to that at the Dolfield Road wetland at Soldiers Delight.

A 1979 report by the Chester County Parks and Recreation Department lists other plants of Pennsylvania's serpentine barrens including slender ladies'-tresses (*Spiranthes gracilis*), fameflower (*Talinum teretifolium*), rose pink (*Sabatia angularis*), whorled milkweed (*Asclepias verticillata*), and green milkweed (*Asclepias viridiflora*).

Nottingham Barrens in Nottingham County Park is managed by the Chester County Parks and Recreation Department. The park is located at 150 Park Road, Nottingham, PA 19362; telephone (215)932-9195. Over half of the 650-acre park is maintained as a natural area.

Directions: Take I-95 north from Baltimore about 47 miles. Take MD-272 north across the state line to Nottingham (watch for a sharp left turn at Jim's Market). In Nottingham, cross Old Baltimore Pike and turn left on Herr Drive. At the first crossroads, turn right on Old Baltimore Pike and then right on Park Road. The park entrance is about one-half mile on the left.

Shenk's Ferry Wildflower Preserve

Shenk's Ferry Wildflower Preserve, located southwest of Lancaster, Pennsylvania, is about 75 miles north of Baltimore, but the splendid display of wildflowers in late April is well worth a trip. The 50-acre preserve is set in the deep ravine of Grubb Run, a small stream running into the Susquehanna River above the Conowingo and Holtwood dams. A level, half-mile trail on a ridge above the stream runs below a steep, rocky hill. The trail is easy to walk and offers many chances to admire the cascading stream and the flowering hillsides.

At Shenk's Ferry, the limestone bedrock has produced moist calcareous soils that harbor mature deciduous forests of oaks, beech, and tuliptree. A great diversity of wildflowers is found in this rich habitat, including some species uncommon in the Piedmont region.

The dominant flowering plant of the steep hillsides is the white form of erect trillium (*Trillium erectum*). A few red erect trillium also occur here. The trillium population covers 15 acres and is estimated at several million plants. The trilliums flower among the rocks and are accompanied by Virginia bluebells (*Mertensia virginica*), a species usually found in bottomlands along streams and rivers. The presence of bluebells on the rocky hillside indicates an exceptionally moist soil at Shenk's Ferry.

The entire hillside is like a huge wild rock garden, and every square inch of soil seems to harbor a flowering plant. Mixed in with the trilliums and bluebells are Jack-in-the-pulpit (*Arisaema triphyllum*), wild ginger (*Asarum canadense*), Dutchman's breeches (*Dicentra cucullaria*), squirrel corn (*Dicentra canadensis*), yellow corydalis (*Corydalis flavula*), wild geranium (*Geranium maculatum*), smooth yellow violet (*Viola pensylvanica*), and golden ragwort (*Senecio aureus*).

Miterwort (*Mitella diphylla*) and goldenseal (*Hydrastis canadensis*), mountain plants uncommon in the Piedmont, also grow in the moist soil of this cool ravine. Clyde Gamber, former naturalist at Shenk's Ferry, says that a mixture of northern and southern flora happened because "the southern species came up the stream valleys and the northern species came down the ridgetops."

Even the bare rocks bloom at Shenk's Ferry Wildflower Preserve. Wild columbine (*Aquilegia canadensis*), lyre-leaved rockcress (*Arabis lyrata*), wild stonecrop (*Sedum ternatum*), early saxifrage (*Saxifraga virginiensis*), and green violet (*Hybanthus concolor*) flourish on the exposed limestone.

Near the end of the trail is a large clearing beneath the power line. Almost immediately the woodland flowers disappear, and sun-loving species such as field pansy (*Viola rafinesquii*), henbit (*Lamium amplexicaule*), and corn salad (*Valerianella locusta*) are seen in this open habitat.

Shenk's Ferry Wildflower Preserve is owned and managed by the Pennsylvania Power and Light Company. It is part of the 5,000-acre natural area around Lake Aldred that has been set aside for conservation and recreation.

The power company is very sensitive to the uniqueness of this site and very concerned about its protection. It welcomes visitors to Shenk's Ferry but requests that everyone stay on the main trail and that no one pick the plants or disturb them in any way. For more information, contact the Management Office of Pennsylvania Power and Light Company, 9 New Village Road, Holtwood, PA 17532; telephone (717)284-2278.

Directions: Take I-95 north from Baltimore about 24 miles. Take MD-24 north past Bel Air and Rocks State Park, and go east on MD-165, which changes to PA-74 when it crosses into Pennsylvania. Continue on PA-74 north to PA-372 east, cross the Susquehanna River, and turn left on River Road. After about eight miles, turn left on PA-324 and immediately right on River Road again. Turn left on Shenk's Ferry Road and follow signs to the wildflower preserve.

6

Maryland Coastal Plain

NORTHERN PRINCE GEORGE'S COUNTY

Prince George's County lies east and southeast of Washington. Its western border with Montgomery County is situated near the division between the Piedmont and the Coastal Plain, and its eastern border is the Patuxent River in Anne Arundel and Calvert Counties. The northern part of Prince George's County is heavily developed, with many housing projects, shopping malls, and the towns of Laurel, Beltsville, and Bowie.

On the Coastal Plain, the land is flatter, the soil sandier, and the climate somewhat milder than in the Piedmont. You can tell you are in the Coastal Plain when the forest contains southern trees such as sweet gum and swamp magnolia (*Magnolia virginiana*).

Some herbaceous plants also are more at home in the nutrient-poor, dry soil of this region. Wildflowers likely to be found in this habitat include cut-leaved evening-primrose (*Oenothera laciniata*), blunt-leaved milkweed (*Asclepias amplexicaulis*), and blue toadflax (*Linaria canadensis*).

Coastal Plain bogs were once numerous in Prince George's County; in the early 1900s, there were over 30 bogs filled with beautiful orchids and other rare plants. Now only the tiny Suitland Bog remains of these rich botanical treasures.

Many highways lead from Washington through Prince George's County, including I-95, US-1, and the Baltimore-Washington Parkway to the northeast, US-50 and MD-4 to the east, and MD-5 and MD-210 to the south.

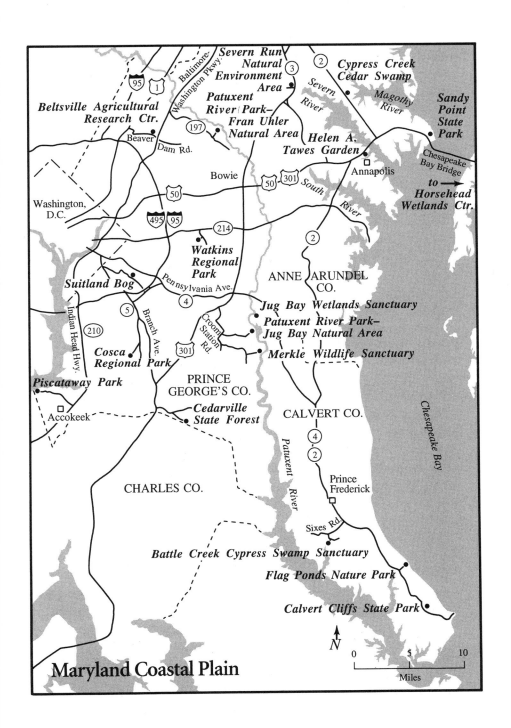

Maryland Coastal Plain

Beltsville Agricultural Research Center

The Beltsville Agricultural Research Center maintains 7,500 acres in northeastern Prince George's County. Most of the land is devoted to gardens and pastures, but some has been left in natural woods and fields. Beltsville is near the site of the old Powder Mill Bogs and the area still has some small wetlands. Much of the research center is off-limits to visitors, but Beaver Dam Road is open and leads to an extensive swamp along Beaverdam Creek.

Records from the research center list typical wetland vegetation such as Turk's-cap lily (*Lilium superbum*), Virginia meadow beauty (*Rhexia virginica*), winged monkey-flower (*Mimulus alatus*), and cardinal flower (*Lobelia cardinalis*).

On a late June visit to Beaver Dam Road, you can find flowers of dry, open fields, including evening lychnis (*Lychnis alba*), bulbous buttercup (*Ranunculus bulbosus*), Carolina cranesbill (*Geranium carolinianum*), rough-fruited cinquefoil (*Potentilla recta*), field pansy (*Viola rafinesquii*), blue toad-flax (*Linaria canadensis*), and Venus's looking-glass (*Triodanis perfoliata*).

Other areas worth exploring are the swamp, filled with the large leaves of skunk cabbage (*Symplocarpus foetidus*), and the oak woods, where partridgeberry (*Mitchella repens*) and spotted wintergreen (*Chimaphila maculata*) flower in deep shade.

Beltsville Agricultural Research Center is managed by the U.S. Department of Agriculture. For more information, contact the Visitor Center, Building 302, BARC-East, Beltsville, MD 20705; telephone (301)344-2483.

Directions: From the Capital Beltway (I-495), take US-1 north for two miles, turn right on Powder Mill Road, right on Edmonston Road, left on Beaver Dam Road, then right on Research Road to the bridge over Beaverdam Creek. From the Baltimore Beltway, take I-95 or US-1 for about 16 miles; turn left on Powder Mill Road and follow above directions.

Patuxent River Park — Fran Uhler Natural Area

The Fran Uhler Natural Area of Patuxent River Park is located on the western shore of the Patuxent River just north of Bowie. Separated by several miles from the main section of the park, this 30-acre bottomland forest can be visited only with permission from the park office.

The main trail is an old road set just below the Amtrak train tracks. Two

Mitchella repens —
Partridgeberry
(height: 1″–3″)

different loop trails wander through the area, traversing bottomlands along the river, moist woodlands, some small swamps, mature upland woods, and old farm fields.

The show of spring wildflowers at the Fran Uhler Area is remarkably diverse for a Coastal Plain forest. In mid-April, the trail along the river blooms with trout-lily (*Erythronium americanum*), Dutchman's breeches (*Dicentra cucullaria*), cut-leaved toothwort (*Dentaria laciniata*), Virginia bluebells (*Mertensia virginica*), and carpets of dwarf ginseng (*Panax trifolius*). In the nearby moist woods are spring beauty (*Claytonia virginica*), star chickweed (*Stellaria pubera*), wood anemone (*Anemone quinquefolia*), and smooth yellow violet (*Viola pensylvanica*).

A small swamp near the main trail contains wetland species such as skunk cabbage (*Symplocarpus foetidus*), spatterdock (*Nuphar advena*), and larger blue flag (*Iris versicolor*). In late summer, look in the swampy areas for Turk's-cap lily (*Lilium superbum*), white turtlehead (*Chelone glabra*), and cardinal flower (*Lobelia cardinalis*).

The open fields and roadsides contain plants of drier habitats such as aborted buttercup (*Ranunculus abortivus*), yellow corydalis (*Corydalis flavula*), mouse-ear cress (*Arabidopsis thaliana*), field pansy (*Viola rafinesquii*), plantain-leaved pussytoes (*Antennaria plantaginifolia*), and coltsfoot (*Tussilago farfara*).

Late summer flowers of the open areas include partridge-pea (*Cassia fasciculata*), blue curls (*Trichostema dichotomum*), black-eyed Susan (*Rudbeckia hirta*), and Maryland golden-aster (*Chrysopsis mariana*).

The Fran Uhler Natural Area of Patuxent River Park is managed by the Maryland National Capital Park and Planning Commission and is located on Lemon's Bridge Road in Bowie. Permission to visit can be obtained by contacting Patuxent River Park, RR Box 3380, Upper Marlboro, MD 20772; telephone (301)627-6074. There are no visitor amenities at the site.

Directions: From the Baltimore-Washington Parkway, take MD-197 (Laurel-Bowie Road) south about five miles and turn left on Lemon's Bridge Road. In about one mile, you will come to a gate and a small parking area.

Patuxent River Park — Jug Bay Natural Area

The Patuxent River Park protects almost 8,000 acres of the Patuxent watershed in Prince George's County. The main area open to the public is the Jug Bay Natural Area, comprising nearly 2,000 acres of freshwater tidal marshes, shrub swamps, upland forests, and open fields. Jug Bay Natural Area is located in eastern Prince George's County near Upper Marlboro. It is just upriver from Merkle Wildlife Sanctuary and across the river from Jug Bay Wetlands Sanctuary in Anne Arundel County.

Several trails wind through the woods and a boardwalk provides easy access to the wetlands. An observation tower overlooks the broad Jug Bay with its expansive growth of wild rice (*Zizania aquatica*) and spatterdock (*Nuphar advena*).

In early April, look for woodland species such as sessile trillium (*Trillium sessile*), round-lobed hepatica (*Hepatica americana*), early saxifrage (*Saxifraga virginiensis*), and trailing arbutus (*Epigaea repens*). In May, Jack-in-the-pulpit (*Arisaema triphyllum*), Canada Mayflower (*Maianthemum canadense*) and showy orchis (*Orchis spectabilis*) bloom in the woods.

In July and August, the wetlands flower with the graceful wild rice, as well as small water-plantain (*Alisma subcordatum*), Virginia dayflower (*Commelina virginica*), pickerelweed (*Pontederia cordata*), Turk's-cap lily (*Lilium superbum*), swamp rose mallow (*Hibiscus moscheutos*), water parsnip (*Sium suave*), swamp milkweed (*Asclepias incarnata*), and cardinal flower (*Lobelia cardinalis*).

Flowering shrubs of this freshwater wetland include swamp magnolia (*Magnolia virginiana*), swamp rose (*Rosa palustris*), silky dogwood (*Cornus amomum*), and buttonbush (*Cephalanthus occidentalis*). Wetland ferns such as royal fern, cinnamon fern, marsh fern, and netted chain fern also grow in abundance here.

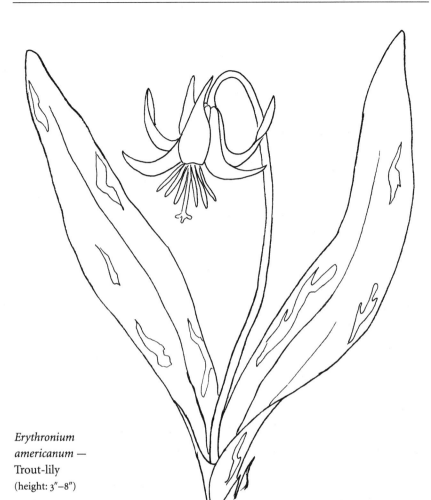

*Erythronium
americanum* —
Trout-lily
(height: 3″–8″)

Some summer flowers in the open fields are Deptford pink (*Dianthus
armeria*), flowering spurge (*Euphorbia corollata*), Queen Anne's lace (*Daucus carota*), narrow-leaved mountain-mint (*Pycnanthemum tenuifolium*),
blue toadflax (*Linaria canadensis*), and sweet everlasting (*Gnaphalium obtusifolium*).

Jug Bay Natural Area in Patuxent River Park is managed by the Maryland National Capital Park and Planning Commission. Facilities available
include canoe rentals and a boat ramp. All activities require a permit or
advance reservation. For more information, contact Patuxent River Park,
R.R. Box 3380, Upper Marlboro, MD 20772; telephone (301)627-6074.

Directions: From the Capital Beltway (I-495), take MD-4 (Pennsylvania Avenue) east for eight miles. Go south on US-301 for almost two miles, turn left on Croom Station Road, left on Croom Road, and left again on Croom Airport Road. Follow the signs to the park office.

Merkle Wildlife Sanctuary

Merkle Wildlife Sanctuary is located on the Patuxent River just south of Patuxent River Park. Merkle was established to provide wintering grounds for Canada geese on the western shore of the Chesapeake Bay. Over 1,500 acres of freshwater tidal wetlands, old fields, and oak-pine woodlands have been preserved at the sanctuary. The Chesapeake Bay Critical Areas Driving Tour, open only on Sundays, links Merkle with Patuxent River Park.

In May, the woodlands have flowers such as pink lady's-slipper (*Cypripedium acaule*), wild columbine (*Aquilegia canadensis*), Mayapple (*Podophyllum peltatum*), primrose-leaved violet (*Viola primulifolia*), and golden ragwort (*Senecio aureus*).

June brings flowers of Coastal Plain fields, including thyme-leaved sandwort (*Arenaria serpyllifolia*), tall buttercup (*Ranunculus acris*), frostweed (*Helianthemum canadense*), blue toadflax (*Linaria canadensis*), and Mayweed (*Anthemis cotula*). The fields continue to bloom in July with partridge-pea (*Cassia fasciculata*) and butterfly pea (*Clitoria mariana*).

August flowers in the dry fields include lance-leaved goldenrod (*Solidago graminifolia*), white heath aster (*Aster pilosus*), camphorweed (*Heterotheca subaxillaris*), and crownbeard (*Verbesina occidentalis*).

July and August are the best months to visit the wetlands. The driving tour goes on a long wooden bridge across the extensive marshes and shrub swamps of Mattaponi Creek. The wetland vegetation here, very similar to that upriver at Jug Bay Natural Area, includes wild rice (*Zizania aquatica*), Turk's-cap lily (*Lilium superbum*), spatterdock (*Nuphar advena*), swamp rose mallow (*Hibiscus moscheutos*), Virginia meadow beauty (*Rhexia virginica*), cardinal flower (*Lobelia cardinalis*), hollow Joe-Pye-weed (*Eupatorium fistulosum*), and climbing hempweed (*Mikania scandens*).

Merkle Wildlife Sanctuary is managed by the Maryland Department of Natural Resources, Wildlife Division. A beautiful new visitor center has informative displays and attractive herb and butterfly gardens. The sanctuary is located at 11704 Fenno Road, Upper Marlboro, MD 20772; telephone (301)889-1410.

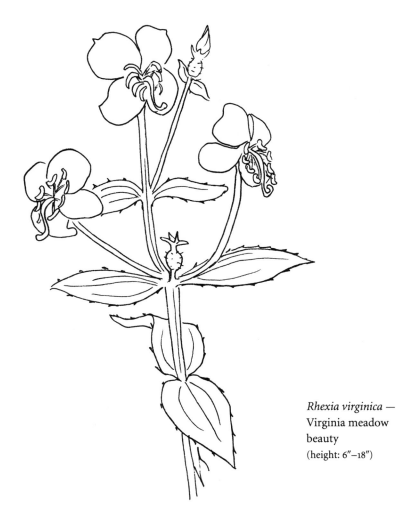

Rhexia virginica —
Virginia meadow
beauty
(height: 6″–18″)

Directions: From the Capital Beltway (I-495), take MD-4 (Pennsylvania Avenue) east for eight miles. Go south on US-301 for almost two miles, turn left on Croom Station Road, and left again on Croom Road. Turn left on Old Thomas Church Road for two and one-half miles, turn right on Fenno Road and left at the sign for Merkle. To take the Critical Areas Driving Tour on Sundays, follow directions to Jug Bay Natural Area and continue to the end of Croom Airport Road where the driving tour begins. Call (301)889-1410 for more information on the driving tour.

SOUTHERN PRINCE GEORGE'S COUNTY

The southern part of Prince George's County is more rural than the northern section, but is rapidly being developed as population increases in the metropolitan area. The natural terrain is typical of the southern Coastal Plain with old tobacco and corn fields, dry oak-pine woodlands, and rolling hillsides along the streams and rivers.

Suitland Bog, the only remaining Coastal Plain bog in Prince George's County, contains many rare plants such as the beautiful rose pogonia (*Pogonia ophioglossoides*), red milkweed (*Asclepias rubra*), and cross-leaved milkwort (*Polygala cruciata*). Other state-rare plants found in southern Prince George's County are Wister's coralroot (*Corallorhiza wisteriana*), Coville's phacelia (*Phacelia ranunculacea*) and nemophila (*Nemophila triloba*).

South of Washington, Prince George's County is bounded by the Potomac River on the west and Charles County on the south. Highways traversing the county to the south include MD-210, MD-5, and US-301.

Watkins Regional Park

Watkins Regional Park is located a few miles north of Upper Marlboro. Most of its 400 acres are devoted to recreational facilities such as ballfields and picnic areas, but some natural areas remain around the nature center, the stream valley, and the floodplain and wetlands along Western Branch.

In mid-April, the oak woodlands of the park burst into flower with spring beauty (*Claytonia virginica*), round-lobed hepatica (*Hepatica americana*), rue-anemone (*Anemonella thalictroides*), bloodroot (*Sanguinaria canadensis*), yellow corydalis (*Corydalis flavula*), and trailing arbutus (*Epigaea repens*). Recently a population of Coville's phacelia (*Phacelia ranunculacea*) was found in the park. This midwestern species previously was known only along the Potomac River in our area.

Damper areas provide habitat for Jack-in-the-pulpit (*Arisaema triphyllum*), wild ginger (*Asarum canadense*), purple cress (*Cardamine douglassii*), pale violet (*Viola striata*), and smooth yellow violet (*Viola pensylvanica*).

Just south of the park boundary, near the intersection of Largo Road and Whitehouse Road, is a wide floodplain along Southwest Branch. Masses of Virginia bluebells (*Mertensia virginica*), as well as trout-lily (*Erythronium americanum*), Dutchman's breeches (*Dicentra cucullaria*), and cut-leaved toothwort (*Dentaria laciniata*) grow here amidst the brush and trash of the roadside.

In mid-May, the woods at Watkins Park harbor false Solomon's-seal (*Smilacina racemosa*), perfoliate bellwort (*Uvularia perfoliata*), pink lady's-slipper (*Cypripedium acaule*), showy orchis (*Orchis spectabilis*), puttyroot (*Aplectrum hyemale*), and the rare Wister's coralroot (*Corallorhiza wisteriana*).

June flowers in the upland woods include pipsissewa (*Chimaphila umbellata*), spotted wintergreen (*Chimaphila maculata*), and round-leaved pyrola (*Pyrola rotundifolia*).

The wetlands bloom in late summer with seedbox (*Ludwigia alternifolia*), square-stemmed monkey-flower (*Mimulus ringens*), cardinal flower (*Lobelia cardinalis*), and yellow sneezeweed (*Helenium autumnale*). The dry fields under the power line have partridge-pea (*Cassia fasciculata*), wild sensitive plant (*Cassia nictitans*), common evening-primrose (*Oenothera biennis*), and cat's-ear (*Hypochoeris radicata*).

Watkins Regional Park is managed by the Maryland National Capital Park and Planning Commission and is located at 301 Watkins Park Road, Upper Marlboro, MD 20772; telephone (301)249-6202. The nature center has live animal displays and regular programs for the public.

Directions: From the Capital Beltway (I-495), take Central Avenue (MD-214) east about three miles to Watkins Park Road. Turn right and go about one mile to the park entrance on the right.

Suitland Bog

"Suitland Bog, a most unique habitat," says the brochure about this small and special place. Indeed, it is hard to believe that this true bog is located inside the Capital Beltway just east of Washington near the town of Suitland.

The last of more than 30 bogs once found in the Beltsville-Suitland area, Suitland Bog was saved from destruction by encroaching development only by attention from concerned citizens. A 20-acre park surrounding the less than one-acre bog was established in 1975.

Although tiny, Suitland Bog is a perfect gem of a bog with a good growth of sphagnum moss, several carnivorous plants, beautiful orchids, and many rare species. The bog is located on a sandy hillside and is fed by groundwater seeps and a small meandering stream.

The bog and its surrounding woods and fields have been studied for many years. Over 200 plant species have been documented, including 20 species considered state-rare by the Maryland Natural Heritage Program. However, some of these rare species have not been seen at Suitland Bog recently. The short walk along the boardwalk through the bog displays many interesting plants. To study the place thoroughly means getting down on hands and knees to see some of the tiny bog species.

Like many other southern Coastal Plain bogs, Suitland Bog is surrounded by swamp magnolia (*Magnolia virginiana*) and so is called a "magnolia bog." Other woody plants prominent in the bog include possum-haw (*Viburnum nudum*), swamp azalea (*Rhododendron viscosum*), maleberry (*Lyonia ligustrina*), highbush blueberry (*Vaccinium corymbosum*), and sheep laurel (*Kalmia angustifolia*), a northern species rare in Maryland.

Mid-June is a good time to visit the bog, for then many shrubs are flowering along with the beautiful bog orchid, rose pogonia (*Pogonia ophioglossoides*). Other species in bloom include swamp dewberry (*Rubus hispidus*), and dwarf St. Johnswort (*Hypericum mutilum*). The pine woods surrounding the bog may have a few fading blossoms of pink lady's-slipper (*Cypripedium acaule*) and many nodding white flowers of spotted wintergreen (*Chimaphila maculata*).

Three species of carnivorous plants are found at Suitland Bog. The only naturally occurring one is spatulate-leaved sundew (*Drosera intermedia*). Round-leaved sundew (*Drosera rotundifolia*) did occur but has not been seen for many years. In the 1930s, thread-leaved sundew (*Drosera filiformis*) and northern pitcher-plant (*Sarracenia purpurea*) were planted in the bog, and they have thrived and multiplied. All three carnivorous plants flower in June, and the specialized leaves with adaptations for catching insects can be seen all summer.

Late June brings the blooming of other rare bog plants such as bunch-flower (*Melanthium virginicum*), ten-angled pipewort (*Eriocaulon decangulare*), and red milkweed (*Asclepias rubra*). Later summer flowers include Virginia meadow beauty (*Rhexia virginica*), marsh St. Johnswort (*Hypericum virginicum*), and cross-leaved milkwort (*Polygala cruciata*).

The bog contains other interesting plants, including several rare sedges, an unusual clubmoss, and many wetland ferns.

The surrounding terrain has been degraded by nearby sand and gravel operations and by housing developments right on the border of the pro-

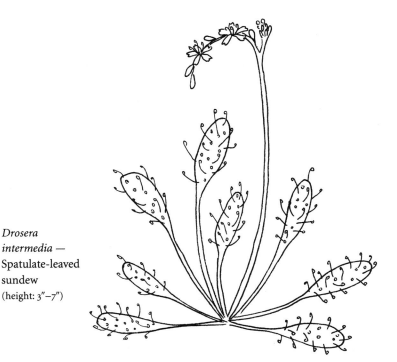

Drosera intermedia — Spatulate-leaved sundew (height: 3″–7″)

tected area. However, even the open fields around the bog are worth exploring. In mid-June, you can find flowers that flourish in nutrient-poor, sandy
soil, such as wild yellow flax (*Linum virginianum*), cut-leaved evening-
primrose (*Oenothera laciniata*), hyssop skullcap (*Scutellaria integrifolia*),
blue toadflax (*Linaria canadensis*), bracted plantain (*Plantago aristata*),
Venus's looking-glass (*Triodanis perfoliata*), cat's-ear (*Hypochoeris radicata*),
and whorled coreopsis (*Coreopsis verticillata*).

Suitland Bog is managed by the Maryland National Capital Parks and
Planning Commission. In order to protect the bog, the park is barred by a
locked gate at the entrance. To obtain information on walks or to arrange a
visit to the bog, contact Clearwater Nature Center, 11000 Thrift Road, Clinton, MD 20735; telephone (301)297-4575.

Directions: From the Capital Beltway (I-495), take Allentown Road
toward Andrews Air Force Base. At the entrance to the base, turn the
opposite way onto Suitland Road. Go for a little more than one mile, go
under Suitland Parkway, and look for the sign on the right. The parking
area is closed unless the gate is open for a scheduled walk.

Cosca Regional Park

Cosca Regional Park is located in southern Prince George's County near Clinton. In the midst of heavy suburban development, the park contains 500 acres, mainly devoted to recreational facilities such as athletic fields, tennis courts, boating and fishing, and picnic/play areas. However, the area around the Clearwater Nature Center has been left natural, and several trails wind through the woods, along the stream, and beside the lake.

In April, the dry woodlands bloom with perfoliate bellwort (*Uvularia perfoliata*), spring beauty (*Claytonia virginica*), star chickweed (*Stellaria pubera*), bloodroot (*Sanguinaria canadensis*), trailing arbutus (*Epigaea repens*), and bluets (*Houstonia caerulea*).

In May, the trail edges and open fields flower with wild pink (*Silene caroliniana*), thyme-leaved sandwort (*Arenaria serpyllifolia*), cut-leaved evening-primrose (*Oenothera laciniata*), blunt-leaved milkweed (*Asclepias amplexicaulis*), blue toadflax (*Linaria canadensis*), Mayweed (*Anthemis cotula*), and field hawkweed (*Hieracium caespitosum*).

Several orchids are found at Cosca in May, including pink lady's-slipper (*Cypripedium acaule*), showy orchis (*Orchis spectabilis*), puttyroot (*Aplectrum hyemale*), and lily-leaved twayblade (*Liparis lilifolia*).

Among the summer flowers in the fields are Deptford pink (*Dianthus armeria*), thimbleweed (*Anemone virginiana*), spotted St. Johnswort (*Hypericum punctatum*), pineweed (*Hypericum gentianoides*), butterflyweed (*Asclepias tuberosa*), and black-eyed Susan (*Rudbeckia hirta*).

The dry upland woods have some summer-flowering species including St. Andrew's cross (*Ascyrum hypericoides*), clammy cuphea (*Cuphea viscosissima*), and blue curls (*Trichostema dichotomum*).

Summer brings flowers to the wetlands around the lake also. Look for Turk's-cap lily (*Lilium superbum*), swamp rose mallow (*Hibiscus moscheutos*), swamp milkweed (*Asclepias incarnata*), square-stemmed monkey flower (*Mimulus ringens*), and purple-headed sneezeweed (*Helenium flexuosum*).

Cosca Regional Park is managed by the Maryland National Capital Park and Planning Commission and is located at 11000 Thrift Road, Clinton, MD 20735; telephone (301)297-4575 for the Clearwater Nature Center. The nature center staff also manages the nearby Cheltenham Wetlands Park and Suitland Bog, both open by reservation only.

Directions: From the Capital Beltway (I-495 and I-95), take Branch Avenue (MD-5) south for about three miles, bear right on Old Branch Avenue for another three miles, and turn right on Thrift Road. Watch for park signs on the right.

Piscataway Park

Piscataway Park, established to protect the view from Mount Vernon across the Potomac River, is located near the town of Accokeek in southwestern Prince George's County. With over 1,500 acres of park land and scenic easements, the park has varied habitats that include river shores, tidal freshwater marshes, shrub swamps, forested wetlands, open fields, and dry oak woodlands. Where Accokeek Creek enters the Potomac River, a beautiful freshwater marsh is crossed by a fine boardwalk. A trail continues along the river, past the open fields and wetlands of Hard Bargain Farm Environmental Center, all the way to Mockley Point on Piscataway Creek.

Flowering in the bottomland woods begins in April with the introduced lesser celandine (*Ranunculus ficaria*), as well as native plants such as trout-lily (*Erythronium americanum*), spring beauty (*Claytonia virginica*), Dutchman's breeches (*Dicentra cucullaria*), and Virginia bluebells (*Mertensia virginica*). In the moist uplands are sessile trillium (*Trillium sessile*), star chickweed (*Stellaria pubera*), bloodroot (*Sanguinaria canadensis*), yellow corydalis (*Corydalis flavula*), and cut-leaved toothwort (*Dentaria laciniata*).

May flowers in the rich woodlands include spring forget-me-not (*Myosotis verna*) and nemophila (*Nemophila triloba*). The drier woods have pinxter flower (*Rhododendron periclymenoides*), deerberry (*Vaccinium stamineum*), bluets (*Houstonia caerulea*), and rattlesnake-weed (*Hieracium venosum*).

In May, the Accokeek Creek marsh flowers with sweetflag (*Acorus calamus*), yellow iris (*Iris pseudacorus*), silky dogwood (*Cornus amomum*), and arrowwood (*Viburnum dentatum*).

Early summer species of the marsh include arrow arum (*Peltandra virginica*), larger blue flag (*Iris versicolor*), spatterdock (*Nuphar advena*), and tall meadowrue (*Thalictrum pubescens*).

The marsh continues to bloom in late summer with broad-leaved arrowhead (*Sagittaria latifolia*), swamp rose mallow (*Hibiscus moscheutos*), winged monkey-flower (*Mimulus alatus*), buttonbush (*Cephalanthus occi-*

dentalis), cardinal flower (*Lobelia cardinalis*), larger bur-marigold (*Bidens laevis*), and New York ironweed (*Vernonia noveboracensis*).

Summer flowers of the river shore are fog-fruit (*Lippia lanceolata*), wild mint (*Mentha arvensis*), and false pimpernel (*Lindernia dubia*). Additional wetland species at Mockley Point are pickerelweed (*Pontederia cordata*) and halberd-leaved rose mallow (*Hibiscus laevis*).

In early summer, the open fields flower with evening lychnis (*Lychnis alba*), narrow-leaved vetch (*Vicia angustifolia*), small-flowered cranesbill (*Geranium pusillum*), cut-leaved evening-primrose (*Oenothera laciniata*), corn salad (*Valerianella locusta*), and yellow passion flower (*Passiflora lutea*).

Late summer bloomers in the fields include elephant's-foot (*Elephantopus carolinianus*), hollow Joe-Pye-weed (*Eupatorium fistulosum*), mistflower (*Eupatorium coelestinum*), and tickseed-sunflower (*Bidens polylepis*).

Piscataway Park is managed by the National Park Service, National Capital Parks East. There are no visitor facilities at the marsh or along the river. For more information on the park, contact the National Capital Parks East, 1099 Anacostia Drive SE, Washington, DC 20020; telephone (202)763-4601.

Directions: From the Capital Beltway (I-495), take Indian Head Highway (MD-210) south for ten miles. Turn right on Bryan Point Road. Go for three miles to the park sign on the right, and take the gravel road to the parking lot.

Cedarville State Forest

Cedarville State Forest is located on the Prince George's–Charles County line at the headwaters of the large Zekiah Swamp. The 3,500 acres contain typical Coastal Plain trees such as Virginia pine, willow oak, sweet gum, and red maple. Several areas are available to the public, including campgrounds, hiking trails, and the Cedarville Pond near Zekiah Swamp Run.

In mid-June, the open fields bloom with sundrops (*Oenothera fruticosa*), fringed loosestrife (*Lysimachia ciliata*), blue toadflax (*Linaria canadensis*), cow-wheat (*Melampyrum lineare*), and large-leaved houstonia (*Houstonia purpurea*).

Two carnivorous plants have been introduced at Cedarville Pond. Northern pitcher-plant (*Sarracenia purpurea*) has naturalized in a marshy

Oenothera fruticosa —
Sundrops
(height: 1′–3′)

area near the dam and spatulate-leaved sundew (*Drosera intermedia*) grows at the edge of the pond.

Orchids reported from Cedarville State Forest include pink lady's-slipper (*Cypripedium acaule*), cranefly orchid (*Tipularia discolor*), and downy rattlesnake-plantain (*Goodyera pubescens*) in dry woods and ragged fringed orchid (*Habenaria lacera*) in wet meadows. Closed gentian (*Gentiana clausa*) has been found in a marshy area near the pond.

Cedarville State Forest is managed by the Maryland Department of Natural Resources, State Forest and Park Service. For more information, contact Cedarville State Forest, Route 4, Box 106A, Brandywine, MD 20613; telephone (301)888-1622.

Directions: From the Capital Beltway (I-495), take Branch Avenue (MD-5) south for about eleven miles, turn left on Cedarville Road, go two and one-half miles and turn right at the park entrance on Bee Oak Road. Continue past the office and turn right on Forest Road for Cedarville Pond and the Swamp Trail.

ANNE ARUNDEL COUNTY

Anne Arundel County lies east of Prince George's County, with Baltimore County to the north and the Chesapeake Bay to the east. Although the northern part of the county is urbanized, the southern part is still largely rural. Annapolis, the state capitol, is a charming city on the Severn River near the bay.

Natural habitats in Anne Arundel County are dominated by tidal estuaries of the bay and its tributaries. Habitats include freshwater, brackish, and salt marshes, swamps and bogs, fields of sandy soil, and dry oak-pine woodlands.

Wetland plants of the brackish and salt marshes are adapted to high saline conditions and daily fluctuations of water level. Some species found in Anne Arundel County's brackish wetlands are narrow-leaved cattail (*Typha angustifolia*) and salt-marsh fleabane (*Pluchea odorata*).

Upland plants of this region grow well in the light, sterile soil and the hot, humid summers. Wildflowers found here more often than in counties to the west include frostweed (*Helianthemum canadense*) and horsemint (*Monarda punctata*), as well as two state-rare species, angle-pod (*Matelea carolinensis*) and red turtlehead (*Chelone obliqua*).

MD-2 and MD-3 (I-97) reach Anne Arundel County from the Baltimore area and US-50 and MD-214 lead there from Washington. US-50/301 is the major highway going east and the route of the Chesapeake Bay Bridge to the eastern shore of Maryland.

Jug Bay Wetlands Sanctuary

Jug Bay Wetlands Sanctuary in Anne Arundel County is a 350-acre nature preserve protecting a large tidal freshwater marsh on the Patuxent River. It is located east of Upper Marlboro and directly across the river from Patuxent River Park–Jug Bay Natural Area in Prince George's County. Jug Bay Wetlands Sanctuary has been designated a component of the Chesapeake Bay National Estuarine Research Reserve in Maryland.

Habitats here include an extensive tidal marsh dominated by wild rice (*Zizania aquatica*) and spatterdock (*Nuphar advena*), a small shrub swamp on the edge of the marsh, dry oak woods, and open fields with sandy soil. Several trails wind through the woods, a short boardwalk makes the marsh and swamp accessible, and a longer trail passes through the wetlands to the open river.

In early May, the woodlands and open fields are in bloom. Species flowering in the woods include pink lady's-slipper (*Cypripedium acaule*), false Solomon's-seal (*Smilacina racemosa*), Indian cucumber-root (*Medeola virginiana*), and spring beauty (*Claytonia virginica*). In the fields and open areas along the trails are thyme-leaved sandwort (*Arenaria serpyllifolia*), lyre-leaved rockcress (*Arabis lyrata*), mouse-ear cress (*Arabidopsis thaliana*), frostweed (*Helianthemum canadense*), blue toadflax (*Linaria canadensis*), dwarf dandelion (*Krigia virginica*), and rattlesnake-weed (*Hieracium venosum*).

The wetlands do not come into full flower until late summer, but some early-blooming species are found in May, including swamp buttercup (*Ranunculus septentrionalis*), marsh blue violet (*Viola cucullata*), and swamp azalea (*Rhododendron viscosum*).

By July, the tidal wetlands are in bloom with the flowering sprays of wild rice, as well as broad-leaved arrowhead (*Sagittaria latifolia*), arrow arum (*Peltandra virginica*), pickerelweed (*Pontederia cordata*), Turk's-cap lily (*Lilium superbum*), swamp rose (*Rosa palustris*), swamp rose mallow (*Hibiscus moscheutos*), and square-stemmed monkey-flower (*Mimulus ringens*).

Summer flowers of the uplands include partridge-pea (*Cassia fasci-*

culata), St. Andrew's cross (*Ascyrum hypericoides*), yellow passionflower (*Passiflora lutea*), butterflyweed (*Asclepias tuberosa*), horsemint (*Monarda punctata*), blue curls (*Trichostema dichotomum*), and buttonweed (*Diodia teres*).

Several plants have been found at Jug Bay Wetlands Sanctuary that are near the northern edge of their range and thus are rare in Maryland. Among the showier of these plants are velvety tick-trefoil (*Desmodium viridiflorum*), angle-pod (*Matelea carolinensis*), and red turtlehead (*Chelone obliqua*). These and other rare species are closely monitored and protected at the sanctuary.

Jug Bay Wetlands Sanctuary is managed by the Anne Arundel County Department of Parks and Recreation. It is a limited access facility, open to the public for educational programs or by advance request. An attractive visitor center has interesting displays and hands-on activities. For more information or to schedule a visit, call (410)741-9330.

Directions: From the Capital Beltway (I-495), take Pennsylvania Avenue (MD-4) east past Upper Marlboro and cross the Patuxent River. Call the above number for directions.

Cypress Creek Cedar Swamp

Cypress Creek Cedar Swamp is located in eastern Anne Arundel County a few miles north of Annapolis. This small swamp contains a stand of Atlantic white-cedar, a Coastal Plain tree that is uncommon on the western shore of the Chesapeake Bay.

The hillside above the swamp has several wetland shrubs including swamp magnolia (*Magnolia virginiana*), sweet pepperbush (*Clethra alnifolia*), and swamp azalea (*Rhododendron viscosum*). Wetland ferns such as netted chain fern, cinnamon fern, and royal fern carpet the wooded swamp.

In early August, look along the edge of the swamp for yellow fringed orchid (*Habenaria ciliaris*) and swamp loosestrife (*Decodon verticillata*).

In the more open wetland near the Magothy River are scythe-fruited arrowhead (*Sagittaria lancifolia*), swamp rose mallow (*Hibiscus moscheutos*), seashore mallow (*Kosteletzkya virginica*), mock bishop's-weed (*Ptilimnium capillaceum*), rattlesnake-master (*Eryngium aquaticum*), water parsnip (*Sium suave*), swamp milkweed (*Asclepias incarnata*), cardinal flower (*Lobelia cardinalis*), and salt-marsh fleabane (*Pluchea odorata*).

The Cypress Creek Cedar Swamp is owned by the Anne Arundel County Department of Utilities. There is no parking area to access the swamp, and there are no trails on the property.

Directions: On US-50/301 at the Severn River Bridge, continue east for about one mile, and then take MD-2 north for four and one-half miles. Park at the pumping station on the right side of the highway and walk down the hill to the swamp, or park at the shopping center on the left side of the highway and cross over.

Severn Run Natural Environment Area

Located near the headwaters of the Severn River in northern Anne Arundel County, the Severn Run Natural Environment Area is an undeveloped park protecting the watershed of Severn Run.

Also protected here is a population of climbing fern, an unusual and rare fern in Maryland. Other ferns found here include New York fern and sensitive fern. In August, the wet meadows along the stream flower with mad-dog skullcap (*Scutellaria lateriflora*), sweet Joe-Pye-weed (*Eupatorium purpureum*), and other species.

Severn Run Natural Environment Area is managed by the Maryland Department of Natural Resources, State Forest and Park Service. For more information, contact Sandy Point State Park, 800 Revell Highway, Annapolis, MD 21401; telephone (410)757-1841.

Directions: From US-50 at Bowie, take MD-3 north for almost 11 miles, turn left on Dicus Mill Road for about one-half mile to a small parking area on the left, and walk upstream on the right. From the Baltimore Beltway (I-695), take MD-3 for about nine miles, turn right on Dicus Mill Road and follow above directions.

Helen Avalynne Tawes Garden

The Helen Avalynne Tawes Garden is a six-acre botanical garden located at the headquarters of the Maryland Department of Natural Resources in Annapolis. The garden features cultivated plantings, pleasant ponds, and representations of several natural habitats of Maryland, including eastern shore wetlands, a Piedmont stream valley, and a western Maryland forest.

In a large pond near the office building are flowering aquatic plants such as larger blue flag (*Iris versicolor*) and fragrant water-lily (*Nymphaea odorata*).

The eastern shore community is planted with loblolly pine, bayberry, and beach plum. Along a short boardwalk grow broad-leaved cattail (*Typha latifolia*) and swamp rose mallow (*Hibiscus moscheutos*).

A tiny representation of a bald cypress swamp contains sweet pepper-bush (*Clethra alnifolia*), white turtlehead (*Chelone glabra*), cardinal flower (*Lobelia cardinalis*), and hollow Joe-Pye-weed (*Eupatorium fistulosum*).

The Piedmont streambank community is a deciduous woodland with spring wildflowers such as Mayapple (*Podophyllum peltatum*) and Virginia bluebells (*Mertensia virginica*).

A hillside planted with eastern hemlock, white pine, black birch, and striped maple features a small waterfall and gives an impression of the forests in western Maryland. Wildflowers here include Jack-in-the-pulpit (*Arisaema triphyllum*), foamflower (*Tiarella cordifolia*), and Virginia water-leaf (*Hydrophyllum virginianum*).

The Tawes Garden is reached from the lobby of the Tawes State Office Building, 580 Taylor Avenue, Annapolis, MD 21401. For more information, call the naturalist at (410)947-3717.

Directions: From US-50/301 just north of Annapolis, go south on Rowe Boulevard. At the second light, turn right on Taylor Avenue and left into the parking lot for the Tawes State Office Building.

Sandy Point State Park

Sandy Point State Park, located in Anne Arundel County at the western end of the Chesapeake Bay Bridge, is well known to boaters, fishermen, and beach-goers. It is also a favorite spot for birders, who regularly sight rare species here, including the peregrine falcons who nest on the pillars of the Bay Bridge. Botanists enjoy exploring the sandy beach, brackish marsh, and old fields of this 800-acre park.

Coming into the park, do not turn toward the tollgate but continue on the road straight ahead. At the sewer line crossing is a meadow habitat that in early August flowers with Deptford pink (*Dianthus armeria*), partridge-pea (*Cassia fasciculata*), rough-fruited cinquefoil (*Potentilla recta*), spotted St. Johnswort (*Hypericum punctatum*), rose pink (*Sabatia angularis*), horse nettle (*Solanum carolinense*), black-eyed Susan (*Rudbeckia hirta*), and ox-eye daisy (*Chrysanthemum leucanthemum*). In a wet ditch along the road is false pimpernel (*Lindernia dubia*).

Continue on the road to the headquarters office. A pond behind the office is ringed with hyssop-leaved boneset (*Eupatorium hyssopifolium*) and early goldenrod (*Solidago juncea*) and is filled with swamp rose mallow (*Hibiscus moscheutos*) and purple loosestrife (*Lythrum salicaria*).

Returning to the main entrance road, go through the tollgate and turn right to take a hiking trail through the brackish marsh. The marsh is dominated by the invasive reedgrass (*Phragmites australis*), and only a few native wetland species such as New York ironweed (*Vernonia noveboracensis*) and groundsel-tree (*Baccharis halimifolia*) are found.

At the old Sandy Point farmhouse, the garden contains peppermint (*Mentha piperita*), common burdock (*Arctium minus*), and the striking blooms of passion flower (*Passiflora incarnata*). This southern species, rare in Maryland, probably was planted here along the fence.

Sandy Point State Park is managed by the Maryland Department of Natural Resources, State Forest and Park Service. The office is located at 800 Revell Highway, Annapolis, MD 21401; telephone (410)757-1841. The Corcoran Tract, a special nature study area, can be visited with permission from the park office.

Directions: On US-50/301 north of Annapolis, continue east almost to the Chesapeake Bay Bridge. Take the last exit before the bridge (clearly marked for the park). Cross the overpass and continue straight ahead for the meadow and pond, or turn right through the tollgate for the marsh trail and the farmhouse.

THE EASTERN SHORE

Although the western shore of the Chesapeake Bay was chosen as the eastern boundary of the area covered in this book, the Horsehead Wetlands Center just across the Chesapeake Bay Bridge is so easily accessible that it is included.

On the eastern shore of Maryland, you can find true salt-marsh habitat with typical plants such as salt-marsh cordgrass (*Spartina alterniflora*), salt-meadow hay (*Spartina patens*), spikegrass (*Distichlis spicata*), sea lavender (*Limonium carolinianum*), and groundsel-tree (*Baccharis halimifolia*).

The eastern shore is famous for boating, fishing, hunting, and relaxing and is an excellent area for birding and botanizing. However, you have to be willing to get wet, hot, and mosquito-bitten to explore some of the best places.

US-50/301 across the Chesapeake Bay Bridge is the only route to the eastern shore in the Washington-Baltimore area.

Horsehead Wetlands Center

Horsehead Wetlands Center is located on the eastern shore of the Chesapeake Bay near Grasonville in Queen Anne's County. It is a natural eastern shore community close to the Washington-Baltimore area and contains excellent examples of habitats, plants, birds, and other animals typical of this region.

A tract of 300 acres on a large peninsula jutting out into the Chesapeake Bay has been preserved as a waterfowl sanctuary, with exhibits of resident birds and programs on wetlands, waterfowl, and the ecology of the bay. Several trails traverse the different habitats including old farm fields, brackish marshes, salt marshes, and open beaches of the bay.

The habitats found at Horsehead are typical of the Eastern Shore Coastal Plain, with fields of nutrient-poor, sandy soil and broad, expansive saline wetlands. Spring wildflowers are not abundant here; summer and fall are the times to enjoy these fields and marshes.

From August through September, the fields bloom with downy lobelia (*Lobelia puberula*), black-eyed Susan (*Rudbeckia hirta*), panicled hawkweed (*Hieracium paniculatum*), lance-leaved coreopsis (*Coreopsis lanceolata*), lance-leaved goldenrod (*Solidago graminifolia*), and late-flowering boneset (*Eupatorium serotinum*).

In very dry, sandy fields grow several plants characteristic of this sterile habitat, including slender ladies'-tresses (*Spiranthes gracilis*), blunt-leaved milkweed (*Asclepias amplexicaulis*), blue toadflax (*Linaria canadensis*), hyssop-leaved boneset (*Eupatorium hyssopifolium*), sweet everlasting (*Gnaphalium obtusifolium*), and seaside goldenrod (*Solidago sempervirens*).

A boardwalk trail across the brackish marsh takes you by wetland plants including swamp rose mallow (*Hibiscus moscheutos*), seashore mallow (*Kosteletzkya virginica*), Virginia meadow beauty (*Rhexia virginica*), purple gerardia (*Agalinis purpurea*), cardinal flower (*Lobelia cardinalis*), and yellow sneezeweed (*Helenium autumnale*).

In the salt marshes and sandy beaches of the bay are several species not found in freshwater wetlands, such as sea lavender (*Limonium carolini-*

anum), salt-marsh fleabane (*Pluchea odorata*), and large salt-marsh aster (*Aster tenuifolius*).

Owned by The Wildfowl Trust of North America, Horsehead Wetlands Center welcomes visitors. A new visitor center, informative exhibits, and rest rooms are near the office. For more information, contact the Horsehead Wetlands Center, P.O. Box 519, Grasonville, MD 21628; telephone (410)827-6694.

Directions: From the east side of the Chesapeake Bay Bridge, continue on US-50/301 east for about seven miles. Turn right through Grasonville on MD-18 for almost one mile, turn right on Perry Corner Road for one-half mile, and turn right at the sign for Horsehead Wetlands Center.

CALVERT COUNTY

Calvert County lies south of Anne Arundel County with the Patuxent River on the west and the Chesapeake Bay on the east. It is still mostly rural with old farms, small towns, beaches along the bay, and some resort areas. The cliffs along the bay shore are well known for an abundance of fossils such as shark teeth and mammal bones.

Calvert County has a wide variety of wetlands including tidal brackish marshes, freshwater ponds, and a small bald cypress swamp. Red turtlehead (*Chelone obliqua*) is among the Maryland rare plants found in the county.

Prince Frederick, the county seat, is the largest town in Calvert County. To reach Calvert County from the metropolitan areas, take Maryland Highways 2 and 4.

Battle Creek Cypress Swamp Sanctuary

The Battle Creek Cypress Swamp near Prince Frederick is considered the most northwestern bald cypress swamp in the United States. Although not uncommon on Maryland's eastern shore, bald cypress trees are not known to occur naturally elsewhere on the western shore or in other regions of Maryland.

This unique cypress swamp has been declared a registered natural landmark by the National Park Service and was the first Maryland preserve purchased by The Nature Conservancy. Pine woods and open farm fields surround the 100-acre swamp dominated by the tall, majestic bald cypress trees.

A short boardwalk trail winds through the heart of the swamp. The canopy of cypress trees creates a dark primeval atmosphere even in winter when the trees are bare, and the swamp is cool and quiet in the heat of summer. Sweet gum and red maple are other trees in the swamp, and flowering shrubs include silky dogwood (*Cornus amomum*) and arrowwood (*Viburnum dentatum*). Numerous ferns flourish in the damp environment, including marsh fern, netted chain fern, cinnamon fern, and royal fern.

In early spring, the hooded flowers and then the large leaves of skunk cabbage (*Symplocarpus foetidus*) appear in the swamp. Later come golden club (*Orontium aquaticum*), false hellebore (*Veratrum viride*), cursed crowfoot (*Ranunculus sceleratus*), Pennsylvania bittercress (*Cardamine pensylvanica*), and marsh blue violet (*Viola cucullata*).

On the edges of the swamp grow Jack-in-the-pulpit (*Arisaema triphyllum*), spring beauty (*Claytonia virginica*), cut-leaved toothwort (*Dentaria laciniata*), golden Alexanders (*Zizia aurea*), and golden ragwort (*Senecio aureus*).

In early May, pink lady's-slipper (*Cypripedium acaule*) flowers in the pine woods. Growing in the poor sandy soil of dry open fields are small-flowered cranesbill (*Geranium pusillum*), field pansy (*Viola rafinesquii*), prickly pear (*Opuntia humifusa*), and blue toadflax (*Linaria canadensis*).

Summer-flowering species are not abundant in the swamp because of the lack of sunlight. However, some plants are able to grow in the deep shade, such as lizard's-tail (*Saururus cernuus*), spotted jewelweed (*Impatiens capensis*), cardinal flower (*Lobelia cardinalis*), and the rare red turtlehead (*Chelone obliqua*).

Late summer brings blooms of the open fields, including wild sensitive plant (*Cassia nictitans*), common mullein (*Verbascum thapsus*), moth mullein (*Verbascum blattaria*), chicory (*Cichorium intybus*), lance-leaved goldenrod (*Solidago graminifolia*), and rough-stemmed goldenrod (*Solidago rugosa*).

The Battle Creek Cypress Swamp Sanctuary is managed by the Calvert County Natural Resources Division. The attractive nature center has interesting exhibits about the cypress swamp community. For more information, contact Battle Creek Cypress Swamp Sanctuary, Calvert County Courthouse, Prince Frederick, MD 20678; telephone (410)535-5327.

Directions: On MD-2/4 east, go south past Prince Frederick for about one mile and turn right on Sixes Road (MD-506). Go for almost two miles and turn left on Gray's Road. Look for the sign to the sanctuary on the right. A visit to Battle Creek Cypress Swamp can be combined with a visit to Flag Ponds Nature Park and/or Calvert Cliffs State Park.

Flag Ponds Nature Park

Flag Ponds Nature Park is a 330-acre park on the western shore of the Chesapeake Bay southeast of Prince Frederick. The park is named for several freshwater ponds where the beautiful larger blue flag (*Iris versicolor*) is found. Habitats of the park include the ponds, upland woods, high clay cliffs, forested wetlands, and sandy beaches on the bay. Three miles of trails, a wetlands boardwalk, and observation platforms add to the pleasure of exploring this park.

In mid-April, the uplands flower with wild ginger (*Asarum canadense*), round-lobed hepatica (*Hepatica americana*), spring beauty (*Claytonia virginica*), bloodroot (*Sanguinaria canadensis*), Dutchman's breeches (*Dicentra cucullaria*), and cut-leaved toothwort (*Dentaria laciniata*).

In May, Jack-in-the-pulpit (*Arisaema triphyllum*), false Solomon's-seal (*Smilacina racemosa*), showy orchis (*Orchis spectabilis*), pink lady's-slipper (*Cypripedium acaule*), and Mayapple (*Podophyllum peltatum*) bloom in the woods. Evening lychnis (*Lychnis alba*), wild columbine (*Aquilegia canadensis*), Carolina cranesbill (*Geranium carolinianum*), prickly pear (*Opuntia humifusa*), and blue toadflax (*Linaria canadensis*) flower along the sandy trail that leads to the public beach. Some areas of the beach here have restricted access, as they are habitat for a federally endangered tiger beetle.

June is the time to visit Flag Ponds to see the flowering of the blue flag in the ponds. Other species of freshwater wetlands include swamp rose mallow (*Hibiscus moscheutos*), water-pennywort (*Hydrocotyle umbellata*), and swamp loosestrife (*Decodon verticillatus*).

Flag Ponds Nature Park is managed by the Calvert County Natural Resources Division. For more information, contact Flag Ponds Nature Park, Calvert County Courthouse, Prince Frederick, MD 20678; telephone (401)535-5327.

Directions: On MD-2/4 east, go south past Prince Frederick for ten miles, then look for the sign and turn left to the park. Flag Ponds Nature Park is about 12 miles south of Battle Creek Cypress Swamp and four miles north of Calvert Cliffs State Park.

Calvert Cliffs State Park

Known best as an excellent place to find Miocene Age fossils such as shark teeth and mollusk shells, Calvert Cliffs State Park is an undeveloped park of over 1,200 acres on the western shore of the Chesapeake Bay. The varied habitats include dry fields, oak woodlands, stream valleys, swamps and a bay beach. The trail to the beach and the fossil-filled cliffs is almost two miles long; there are other trails through the deep woodlands.

The mature forest contains pitch pine, swamp chestnut oak, American beech, and American holly. Spring flowers in these upland woods include trailing arbutus (*Epigaea repens*), pinxter flower (*Rhododendron periclymenoides*), mountain laurel (*Kalmia latifolia*), lowbush blueberry (*Vaccinium vacillans*), Indian cucumber-root (*Medeola virginiana*), puttyroot (*Aplectrum hyemale*), showy orchis (*Orchis spectabilis*), and pink lady's-slipper (*Cypripedium acaule*).

Along the lowland streams are wet areas with swamp magnolia (*Magnolia virginiana*), sweet pepperbush (*Clethra alnifolia*), and several wetland ferns. In May, these swampy places bloom with false hellebore (*Veratrum viride*), marsh blue violet (*Viola cucullata*), and northern white violet (*Viola pallens*). In summer, they are filled with lizard's-tail (*Saururus cernuus*) and the large leaves of skunk cabbage (*Symplocarpus foetidus*).

The open fields flower in early May with cut-leaved evening-primrose (*Oenothera laciniata*), yellow wood-sorrel (*Oxalis stricta*), blue toadflax (*Linaria canadensis*), wild strawberry (*Fragaria virginiana*), and narrow-leaved vetch (*Vicia angustifolia*).

Calvert Cliffs State Park is managed by the Maryland Department of Natural Resources, State Forest and Park Service. For more information, contact Calvert Cliffs State Park, Route 4, Box 106A, Brandywine, MD 20613; telephone (301)888-1622.

Directions: On MD-4 east, go south past Prince Frederick for 14 miles, look for the sign and turn left into the park. Calvert Cliffs can easily be visited on the same day as the nearby Flag Ponds and can also be combined with Battle Creek Cypress Swamp.

NEAR BALTIMORE

I-95 runs northeast from Baltimore through Baltimore County and Harford County near the western shore of the Chesapeake Bay. The highway nearly parallels the fall line, the line between the hard rocks of the Piedmont and the unconsolidated sediments of the younger Coastal Plain.

Where the Patapsco, Gunpowder, and Susquehanna rivers drop to the flatter terrain of the Coastal Plain, they become estuaries of the upper Chesapeake Bay. They are wider, slower, and saltier and are subject to daily tides.

This part of Maryland contains broad, flat peninsulas, winding creeks and rivers, and expansive freshwater and brackish marshes. Species of the brackish tidal marshes include big cordgrass (*Spartina cynosuroides*), seashore mallow (*Kosteletzkya virginica*), and salt-marsh fleabane (*Pluchea odorata*).

Much of the shore line is privately held, and the great majority of it is owned by the Army's Aberdeen Proving Ground. However, public access to the estuaries and the bay is found in some places. I-95 and US-40 are the major highways through the Coastal Plain region north of Baltimore.

Black Marsh

Black Marsh is a 1,300-acre park in a highly industrial area along the Patapsco River southeast of Baltimore. Once owned by Bethlehem Steel, the marsh was recently bought by the Maryland Chapter of The Nature Conservancy and then transferred to the state of Maryland. The authors of Baltimore County's master plan have described Black Marsh as "the finest area of tidal wetlands in the whole upper Chesapeake Bay."

Habitats at Black Marsh include mature forests, old fields, freshwater wetlands, brackish marshes, and four miles of Chesapeake Bay coastline. Black Marsh is relatively undisturbed and is habitat for egrets, American bittern, and black rail, as well as several state-rare plants. There is concern that some proposed recreational developments may have an adverse effect on the environmental quality of the park.

The main trail follows an old road through the woods. The left fork leads to an old concrete pier on the bay and then loops around through forested wetlands and extensive brackish marshes. There is no boardwalk through the marsh, so you must return on the trail around the freshwater ponds.

In late summer, the marsh is filled with the high stalks of big cordgrass (*Spartina cynosuroides*), reedgrass (*Phragmites australis*), and narrow-leaved cattail (*Typha angustifolia*). Showier flowers include swamp rose mallow

(*Hibiscus moscheutos*), seashore mallow (*Kosteletzkya virginica*), and swamp loosestrife (*Decodon verticillatus*). Smaller plants of the brackish marsh include whorled water-pennywort (*Hydrocotyle verticillata*) and water pimpernel (*Samolus floribundus*).

Black Marsh is managed by the Maryland Department of Natural Resources, State Forest and Park Service. There are no visitor facilities at present. For more information, contact the State Forest and Park Service, Tawes State Office Building, 580 Taylor Avenue, Annapolis, MD 21401; telephone (410)974-3771.

Directions: From the Baltimore Beltway (I-695) east, take MD-151 south toward Sparrows Point, then bear right on MD-20 to Edgemere. Go about two and one-half miles to the park entrance on the left. On your return, take time to turn right on Miller Island Road to view the extensive brackish marshes and the islands in the bay. (Although located on the Coastal Plain, this site is shown on the map of Maryland Piedmont: Baltimore and Nearby Counties.)

Gunpowder Falls State Park — Hammerman Area

The Gunpowder River and the Little Gunpowder River wind through Baltimore County and come together just before emptying into the Chesapeake Bay. The 14,000-acre Gunpowder Falls State Park protects most of this watershed. Many areas along these rivers are in the Piedmont region, but one of the most popular, the Hammerman Area, is in the Coastal Plain region east of Baltimore.

Extensively developed for swimming, boating, fishing, and picnicking, the Hammerman Area also has a beautiful freshwater tidal marsh. The Muskrat Trail, at the first picnic area, is a one-mile circuit with short boardwalks across the marsh and an observation booth overlooking a tidal creek.

Late summer is a good time to see the marsh in bloom, but early September is also a fine time to visit this park and also avoid the beach traffic. Freshwater marsh species found here are arrow arum (*Peltandra virginica*), arrow-leaved tearthumb (*Polygonum sagittatum*), swamp rose mallow (*Hibiscus moscheutos*), water hemlock (*Cicuta maculata*), water horehound (*Lycopus americanus*), cardinal flower (*Lobelia cardinalis*), swamp beggarticks (*Bidens connata*), tickseed-sunflower (*Bidens polylepis*), and climbing hempweed (*Mikania scandens*). Small plants in shallow areas of the marsh include water-pennywort (*Hydrocotyle umbellata*) and moneywort (*Lysimachia nummularia*).

At the observation booth is a small population of salt-marsh fleabane (*Pluchea odorata*), a species usually found in brackish or salt marshes. Other indicators of brackish water here are big cordgrass (*Spartina cynosuroides*), and narrow-leaved cattail (*Typha angustifolia*).

Late summer bloomers in the open fields and woodland edges include panicled tick-trefoil (*Desmodium paniculatum*), white snakeroot (*Eupatorium rugosum*), hollow Joe-Pye-weed (*Eupatorium fistulosum*), early goldenrod (*Solidago juncea*), rough-stemmed goldenrod (*Solidago rugosa*), crownbeard (*Verbesina occidentalis*), and New York ironweed (*Vernonia noveboracensis*).

Managed by the Maryland Department of Natural Resources, State Forest and Park Service, the Hammerman Area of Gunpowder Falls State Park has a large bathing pavilion, snack bar, and other amenities open in summer. For more information, contact Gunpowder Falls State Park, P.O. Box 172, Glen Arm, MD 21057; telephone (410)592-2897.

Directions: From the Baltimore Beltway (I-695), take US-40 north for about five miles to White Marsh, turn right on Ebenezer Road for about four miles to the sign for the Hammerman Area. (Although located on the Coastal Plain, this site is shown on the map of Maryland Piedmont: Baltimore and Nearby Counties.)

Bosely Wildlife Conservancy — Otter Point Creek

The Melvin G. Bosely Wildlife Conservancy, on Otter Point Creek near Edgewood in southern Harford County, is owned by the Izaak Walton League of America. It is part of the 400-acre freshwater tidal wetlands designated as the Otter Point Creek site of the Chesapeake Bay National Estuarine Research Reserve in Maryland. Habitats include forested wetlands, meandering streams, wet meadows, and open marshes.

Spring flowering species in the tidal marsh include sweetflag (*Acorus calamus*), yellow iris (*Iris pseudacorus*), larger blue flag (*Iris versicolor*), swamp buttercup (*Ranunculus septentrionalis*), and spring cress (*Cardamine rhomboidea*).

Summer and fall blooming plants are more numerous. In the high marsh grow both broad-leaved cattail (*Typha latifolia*) and narrow-leaved cattail (*Typha angustifolia*), wild rice (*Zizania aquatica*), halberd-leaved tearthumb (*Polygonum arifolium*), climbing false buckwheat (*Polygonum scandens*), swamp milkweed (*Asclepias incarnata*), cardinal flower (*Lobelia cardinalis*), purple-stemmed aster (*Aster puniceus*), yellow sneezeweed (*Helenium autumnale*), and larger bur-marigold (*Bidens laevis*).

In the low marsh are broad-leaved aquatics such as broad-leaved arrowhead (*Sagittaria latifolia*), arrow arum (*Peltandra virginica*), pickerel-weed (*Pontederia cordata*), and spatterdock (*Nuphar advena*).

In late summer, look in the wet meadows for virgin's bower (*Clematis virginiana*), panicled aster (*Aster lanceolatus*), calico aster (*Aster lateriflorus*), New York ironweed (*Vernonia noveboracensis*), Jerusalem artichoke (*Helianthus tuberosus*), and green-headed coneflower (*Rudbeckia laciniata*).

The Bosely Conservancy is managed by the Izaak Walton League of America and the Chesapeake Bay National Estuarine Research Reserve in Maryland (CBNERR-MD). At present there are no visitor facilities. Trails to the marsh are unmarked but are easy to follow. For more information, contact the CBNERR-MD, Tidewater Administration, Tawes State Office Building, 580 Taylor Avenue, Annapolis, MD 21401; telephone (410) 974-2784.

Directions: From I-95 north from Baltimore, take MD-24 south. Soon bear right onto Edgewood Road and continue for about two miles, crossing US-40. Turn left on Hanson Road and left again on Perry Avenue. Parking is at the end of Perry Avenue. (Although located on the Coastal Plain, this site is shown on the map of Maryland Piedmont: Baltimore and Nearby Counties.)

7

Maryland Mountains

THE BLUE RIDGE:
FREDERICK AND WASHINGTON COUNTIES

North and west of the Washington-Baltimore metropolitan area lie the Blue Ridge Mountains of Maryland. The Catoctin Mountains run through the center of Frederick County and the high ridge of South Mountain marks the Frederick–Washington County line.

Much lower than their counterparts in the southern Appalachians or in New England, these rolling hills are formed of greenstone, granite, quartzite, and other erosion-resistant rocks.

Many plants that occur in the Piedmont region to the east also grow in the Blue Ridge. And several species that prefer cooler, moister conditions can be found in the mountains, including purple fringed orchid (*Habenaria fimbriata*), nodding trillium (*Trillium cernuum*), Canada lily (*Lilium canadense*), marsh marigold (*Caltha palustris*), and swamp saxifrage (*Saxifraga pensylvanica*).

This is a rural region with many farms, small towns, forested areas with swift-running streams, and several state and national parks. The major population centers are Frederick in Frederick County and Hagerstown in Washington County. Frederick is reached via I-270 from Washington and I-70 from Baltimore. From Frederick, US-15 leads north to the Catoctins and I-70, US-40, and US-Alt.40 lead west toward South Mountain.

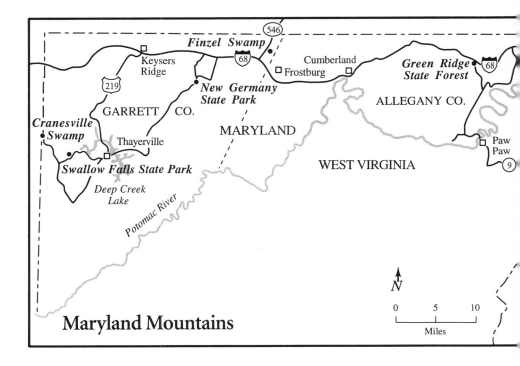

Maryland Mountains

Sugarloaf Mountain

Sugarloaf Mountain is a 1,300-foot-high monadnock rising above the rolling terrain of northern Montgomery and southern Frederick counties. Although several miles east of the main Blue Ridge Mountains, Sugarloaf is formed of the same quartzite rock that caps these mountains in Maryland.

Owned by the late Gordon Strong, the 3,200-acre mountain was left to a private corporation, with the stipulation that it be maintained in a natural state for the enjoyment of the public. A paved road runs almost to the summit, and several old roads and hiking trails criss-cross the mountain. Mt. Ephraim Road on the west side is especially interesting because of several seeps and seepage swamps.

The forest is dominated by oaks and hickories, and northern trees such as eastern hemlock, white pine, and black birch grow here in the cooler microclimates of the higher elevations.

April flowers in the woods include spring beauty (*Claytonia virginica*), round-lobed hepatica (*Hepatica americana*), rue-anemone (*Anemonella thalictroides*), cut-leaved toothwort (*Dentaria laciniata*), spring cress (*Car-*

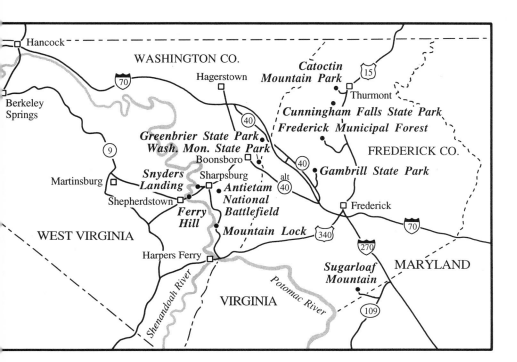

damine rhomboidea), spring avens (*Geum vernum*), sweet white violet (*Viola blanda*), dog violet (*Viola conspersa*), marsh blue violet (*Viola cucullata*), trailing arbutus (*Epigaea repens*), and robin's plantain (*Erigeron pulchellus*).

Among the species flowering in May are orchids such as large whorled pogonia (*Isotria verticillata*), lily-leaved twayblade (*Liparis lilifolia*), pink lady's-slipper (*Cypripedium acaule*) and showy orchis (*Orchis spectabilis*). Also blooming in May are Canada Mayflower (*Maianthemum canadense*), yellow stargrass (*Hypoxis hirsuta*), wild columbine (*Aquilegia canadensis*), celandine (*Chelidonium majus*), wild geranium (*Geranium maculatum*), pennywort (*Obolaria virginica*), four-leaved milkweed (*Asclepias quadrifolia*), and showy skullcap (*Scutellaria serrata*).

In summer, these cool woods harbor starry campion (*Silene stellata*), enchanter's nightshade (*Circaea lutetiana*), poke milkweed (*Asclepias exaltata*), wild bergamot (*Monarda fistulosa*), and bee balm (*Monarda didyma*). Look in seepage areas for purple fringed orchid (*Habenaria fimbriata*), green wood orchid (*Habenaria clavellata*), Canada lily (*Lilium canadense*), Turk's-cap lily (*Lilium superbum*), tall meadowrue (*Thalictrum pubescens*), and mad-dog skullcap (*Scutellaria lateriflora*).

Viola cucullata —
Marsh blue violet
(height: 5″–10″)

Sugarloaf Mountain is owned and managed by Stronghold, Inc. Picnic tables and rest rooms are located at the parking lots near the summit. For more information, contact Stronghold, Inc., 7901 Comus Road, P.O. Box 55, Dickerson, MD 20842; telephone (301)874-2024.

Directions: From I-270 south of Frederick, take MD-109 southwest for three miles to Comus and there turn right on Comus Road (MD-95) for another three miles to the foot of the mountain.

Frederick Municipal Forest

The Frederick Municipal Forest, on the east slopes of the Catoctin Mountains just north of Frederick, is located between Gambrill State Park and Cunningham Falls State Park. Old logging roads and fire roads wander through this area of low mountains, second-growth woodlands, and sparkling streams.

May flowers of the mountain hillsides include Indian cucumber-root (*Medeola virginiana*), large whorled pogonia (*Isotria verticillata*), Canada Mayflower (*Maianthemum canadense*), miterwort (*Mitella diphylla*), wild sarsaparilla (*Aralia nudicaulis*), spotted wintergreen (*Chimaphila maculata*), round-leaved pyrola (*Pyrola rotundifolia*), and shinleaf (*Pyrola elliptica*).

Seepage swamps along the streams have species typical of this cool wet habitat, such as false hellebore (*Veratrum viride*), marsh marigold (*Caltha palustris*), swamp saxifrage (*Saxifraga pensylvanica*), and marsh blue violet (*Viola cucullata*).

In mid-June, plants flowering in the forest area include purple fringed orchid (*Habenaria fimbriata*), yellow fringed orchid (*Habenaria ciliaris*), and Canada lily (*Lilium canadense*). Along the roadsides are wild indigo (*Baptisia tinctoria*), whorled loosestrife (*Lysimachia quadrifolia*), poke milkweed (*Asclepias exaltata*), white beardtongue (*Penstemon digitalis*), and cow-wheat (*Melampyrum lineare*).

Two unusual orchids that flower later in the summer are spotted coralroot (*Corallorhiza maculata*) and helleborine (*Epipactus helleborine*), an introduced European species.

The Frederick Municipal Forest is owned by the city of Frederick. There are no visitor amenities and no information is available about trails or other resources. An adventurous spirit and a front-wheel drive vehicle are needed to explore this back area.

Caltha pulustris —
Marsh marigold
(height: 1′–2′)

Directions: From Frederick, take MD-15 north for about ten miles and turn left on Mountaindale Road. Continue up the mountain to Gambrill Park Road or turn right or left on Fishing Creek Road. Park anywhere on the ridge and explore.

Gambrill State Park

Gambrill State Park near Frederick consists of over 1,000 forested acres in the southern part of the Catoctin Mountains. From the 1,600-foot elevation of High Knob, there are sweeping views of Frederick County farmlands and towns to the east and South Mountain to the west. Picnic areas and hiking trails are found along the park road and at the summit. The Lost Chestnut Trail is a one-mile self-guiding nature trail.

The forests are mostly oak, with some eastern hemlock and white pine on the higher slopes. Flowers of late April include rue-anemone (*Anemonella thalictroides*), cut-leaved toothwort (*Dentaria laciniata*), early saxifrage (*Saxifraga virginiensis*), wild geranium (*Geranium maculatum*), and plantain-leaved pussytoes (*Antennaria plantaginifolia*). In May, the woods are bright with flowering shrubs such as mountain laurel (*Kalmia latifolia*), redbud (*Cercis canadensis*), and flowering dogwood (*Cornus florida*).

Gambrill State Park is managed by the Maryland Department of Natural Resources, State Forest and Park Service. For more information, contact Gambrill State Park, 8602 Gambrill Park Road, Frederick, MD 21701; telephone (301)473-8360.

Directions: From I-70 west of Frederick, take US-40 about one and one-half miles west to the entrance road on the right.

Catoctin Mountain Park and Cunningham Falls State Park

These side-by-side parks protect over 10,000 acres of beautiful forest in the Catoctin Mountains north of Frederick. Catoctin Mountain Park is a national park known for great fishing, hiking, and cross-country skiing and as the home of Camp David, the presidential retreat. Cunningham Falls is a state park with a lovely waterfall, a fine lake, and several camping areas.

Heavily logged and farmed until the 1930s, the parklands have now reverted to forest dominated by oaks and hickories. Northern trees such as eastern hemlock, white pine, sugar maple, black birch, and yellow birch also grow in this cool climate. Well-marked trails run along bubbling streams and climb to overlooks on the ridgetops of erosion-resistant greenstone and quartzite.

April wildflowers in the Catoctins include early bloomers such as round-lobed hepatica (*Hepatica americana*), wood anemone (*Anemone quinquefolia*), bloodroot (*Sanguinaria canadensis*), Dutchman's breeches (*Dicentra cucullaria*), and trailing arbutus (*Epigaea repens*).

In mid-May, the Whiskey Still Trail is full of spring flowers, including showy orchis (*Orchis spectabilis*), rue-anemone (*Anemonella thalictroides*), hispid buttercup (*Ranunculus hispidus*), hooked crowfoot (*Ranunculus recurvatus*), miterwort (*Mitella diphylla*), dog violet (*Viola conspersa*), dwarf ginseng (*Panax trifolius*), lousewort (*Pedicularis canadensis*), and bluets (*Houstonia caerulea*). The rock outcrop at the end of the trail is carpeted with yellow corydalis (*Corydalis flavula*) and small-flowered phacelia (*Phacelia dubia*).

The Cunningham Falls Trail has perfoliate bellwort (*Uvularia perfoliata*), yellow lady's-slipper (*Cypripedium calceolus*), wild pink (*Silene caroliniana*), wild geranium (*Geranium maculatum*), heart-leaved Alexanders (*Zizia aptera*), yellow pimpernel (*Taenidia integerrima*), and pennywort (*Obolaria virginica*).

Seepage areas along Owens Creek are habitat for uncommon species such as nodding trillium (*Trillium cernuum*) and purple fringed orchid (*Habenaria fimbriata*), as well as false hellebore (*Veratrum viride*), Canada Mayflower (*Maianthemum canadense*), spring cress (*Cardamine rhomboidea*), swamp saxifrage (*Saxifraga pensylvanica*), and golden ragwort (*Senecio aureus*).

In early June, old fields and open roadsides bloom with sun-loving plants such as dame's rocket (*Hesperis matronalis*), yellow sweet clover (*Melilotus officinalis*), hairy beardtongue (*Penstemon hirsutus*), common fleabane (*Erigeron philadelphicus*), and ox-eye daisy (*Chrysanthemum leucanthemum*).

Catoctin Mountain Park is managed by the National Park Service. For more information, contact Catoctin Mountain Park, Thurmont, MD 21788; telephone (301)663-9388. Cunningham Falls State Park is managed by the Maryland Department of Natural Resources, State Forest and Park Service. For information, contact Cunningham State Park, 14039 Catoctin Hollow Road, Thurmont, MD 21788; telephone (301)271-7574. The Catoctin Mountain Park visitor center has historical exhibits and pamphlets on the various areas of the park. A wildflower checklist also is available.

Directions: From Frederick, take US-15 north to Thurmont. Then take MD-77 west about one mile to the entrance to Catoctin Mountain Park. Cunningham Falls can be reached from the visitor center at Catoctin Park.

Greenbrier State Park

Greenbrier State Park lies on the high ridge of South Mountain in Washington County north of Boonsboro. It is a few miles north of Washington Monument State Park on the Appalachian Trail. Greenbrier has been developed as a multi-use area with a large lake, swimming beach, and grassy picnic areas. Camping, fishing, and boating also are popular here.

Away from the developed areas, Greenbrier has some natural woodlands with streams and seeps that are worth exploring. In February, skunk cabbage (*Symplocarpus foetidus*) emerges in the seepage swamps. In late April and early May, these cool wet areas harbor false hellebore (*Veratrum viride*), nodding trillium (*Trillium cernuum*), spring cress (*Cardamine rhomboidea*), and marsh blue violet (*Viola cucullata*).

In April, trailing arbutus (*Epigaea repens*) blooms on the dry hillsides. In May, mountain laurel (*Kalmia latifolia*) flowers in the same habitat, and Canada Mayflower (*Maianthemum canadense*) carpets the woodland floor. Look for the leaves of later-blooming species such as downy rattlesnake-plantain (*Goodyera pubescens*) and round-leaved pyrola (*Pyrola rotundifolia*).

Greenbrier State Park is managed by the Maryland Department of Natural Resources, State Forest and Park Service. For more information, contact Greenbrier State Park, Route 2, Box 235, Boonsboro, MD 21713; telephone (301)791-4767.

Directions: From Frederick, take I-70 west for about 11 miles to the Myersville exit. From Myersville, take MD-17 north, and then US-40 west for three miles to the park entrance. Greenbrier also can be reached from Washington Monument State Park via Monument Road and Grindstone Road.

Washington Monument State Park

Washington Monument State Park is located on the Frederick County–Washington County line on the high crest of South Mountain just east of Boonsboro. The park surrounds a small monument honoring George Washington. This monument was built earlier than the famous one in the

Viola pedata —
Birdfoot violet
(height: 4″–8″)

capital city and now is known as an excellent site for watching hawk migrations in the fall.

The Appalachian Trail runs through the park, and other trails wind through old fields and second-growth woodlands. The area has been recently farmed, so a mature forest has not yet developed.

A power line cutting across the ridge has a nice display of wildflowers in late April. On the edges of the woodlands grow rue-anemone (*Anemonella thalictroides*) and dog violet (*Viola conspersa*). In the sunny, open area are wild strawberry (*Fragaria virginiana*), dwarf cinquefoil (*Potentilla canadensis*), ovate-leaved violet (*Viola fimbriatula*), masses of birdfoot violet (*Viola pedata*), and plantain-leaved pussytoes (*Antennaria plantaginifolia*).

Washington Monument State Park is managed by the Maryland Department of Natural Resources, State Forest and Park Service. There are rest rooms and picnic areas but no other visitor facilities. For more information, contact Washington Monument State Park, Route 1, Middletown, MD 21769; telephone (301)432-8065.

Directions: From I-70 just west of Frederick, take US-Alt.40 (Old National Pike) west for about nine miles to the top of South Mountain. Turn right on Monument Road to the park entrance.

LIMESTONE REGION: WASHINGTON COUNTY

On the western edge of the Blue Ridge Mountains lies a narrow belt of limestone formations called the Great Valley or, locally, the Hagerstown Valley. Limestone regions are known for fertile soil rich in calcium and for springs, caves, and sinkholes in the water-soluble rock. In Washington County, the limestone bluffs along the Potomac River have fine examples of this karst topography.

The calcareous soil of this region provides excellent habitat for many plants that are rare in the Piedmont or Blue Ridge. An especially rich environment occurs on the cool, moist, north-facing bluffs. Uncommon species associated with these limestone formations are dwarf larkspur (*Delphinium tricorne*), goldenseal (*Hydrastis canadensis*), green violet (*Hybanthus concolor*), spreading rockcress (*Arabis patens*), and shooting star (*Dodecatheon meadia*).

This western part of Washington County is just upriver from Harpers Ferry near the town of Sharpsburg. Access to the limestone region is via US-340 and MD-34.

C&O Canal National Historical Park: Beyond Harpers Ferry

Sixty miles from its beginning in Washington, the C&O Canal passes through the Blue Ridge and then the Great Valley. Just beyond Harpers Ferry, the Potomac River and the accompanying canal and towpath make a series of wide loops as the river winds its way through different types of rocks.

This section of the C&O Canal National Historical Park is a naturalist's delight. As you walk west on the towpath, high limestone bluffs alternate with moist bottomland forests, and the broad river often is in view. Limited access to the towpath, the rural nature of the surrounding countryside, and the larger acreage under federal protection give a sense of wilderness to this part of the park. The area is also rich in human history, with old quarries, limekilns, boat landings, and even a cave where residents of Sharpsburg hid during the Battle of Antietam.

In mid-April, the bottomlands along the canal are carpeted with sessile trillium (*Trillium sessile*), Dutchman's breeches (*Dicentra cucullaria*), and squirrel corn (*Dicentra canadensis*). Uncommon species found in this section of the park include harbinger-of-spring (*Erigenia bulbosa*), ellisia (*Ellisia nyctelea*), and smooth ruellia (*Ruellia strepens*).

Areas along this part of the towpath of particular interest to botanists include Mountain Lock, Ferry Hill, and Snyders Landing. For more information, contact the C&O Canal National Historical Park, Box 158, Sharpsburg, MD 21782; telephone (301)432-5124.

Mountain Lock

Mountain Lock is located on the C&O Canal a few miles above Harpers Ferry in southern Washington County. Named for the old lockhouse at the foot of Elk Ridge, the area has high limestone bluffs, wooded hillsides, seepage springs, and rich alluvial bottomlands in the canal bed and along the river. The best wildflower displays are downriver from the lockhouse. The only real trail is the towpath along the canal, but a few steep paths lead up the bluffs.

Mountain Lock is an excellent example of Maryland's limestone habitats. The north-facing slope, shaded and cool even in summer, and the well-developed calcareous soil have created conditions hospitable to plants usually found farther north or west. Several plants uncommon in Mary-

*Sanguinaria
canadensis* —
Bloodroot
(height: 3″–6″)

land, including green violet (*Hybanthus concolor*) and shooting star (*Dode-catheon meadia*), occur on the almost inaccessible high bluffs. Like other areas in the limestone region, such as Ferry Hill and Snyders Landing, Mountain Lock is known for a rich diversity of plant species.

In late March, the tiny harbinger-of-spring (*Erigenia bulbosa*) flowers in the bottomlands along the canal, and masses of round-lobed hepatica (*Hepatica americana*) bloom on the rocky hillsides.

In early April, the woods are filled with twinleaf (*Jeffersonia diphylla*), bloodroot (*Sanguinaria canadensis*), Dutchman's breeches (*Dicentra cucul-laria*), yellow corydalis (*Corydalis flavula*), cut-leaved toothwort (*Dentaria laciniata*), and slender toothwort (*Dentaria heterophylla*).

By mid-April, the hillsides are flowering with both the maroon and green forms of sessile trillium (*Trillium sessile*), trout-lily (*Erythronium americanum*), wild ginger (*Asarum canadense*), spring beauty (*Claytonia virginica*), early meadowrue (*Thalictrum dioicum*), rue-anemone (*Anemonella thalictroides*), blue cohosh (*Caulophyllum thalictroides*), squirrel corn (*Dicentra canadensis*), and smooth yellow violet (*Viola pensylvanica*).

The limestone outcrops are a veritable rock garden with wild columbine (*Aquilegia canadensis*), lyre-leaved rockcress (*Arabis lyrata*), smooth rockcress (*Arabis laevigata*), spreading rockcress (*Arabis patens*), early saxifrage (*Saxifraga virginiensis*), alumroot (*Heuchera americana*), miterwort (*Mitella diphylla*), wild stonecrop (*Sedum ternatum*), and green violet. High up on the bluffs are hispid buttercup (*Ranunculus hispidus*), heart-leaved Alexanders (*Zizia aptera*), wild blue phlox (*Phlox divaricata*), round-leaved ragwort (*Senecio obovatus*), and the beautiful pink shooting star.

By mid-May, the wildflower display slows on the Mountain Lock bluffs, although there are a few late bloomers such as false Solomon's-seal (*Smilacina racemosa*), wild pink (*Silene caroliniana*), Canada violet (*Viola canadensis*), yellow pimpernel (*Taenidia integerrima*), and one-flowered cancerroot (*Orobanche uniflora*).

The Mountain Lock area is part of the C&O Canal National Historical Park and is managed by the National Park Service. There are no visitor facilities. For more information, contact the C&O Canal National Historical Park, Box 158, Sharpsburg, MD 21782; telephone (301)432-5124.

Directions: From I-70 west of Frederick, take the first exit, US-340 west, for about 16 miles. Just before the bridge across the Potomac River, turn left at Keep Tryst Road (signs for Kennedy Farmhouse), and then turn right onto Sandy Hook-Harpers Ferry Road. Go on this road for almost seven miles to Dargan, turn left on Limekiln Road and immediately left again on Mountain Lock Road. Continue to the end of the road where there is very limited parking at the lockhouse. To visit Ferry Hill or Snyders Landing after Mountain Lock, return to Harpers Ferry Road, turn left and go about six miles to Sharpsburg. Follow the directions to Ferry Hill or Snyders Landing from there.

Ferry Hill

The Ferry Hill Trail is a short loop trail on the grounds of the Ferry Hill Plantation just west of Sharpsburg. The old plantation house, situated on a

Anemonella thalictroides —
Rue-anemone
(height: 4″–8″)

high hill above the Potomac River, now serves as headquarters for the C&O
Canal National Historical Park.

Ferry Hill supports many of the species typical of the limestone region
and is more accessible than Mountain Lock and Snyders Landing. The trail
winds down from the mansion through wooded bluffs, levels out at the
canal and towpath, and then returns uphill. A trail guide is available at the
park headquarters, and many plants are identified with labels.

In mid-April, wildflowers of these rich, calcareous bluffs include sessile
trillium (*Trillium sessile*), wild ginger (*Asarum canadense*), early meadowrue
(*Thalictrum dioicum*), rue-anemone (*Anemonella thalictroides*), twinleaf
(*Jeffersonia diphylla*), bloodroot (*Sanguinaria canadensis*), smooth rockcress
(*Arabis laevigata*), spreading rockcress (*Arabis patens*), cut-leaved toothwort
(*Dentaria laciniata*), and early saxifrage (*Saxifraga virginiensis*).

Late April brings the blooming of wild stonecrop (*Sedum ternatum*), palmate-leaved violet (*Viola palmata*), woolly blue violet (*Viola sororia*), pale violet (*Viola striata*), shooting star (*Dodecatheon meadia*), and round-leaved ragwort (*Senecio obovatus*).

The flowering continues in early and mid-May with smooth Solomon's-seal (*Polygonatum biflorum*), false Solomon's-seal (*Smilacina racemosa*), yellow stargrass (*Hypoxis hirsuta*), dwarf larkspur (*Delphinium tricorne*), wild columbine (*Aquilegia canadensis*), alumroot (*Heuchera americana*), hairy-jointed meadow-parsnip (*Thaspium barbinode*), violet wood-sorrel (*Oxalis violacea*), one-flowered cancer-root (*Orobanche uniflora*), and rattlesnake-weed (*Hieracium venosum*).

As the canopy closes over in June, blooming moves to the open areas near the canal. Summer wildflowers along the towpath include common evening-primrose (*Oenothera biennis*), chicory (*Cichorium intybus*), thin-leaved sunflower (*Helianthus decapetalus*), green-headed coneflower (*Rudbeckia laciniata*), and hollow Joe-Pye-weed (*Eupatorium fistulosum*).

The muddy shores of the canal and river are habitat for halberd-leaved rose mallow (*Hibiscus laevis*) and cardinal flower (*Lobelia cardinalis*), as well as ditch stonecrop (*Penthorum sedoides*), toothcup (*Rotala ramosior*), and false pimpernel (*Lindernia dubia*). The shallow river itself hosts mats of water stargrass (*Heteranthera dubia*) and water willow (*Justicia americana*).

Early fall brings a small resurgence of bloom to the woodlands with the flowering of starry campion (*Silene stellata*), dittany (*Cunila origanoides*), Indian tobacco (*Lobelia inflata*), and mistflower (*Eupatorium coelestinum*).

The Ferry Hill Trail is part of the C&O Canal National Historical Park and is managed by the National Park Service. The headquarters has general information and rest rooms. For more information, contact C&O Canal National Historical Park, Box 158, Sharpsburg, MD 21782; telephone (301)432-5124.

Directions: From I-70 west from Frederick, take US-Alt.40 west for about 12 miles to Boonsboro, turn left on MD-34 for about six miles to Sharpsburg, continue through Sharpsburg on MD-34 for another two miles. Ferry Hill is on the right just before the bridge across the Potomac River. A visit to Ferry Hill can be combined with a visit to Snyders Landing or Snavely Ford Trail.

Snyders Landing

Snyders Landing is located on the C&O Canal northwest of Sharpsburg and about four miles upriver from Ferry Hill. Snyders Landing has been identified by many botanists as an important limestone habitat. The north-facing bluffs are cool and moist, with many caves, springs, sinkholes, and other types of karst topography. The low-lying areas along the river as well as the damp canal bed provide a rich bottomland habitat.

Several plants that are not common in Maryland have been found on these limestone bluffs, including northern white-cedar and ferns such as walking fern, bulblet fern, and wall rue.

From the parking area, turn left on the towpath and walk downriver. You are actually walking northwest at this point as the river twists in several S-curves in this area. Because the canal is not filled with water, you can cross over and walk along the base of the high bluffs. A few trails lead up the ravines, but they are very steep and soon lead to private property.

In early April, a large colony of twinleaf (*Jeffersonia diphylla*) flowers in these rich woodlands. Other early bloomers include wild ginger (*Asarum canadense*), spring beauty (*Claytonia virginica*), round-lobed hepatica (*Hepatica americana*), early meadowrue (*Thalictrum dioicum*), rue-anemone (*Anemonella thalictroides*), blue cohosh (*Caulophyllum thalictroides*), Dutchman's breeches (*Dicentra cucullaria*), squirrel corn (*Dicentra canadensis*), yellow corydalis (*Corydalis flavula*), and cut-leaved toothwort (*Dentaria laciniata*).

By late April, the damp canal bed is filled with erect trillium (*Trillium erectum*); here the large red flowers are so heavy that they hang below the leaves. This trillium is not found growing naturally along the Potomac River south of Snyders Landing. Also blooming in the moist bottomlands are sessile trillium (*Trillium sessile*), trout-lily (*Erythronium americanum*), spring cress (*Cardamine rhomboidea*), heart-leaved Alexanders (*Zizia aptera*), and Virginia bluebells (*Mertensia virginica*). False mermaid (*Floerkea proserpinacoides*), a little annual, is abundant on the floodplain.

Along the towpath grows nodding star-of-Bethlehem (*Ornithogalum nutans*), a naturalized escape from gardens. On the steep, rocky bluffs are wild columbine (*Aquilegia canadensis*), smooth rockcress (*Arabis laevigata*), lyre-leaved rockcress (*Arabis lyrata*), spreading rockcress (*Arabis patens*), early saxifrage (*Saxifraga virginiensis*), and miterwort (*Mitella di-*

phylla). On top of the high bluffs are the deep pink shooting star (*Dodecatheon meadia*) and the brilliant blue dwarf larkspur (*Delphinium tricorne*), both uncommon species in Maryland.

Late spring and early summer are not good times to find wildflowers at Snyders Landing. By late May, the invasive, weedy garlic mustard (*Alliaria petiolata*) overruns the bottomlands and, in summer, vines such as Japanese honeysuckle, poison ivy, and wild blackberry cover the bluffs.

In late August, the open areas along the towpath bloom again with pale jewelweed (*Impatiens pallida*), green-headed coneflower (*Rudbeckia laciniata*), thin-leaved sunflower (*Helianthus decapetalus*), white snakeroot (*Eupatorium rugosum*), white wood aster (*Aster divaricatus*), and small-flowered leafcup (*Polymnia canadensis*).

Snyders Landing is part of the C&O Canal National Historical Park and is managed by the National Park Service. There are no visitor facilities at the site. For more information, contact C&O Canal National Historical Park, Box 158, Sharpsburg, MD 21782; telephone (301)432-5124.

Directions: From I-70 west from Frederick, take US-Alt.40 west for about 12 miles to Boonsboro, turn left on MD-34 for about six miles to Sharpsburg. Turn right on North Mechanic Street, go one block, turn left on Snyders Landing Road (Chapline Street), and go about one and one-half miles to the parking area. A visit to Snyders Landing can be combined with a visit to Snavely Ford Trail or Ferry Hill, both near Sharpsburg, or with Mountain Lock, which is on the C&O Canal a few miles downriver.

Antietam National Battlefield: Snavely Ford Trail

Antietam Battlefield in Sharpsburg commemorates a famous Civil War battle. The current bucolic atmosphere of the landscape belies the tragic loss of life that occurred here on September 17, 1862. The fields and streams of the battlefield now are popular for walking, bicycling, and fishing. The Snavely Ford Trail near Burnside Bridge is a pleasant two-mile circuit walk along Antietam Creek and has a fine display of wildflowers.

Here in the limestone valley, the rich, moist, calcareous soil provides lush habitat for April wildflowers including both the maroon and green forms of sessile trillium (*Trillium sessile*), wild ginger (*Asarum canadense*), blue cohosh (*Caulophyllum thalictroides*), Dutchman's breeches (*Dicentra cucullaria*), and pale violet (*Viola striata*).

May bloomers on the hillside are dwarf larkspur (*Delphinium tricorne*)

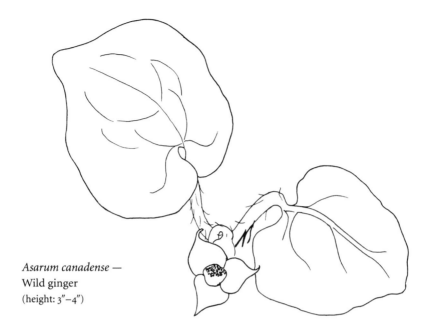

Asarum canadense —
Wild ginger
(height: 3″–4″)

and round-leaved ragwort (*Senecio obovatus*). Along the creek are Jack-in-the-pulpit (*Arisaema triphyllum*), Mayapple (*Podophyllum peltatum*), wild blue phlox (*Phlox divaricata*), Virginia waterleaf (*Hydrophyllum virginianum*), and broad-leaved waterleaf (*Hydrophyllum canadense*). Several garden plants have naturalized along this trail, including nodding star-of-Bethlehem (*Ornithogalum nutans*), celandine (*Chelidonium majus*), and dame's rocket (*Hesperis matronalis*).

In June, look in the woods for early summer bloomers such as black cohosh (*Cimicifuga racemosa*), thimbleweed (*Anemone virginiana*), and tall bellflower (*Campanula americana*). In the open fields are Deptford pink (*Dianthus armeria*), fringed loosestrife (*Lysimachia ciliata*), and yellow goatsbeard (*Tragopogon pratensis*).

Antietam National Battlefield is managed by the National Park Service. Excellent displays in the visitor center explain the drama of this bloodiest of battles. For more information, contact Antietam National Battlefield, Box 158, Sharpsburg, MD 21782; telephone (301)432-5124.

Directions: From I-70 west from Frederick, take US-Alt.40 west for about 12 miles over South Mountain to Boonsboro. At the light, turn left on MD-34 toward Sharpsburg and go almost six miles. Turn left on a one-way road through Antietam Battlefield. This turn is about one-half mile beyond the bridge over Antietam Creek. Follow the park road and turn left again at the Sherrick Farmhouse to reach the parking area for Snavely Ford Trail.

RIDGE AND VALLEY: ALLEGANY COUNTY

Allegany County lies west of Washington County in the panhandle of Maryland and is the heart of Maryland's Ridge and Valley province. The rolling hills rise higher and higher as one goes west from Sideling Hill at 1,760 feet to Dan's Mountain at almost 2,900 feet.

Ancient sedimentary rocks, such as shale, sandstone, and siltstone, underlie these mountains and the soils are thin and dry. The Ridge and Valley province contains good examples of mid-Appalachian shale barrens, very hot dry habitats that support a distinct community of plants. Shale barrens, occurring mostly on hard shales of the Devonian period, can be found on steep, south-facing slopes of crumbling shale.

Allegany County shale barrens are habitat for several state-rare plants, including Kate's Mountain clover (*Trifolium virginicum*), mountain pimpernel (*Taenidia montana*), and pussytoes ragwort (*Senecio antennariifolius*).

Allegany County is still very rural, with dairy farms and scattered small villages. Cumberland is the largest city, a center of the railroad industry and the terminus of the C&O Canal. The major highways run east and west, including the new I-68 and the old US-Alt.40.

Green Ridge State Forest

Green Ridge State Forest is about 130 miles from the Washington-Baltimore area but is easily reached via major highways. Containing about 34,000 acres of second-growth woodlands, the forest has campgrounds, hiking trails, and old logging roads. It adjoins the C&O Canal National Historical Park near the Paw Paw bends of the Potomac River.

Used extensively for timbering, hunting, and fishing, the forest also harbors fine examples of Maryland's shale barrens. Many of these barrens are found on the eastern side of the ridge along bumpy back roads. An excellent shale barren that was easily accessible was destroyed in 1987 by highway construction.

Look for shale barrens on steep, open, south-facing slopes that are

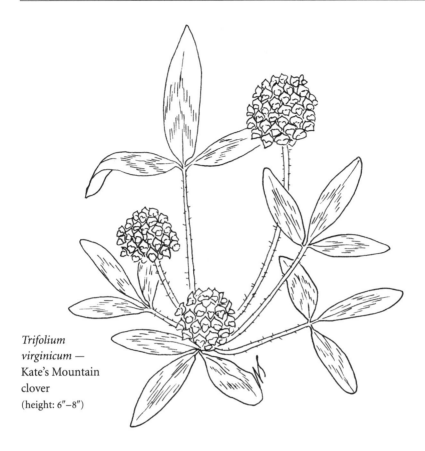

*Trifolium
virginicum* —
Kate's Mountain
clover
(height: 6″–8″)

undercut by a stream. Shale barrens are not easy to explore, as they are steep
and slippery and have crumbling and sliding rocks. Tucked among the rock
fragments live certain plants that are adapted to this hot, dry, and harsh
environment.

Late April and early May are good times to find shale-barren plants in
flower. Some of the characteristic shale-barren species found in Green Ridge
State Forest are Kate's Mountain clover (*Trifolium virginicum*), mountain
pimpernel (*Taenidia montana*), shale-barren pussytoes (*Antennaria virginica*), pussytoes ragwort (*Senecio antennariifolius*), and shale-barren goldenrod (*Solidago harrisii*). Usually only a few of these shale-barren species are
found at any one site.

Several shale-barren plants are midwestern species, such as bent milk-
vetch (*Astragalus distortus*), a species that in the east is found only on shale
barrens. About 8,000 years ago, the east was hotter and drier than it is now

and prairie species migrated eastward. As the eastern climate turned cooler and wetter, prairie plants moved west again, although a few remained as relict populations in certain very dry habitats such as shale barrens.

Many species that occur on shale barrens in Green Ridge State Forest are not unique to that habitat and are found in other dry rocky places. More common species on the barrens include bastard toadflax (*Comandra umbellata*), wild pink (*Silene caroliniana*), rocktwist (*Draba ramosissima*), birdfoot violet (*Viola pedata*), ovate-leaved violet (*Viola fimbriatula*), moss phlox (*Phlox subulata*), small-flowered phacelia (*Phacelia dubia*), hoary puccoon (*Lithospermum canescens*), and bluets (*Houstonia caerulea*).

The wooded hillsides of Green Ridge State Forest support species typical of eastern deciduous woods. In mid-May, you may find spiderwort (*Tradescantia virginiana*), dwarf larkspur (*Delphinium tricorne*), yellow corydalis (*Corydalis flavula*), violet wood-sorrel (*Oxalis violacea*), three-lobed violet (*Viola triloba*), and round-leaved ragwort (*Senecio obovatus*).

June-flowering species in the woods include lance-leaved wild licorice (*Galium lanceolatum*) and spotted wintergreen (*Chimaphila maculata*). In open areas, look for thimbleweed (*Anemone virginiana*), leatherflower (*Clematis viorna*), goat's-rue (*Tephrosia virginiana*), and gray beardtongue (*Penstemon canescens*).

In July, the dry fields come into bloom with waxy meadowrue (*Thalictrum revolutum*), Deptford pink (*Dianthus armeria*), flowering spurge (*Euphorbia corollata*), common St. Johnswort (*Hypericum perforatum*), butterflyweed (*Asclepias tuberosa*), viper's bugloss (*Echium vulgare*), motherwort (*Leonurus cardiaca*), hoary mountain-mint (*Pycnanthemum incanum*), and ox-eye daisy (*Chrysanthemum leucanthemum*).

The eastern part of Green Ridge State Forest connects with the C&O Canal National Historical Park in several places, including the stretch where the canal and towpath go through the Paw Paw Tunnel. In early June, the damp canal bed upriver from the tunnel is filled with the brilliant blue flowers of larger blue flag (*Iris versicolor*).

Downriver from the tunnel is an area of high rocky bluffs. On these cool, moist hillsides, spring-flowering species such as wild columbine (*Aquilegia canadensis*) and lyre-leaved rockcress (*Arabis lyrata*) still bloom in July along with live-forever (*Sedum telephioides*), harebell (*Campanula rotundifolia*), heart-leaved skullcap (*Scutellaria ovata*), and woodland sunflower (*Helianthus divaricatus*). The canal bed here sports both the small creeping moneywort (*Lysimachia nummularia*) and the tall swamp candles (*Lysimachia terrestris*).

Green Ridge State Forest is managed by the Maryland Department of Natural Resources, State Forest and Park Service. For more information, contact Green Ridge State Forest, Star Route, Flintstone, MD 21530; telephone (301)478-2991.

Directions: From the Washington-Baltimore area, go to Frederick and continue west on I-70. At Hancock, take I-68 west for about 20 miles. Look for the sign for the Green Ridge State Forest office. Interesting forest roads on the east side include Orleans Road, Carroll Road, and Outdoor Club Road. The Paw Paw Tunnel area can be reached via MD-51 at the southern end of Green Ridge State Forest. Signs direct you to the parking lot and access to the towpath and the tunnel.

ALLEGHENY PLATEAU: GARRETT COUNTY

Garrett County, sometimes called "Maryland's Little Switzerland," is located on the high Allegheny Plateau. In this province, the terrain is more rugged and the climate much cooler than in the rest of Maryland. Northern habitats such as coniferous forests, birch-maple woodlands, and mountain peatlands are found here, and the natural communities contain boreal species not found in other regions. Although Garrett County is about 150 miles from Washington or Baltimore, it is well worth a special trip to explore the unusual habitats of this region.

Maryland's highest mountain, the 3,360-foot Backbone Mountain, is located in southern Garrett County near the West Virginia state line. Most of the county, however, is not mountainous as much as it is high and hilly, with many places over 2,500 feet in elevation. Shales and sandstones of the Carboniferous period underlie this region, accompanied by deposits of coal and natural gas.

Although Maryland was never glaciated, the last glacial advance, about 18,000 years ago, had a cooling effect still in evidence on the Allegheny Plateau. Northern plants native to New England and Canada migrated south during glaciation; then as the climate warmed, they moved northward again. However, relict populations of several northern species remained in cool microclimates of the highlands.

Boreal species occurring in Garrett County include American larch, wild calla (*Calla palustris*), yellow clintonia (*Clintonia borealis*), goldthread (*Coptis groenlandica*), small cranberry (*Vaccinium oxycoccus*), and creeping snowberry (*Gaultheria hispidula*). These species are at or near the southern edge of their range in Garrett County, so they are rare in Maryland, although they may be common in northern states.

Garrett County is the most rural of Maryland's counties, with small towns, villages, open farmland, and several state parks and forests. Logging and dairy farming are the main occupations in the county. In the mid-1980s, a recreational boom hit Garrett County with the development of Deep Creek Lake as a boating center in summer and skiing/snowmobiling area in winter. Garrett County is reached via highways I-68 and US-219.

Finzel Swamp

Finzel Swamp is located at the headwaters of the Savage River, near the town of Finzel in the northeastern corner of Garrett County. It contains an excellent example of northern shrub swamp surrounded by northern forest. Because it is considered an exemplary community of this type, over 300 acres have been preserved as a nature sanctuary by the Maryland Chapter of The Nature Conservancy.

Spring comes late to the mountains, so late May is a good time to visit Finzel Swamp. Woody plants in the swamp include northern trees such as American larch, black ash, and mountain-ash and shrubs of cool wetlands such as speckled alder, red chokeberry, and mountain holly. In late May, the rose azalea (*Rhododendron prinophyllum*) brightens the swamp with its fragrant pink flowers.

In the deep water of the swamp is the beautiful wild calla (*Calla palustris*), a plant of northern wetlands at the southern edge of its range here. The open swamp is filled with the large leaves of skunk cabbage (*Symplocarpus foetidus*) and the tall stalks of false hellebore (*Veratrum viride*). Flowers of the swamp edges include marsh blue violet (*Viola cucullata*), northern white violet (*Viola pallens*), and, blooming in late summer, Canadian burnet (*Sanguisorba canadensis*).

The cool woodlands surrounding the swamp are habitat for many northern species not often found in the mid-Atlantic states, including painted trillium (*Trillium undulatum*), goldthread (*Coptis groenlandica*), fringed polygala (*Polygala paucifolia*), and starflower (*Trientalis borealis*). Both the yellow clintonia (*Clintonia borealis*) of the north and the white

Clintonia borealis —
Yellow clintonia
(height: 6″–16″)

clintonia (*Clintonia umbellulata*) of the southern mountains are found in the woods above Finzel Swamp.

Finzel Swamp is owned and managed by the Maryland Chapter of The Nature Conservancy. It is open to the public during daylight hours for nature study and hiking only. For more information, contact the Maryland Field Office, The Nature Conservancy, 2 Wisconsin Circle, Suite 600, Chevy Chase, MD 20815; telephone (301)656-8673.

Directions: From I-68 at Frostburg, continue west about three miles and go north on MD-546 for almost two miles. Turn right onto a dirt road on the north side of a recreation area. Where four driveways converge, take the second one from the left and follow it for about one-half mile to the preserve sign and gate. Park in front of the gate. You may walk on the dirt road between the swamp and the woods or on the trail around the swamp, but please respect the nearby private property and house.

New Germany State Park

A few miles south of Grantsville and within the Savage River State Forest is New Germany State Park. Surrounded by large white pines and eastern hemlocks, a 13-acre lake is the showpiece of this beautiful park. The park is popular in winter for cross-country skiing and in summer for fishing and swimming; cabins and pleasant campsites are available.

The temperature here averages eight to ten degrees cooler than in the Washington-Baltimore area. And many plants found here are more typically found 500 miles north in New England or 2,000 feet higher in the southern Appalachians.

On a late May visit, you can see many mountain wildflowers. Look on the banks of the rushing stream for white clintonia (*Clintonia umbellulata*), foamflower (*Tiarella cordifolia*), and dwarf ginseng (*Panax trifolius*). And walk the roads through the campground to see painted trillium (*Trillium undulatum*), Canada Mayflower (*Maianthemum canadense*), northern white violet (*Viola pallens*), and fringed polygala (*Polygala pauciflora*).

New Germany State Park is managed by the Maryland Department of Natural Resources, State Forest and Park Service. For more information, contact the park office at Route 2, Box 62A, Grantsville, MD 21536; telephone (301)895-5453.

Directions: From I-68 at Frostburg, continue west about 14 miles to Lower New Germany Road just east of Grantsville. Take Lower New Ger-

Maianthemum canadense —
Canada Mayflower
(height: 2″–6″)

many Road south for almost five miles, turn right on Twin Churches Road, then left on New Germany Road to the park entrance.

Swallow Falls State Park

Swallow Falls State Park is located on the Youghiogheny River just west of Deep Creek Lake. It contains a 300-acre old-growth forest of eastern hemlock and yellow birch and features rocky gorges, cascading streams, and a 60-foot waterfall.

In late May, several wildflowers bloom even within the picnic areas and campsites. Fringed polygala (*Polygala paucifolia*) carpets the ground near the park office, along with wild geranium (*Geranium maculatum*) and bluets (*Houstonia caerulea*). On the streambanks grow Canada Mayflower (*Maianthemum canadense*), northern white violet (*Viola pallens*), sweet white violet (*Viola blanda*), and golden ragwort (*Senecio aureus*). Pink lady's-slipper (*Cypripedium acaule*) and common wood-sorrel (*Oxalis montana*) flower in the deep shade of the hemlock forest.

June flowers of these cool, moist woods include Turk's-cap lily (*Lilium superbum*), round-leaved orchid (*Habenaria orbiculata*), and pale Indian plantain (*Cacalia atriplicifolia*).

Swallow Falls State Park is managed by the Maryland Department of Natural Resources, State Forest and Park Service. For more information, contact Swallow Falls State Park, RFD # 5, Box 122, Oakland, MD 21550; telephone (301)334-9180.

Directions: From I-68 at Frostburg, continue west about 20 miles to Keysers Ridge. Take US-219 south through McHenry and Deep Creek Lake for about 19 miles. Just past Thayerville, turn right onto Mayhew Inn Road and follow for about one and one-half miles; then turn left on Bray School Road for one and one-half miles. Turn right on Oakland–Sang Run Road for one mile and turn left on Swallow Falls Road to the entrance of the park. Signs are posted along the way. The approach to Cranesville Swamp is similar and visits to both places can be combined.

Cranesville Swamp

Cranesville Swamp is on the Maryland–West Virginia border just north of Swallow Falls State Park. Despite its name, the area is not a swamp but a true bog, an acidic peatland that is very low in nutrients. Lying at an elevation of over 2,500 feet, Cranesville Swamp is a fine example of a boreal bog where the cold, wet environment provides habitat for northern plants. Many of these plants are rare in our area because they occur as relict populations far south of their normal range.

Over 400 acres of nature preserve owned by the Maryland and West Virginia chapters of The Nature Conservancy protect Cranesville Swamp. A 1,500-foot boardwalk allows easy exploration of the bog. The Nature Conservancy requests that all visitors stay on the boardwalk because the bog habitat is easily damaged.

Surrounding the bog is a coniferous forest of eastern hemlock, white pine, and red spruce. Scattered throughout the bog is American larch, a deciduous conifer of cold northern wetlands, at the southernmost limit of its range here. Shrubs around the bog edges include speckled alder, black chokeberry, mountain holly, and sheep laurel (*Kalmia angustifolia*).

The central area of the bog is an open mass of small plants including spaghnum moss, round-leaved sundew (*Drosera rotundifolia*), and large cranberry (*Vaccinium macrocarpon*). Northern sedges, such as tawny cottongrass, also grow in the bog. Other state-rare species are found in the forest above the bog, including purple fringed orchid (*Habenaria fimbriata*) and goldthread (*Coptis groenlandica*).

Cranesville Swamp is owned jointly by the Maryland and West Virginia chapters of The Nature Conservancy. The preserve is open to the public during daylight hours for passive uses such as hiking and nature study. For more information, contact the Maryland Field Office, The Nature Conservancy, 2 Wisconsin Circle, Suite 600, Chevy Chase, MD 20815; telephone (301)656-8673; or the West Virginia Field Office, The Nature Conservancy, 723 Kanawha Boulevard, Suite 500, Charleston, WV 25337; telephone (304)345-4350.

Directions: From I-68 at Frostburg, continue west about 20 miles to Keysers Ridge. Take US-219 south for 19 miles just past Thayersville. Turn right on Mayhew Inn Road and follow directions to Swallow Falls Park. However, continue past the park entrance, and then turn right on Cranesville Road for about four miles. Turn left on Lake Ford Road, and soon turn right at a fork to the preserve and parking area. A visit to Cranesville Swamp can be combined with a visit to nearby Swallow Falls State Park.

8

Virginia Piedmont

ARLINGTON AND FAIRFAX COUNTIES: POTOMAC PALISADES

Along the Virginia shore of the Potomac River above Washington, there are high rocky palisades, wooded stream valleys, and rich bottomlands beside the river. The hills and ravines are covered with some of the Piedmont region's finest deciduous forests. Several areas along the river present a grand display of early spring wildflowers.

Regular flooding of the river, fertile alluvial soil, and shaded, north-facing hillsides have contributed to habitats that support a particularly diverse flora, especially at places such as Scott's Run Nature Preserve and Great Falls Park.

Several species found here along the Potomac River are rare in Virginia, including starry false Solomon's-seal (*Smilacina stellata*), white trout-lily (*Erythronium albidum*), false rue-anemone (*Isopyrum biternatum*), Coville's phacelia (*Phacelia ranunculacea*), few-flowered valerian (*Valeriana pauciflora*), sweet-scented Indian plantain (*Cacalia suaveolens*), and riverbank goldenrod (*Solidago racemosa*). Botanists theorize that these species may have migrated down the river and found hospitable habitats in the moist hillsides of this area.

Most of the places along the Virginia palisades can be reached from the George Washington Memorial Parkway or from Georgetown Pike (VA-193), which follows the river in Fairfax County. As you move upriver from Arlington, you come to the following parks with river access: Potomac Overlook, Gulf Branch, Turkey Run, Scott's Run, Great Falls, Riverbend, and Fraser Preserve.

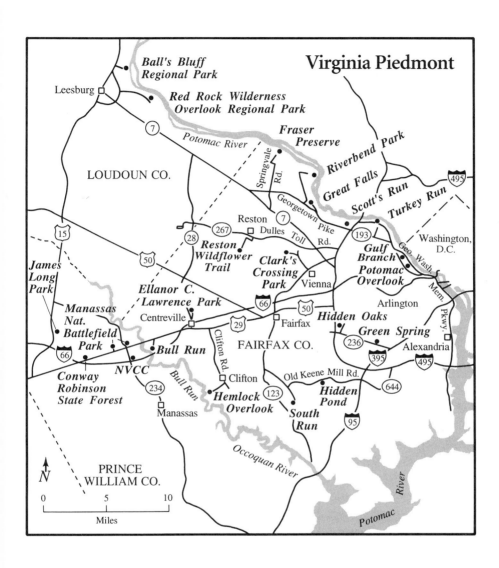

Virginia Piedmont

Ball's Bluff
Regional Park

Leesburg

Red Rock Wilderness
Overlook Regional Park

Fraser
Preserve

Riverbend Park

7

Potomac River

Springvale Rd.

Georgetown Pike

Great Falls

Scott's Run

Turkey Run

495

LOUDOUN CO.

Reston

7

Dulles Toll Rd.

193

Washington,
D.C.

15

267

28

Reston
Wildflower
Trail

Clark's
Crossing
Park

Gulf
Branch
Potomac
Overlook

Geo. Wash.

50

Vienna

James
Long
Park

Ellanor C.
Lawrence Park

66

50

Arlington

Mem. Pkwy.

Manassas
Nat.
Battlefield
Park

Centreville

Hidden Oaks

Green Spring

Alexandria

66

29

Fairfax

236

Bull Run

FAIRFAX CO.

395

495

Conway
Robinson
State Forest

NVCC

Clifton Rd.

Old Keene Mill Rd.

644

234

Clifton

123

Hidden
Pond

Bull Run

Hemlock
Overlook

South
Run

95

Manassas

Occoquan River

N

PRINCE
WILLIAM CO.

0   5   10

Miles

Potomac River

Potomac Overlook Regional Park

Potomac Overlook is a 95-acre park located along the Potomac River near Donaldson Run in Arlington. The hillsides have a mature forest of oaks, beech, and tuliptree, and deep ravines cut down to the river. Although Potomac Overlook is located very close to the city of Washington, an impressive number of wildflowers have been found at the park.

In early April, spring beauty (*Claytonia virginica*), star chickweed (*Stellaria pubera*), round-lobed hepatica (*Hepatica americana*), bloodroot (*Sanguinaria canadensis*), cut-leaved toothwort (*Dentaria laciniata*), and early saxifrage (*Saxifraga virginiensis*) bloom along the Donaldson Run Trail.

By mid-April, trout-lily (*Erythronium americanum*), smooth yellow violet (*Viola pensylvanica*), common blue violet (*Viola papilionacea*), Virginia bluebells (*Mertensia virginica*), and golden ragwort (*Senecio aureus*) flower in the moist bottomland woods. An especially fine display of Jack-in-the-pulpit (*Arisaema triphyllum*) is found in the upland woods. The large-flowered trillium (*Trillium grandiflorum*) and sharp-lobed hepatica (*Hepatica acutiloba*) are mountain species that have been planted in the park.

During May, the hillsides bloom with smooth Solomon's-seal (*Polygonatum biflorum*), false Solomon's-seal (*Smilacina racemosa*), Indian cucumber-root (*Medeola virginiana*), perfoliate bellwort (*Uvularia perfoliata*), and wild geranium (*Geranium maculatum*).

Woodland species flowering in June include the waxy Indian pipe (*Monotropa uniflora*) and round-leaved pyrola (*Pyrola rotundifolia*). In early August, look for cranefly orchid (*Tipularia discolor*) and downy rattlesnake-plantain (*Goodyera pubescens*). Late summer brings the woodland composites such as woodland sunflower (*Helianthus divaricatus*), white wood aster (*Aster divaricatus*), and white snakeroot (*Eupatorium rugosum*).

Potomac Overlook Regional Park is managed by the Northern Virginia Regional Park Authority and is located at 2845 Marcey Road, Arlington, Virginia 22207; telephone (703)528-5406. The attractive nature center has a map of the trails and a wildflower checklist.

Directions: From the George Washington Memorial Parkway, go west on Spout Run Parkway (VA-124) for about one mile. Turn right on Lorcom Lane and then right again on Military Road. Continue to Marcey Road and turn right into the park.

Medeola virginiana —
Indian cucumber-root
(height: 8″–14″)

Gulf Branch Nature Area

Gulf Branch Nature Area is located in a small park in suburban Arlington County about one mile upriver from Potomac Overlook Regional Park. Much of the park is used for recreational purposes, but a trail following Gulf Branch down toward the Potomac River winds through oak woodlands.

In late April and early May, you can find Jack-in-the-pulpit (*Arisaema triphyllum*), smooth Solomon's-seal (*Polygonatum biflorum*), false Solomon's-seal (*Smilacina racemosa*), Indian cucumber-root (*Medeola virginiana*), star chickweed (*Stellaria pubera*), Mayapple (*Podophyllum peltatum*), and common blue violet (*Viola papilionacea*).

Gulf Branch Nature Area is managed by the Arlington County Park Division and is located at 3608 North Military Road, Arlington, VA 22207; telephone (703)558-2340.

Directions: From the George Washington Memorial Parkway, go west on Spout Run Parkway (VA-124) for about one mile. Turn right on Lorcom Lane and right again on Military Road. Continue for a little more than one mile to the nature center on the left.

Turkey Run Park

Turkey Run Park is located just inside the Capital Beltway between the Potomac River and the George Washington Memorial Parkway. Large oaks, beech, tuliptree, basswood, sugar maple, and other mature trees form an exceptionally fine hardwood forest at Turkey Run. A well-developed floodplain, rocky bluffs, and deep ravines are other habitats of this 200-acre park.

Turkey Run is a good place to see the earliest blooming wildflowers. In January and February, look for skunk cabbage (*Symplocarpus foetidus*) in swampy areas along the streams. In March, search the floodplain for the diminutive harbinger-of-spring (*Erigenia bulbosa*), a midwestern species found in the Potomac River watershed in our area. In early April, walk the upland trails to find spring beauty (*Claytonia virginica*), round-lobed hepatica (*Hepatica americana*), twinleaf (*Jeffersonia diphylla*), bloodroot (*Sanguinaria canadensis*), and cut-leaved toothwort (*Dentaria laciniata*).

In mid-April, an explosion of bloom occurs in the rich bottomlands and moist hillsides of this park. Over 25 species flower at this time, including masses of Virginia bluebells (*Mertensia virginica*) on the floodplain.

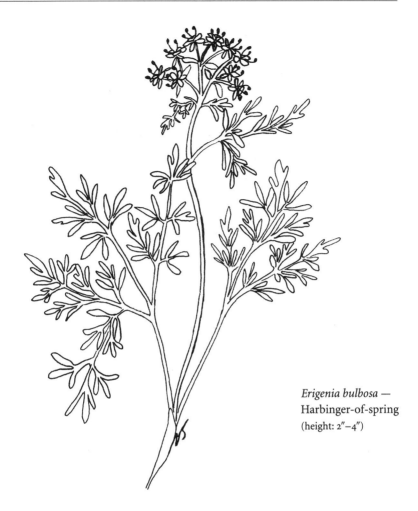

Erigenia bulbosa —
Harbinger-of-spring
(height: 2″–4″)

Other plants found along the riverside trail are wild ginger (*Asarum cana-dense*), swamp buttercup (*Ranunculus septentrionalis*), sessile trillium (*Trillium sessile*), trout-lily (*Erythronium americanum*), and its close relative, white trout-lily (*Erythronium albidum*). White trout-lily is another midwestern species found in our area on floodplains along the Potomac River.

While you are enjoying the beauty of the wildflowers, you might like to taste the leaves of ramps (*Allium tricoccum*). This is the plant made famous by ramps festivals in the southern Appalachians. Considered a spring tonic, this relative of garlic has a strong smell that remains with the eater for a long time.

Upland plants blooming in mid-April are star chickweed (*Stellaria pubera*), rue-anemone (*Anemonella thalictroides*), blue cohosh (*Caulophyllum thalictroides*), Dutchman's breeches (*Dicentra cucullaria*), squirrel corn (*Dicentra canadensis*), early saxifrage (*Saxifraga virginiensis*), and smooth rockcress (*Arabis laevigata*). Coville's phacelia (*Phacelia ranunculacea*), a midwestern species rare in the east, forms carpets on several of the moist hillsides, and dwarf ginseng (*Panax trifolius*) and wild blue phlox (*Phlox divaricata*) flower on the floodplain.

As the trees leaf out in May, the ephemeral early spring flowers disappear, but other species come into bloom, including showy orchis (*Orchis spectabilis*) and puttyroot (*Aplectrum hyemale*) in the uplands. Starry false Solomon's-seal (*Smilacina stellata*), a northern species of moist woods, grows here near the river, and few-flowered valerian (*Valeriana pauciflora*), a species of very limited distribution, occurs on the floodplain.

Only a few plants flower in the deep shade of these mature woods in June and July. Among those that do are leatherflower (*Clematis viorna*), black cohosh (*Cimicifuga racemosa*), and goatsbeard (*Aruncus dioicus*). Cranefly orchid (*Tipularia discolor*) and downy rattlesnake-plantain (*Goodyera pubescens*) bloom in August on the dry hillsides.

By late summer, the open areas on the floodplain begin to flower with fringed loosestrife (*Lysimachia ciliata*), American germander (*Teucrium canadense*), horse-balm (*Collinsonia canadensis*), Culver's-root (*Veronicastrum virginicum*), New York ironweed (*Vernonia noveboracensis*), and thin-leaved sunflower (*Helianthus decapetalus*). Along the river shore and on the rocky shoals are several species of these wet habitats, including halberd-leaved rose mallow (*Hibiscus laevis*), swamp milkweed (*Asclepias incarnata*), winged monkey-flower (*Mimulus alatus*), cardinal flower (*Lobelia cardinalis*), fog-fruit (*Lippia lanceolata*), and masses of water willow (*Justicia americana*).

Turkey Run Park is managed by the National Park Service through the George Washington Memorial Parkway. In the upland woods are three picnic areas and rest rooms. The bottomland woods are reached from the picnic areas via steep trails that connect with the Potomac Heritage Trail along the river. The mile-long trail along Turkey Run crosses the stream several times and is well marked. However, the loop trail to Dead Run is unmarked and not easy to follow. For more information, contact George Washington Memorial Parkway, Turkey Run Park, McLean, VA 22101; telephone (703)285-2598.

Directions: From the George Washington Memorial Parkway, take the exit for the Turkey Run Picnic Area and park at Area C1. A zigzag trail leads down to the Turkey Run Trail and the Potomac Heritage Trail along the river. To approach the riverside trail from the Turkey Run valley, take Georgetown Pike (VA-193) west to Turkey Run Road, turn right and follow for almost one mile. The road ends at a very small parking area near the stream. You can cross over on rocks and walk downstream for about a mile to the river.

Scott's Run Nature Preserve

A favorite place for many wildflower enthusiasts in the Washington area is Scott's Run Nature Preserve, formerly called Dranesville District Park. This park lies just outside the Capital Beltway near McLean and contains almost 400 acres of relatively undisturbed upland woods, moist hillsides, and bottomlands along the Potomac River. The upland forest features large mature specimens of oaks, tuliptree, black birch, and sugar maple. Along the stream, you can walk through a beech-hemlock ravine that resembles areas in the mountains. The bottomland forest has huge sycamore, river birch, and silver maple trees.

Scott's Run Nature Preserve is known for a great diversity of plant life. The variety of soils, moisture conditions, and slope orientations has created several microhabitats that support many different species of plants. Botanist Albert Radford of the University of North Carolina described the area as "the most diverse forest, from a plant community and species viewpoint, seen in the entire Piedmont." In a survey done several years ago, 175 species of flowering plants were found in bloom between March and June, and over 20 species of ferns were identified.

Once known as the "Burling Tract," the park also has an interesting social history. After serving as a rustic retreat for a well-known Washington lawyer, the area was slated to become a housing development until local citizens and students acted to save the natural woodlands. The park has two main trails and many unmarked trails wandering through the uplands, hillsides, ravines, and bottomlands.

Early April wildflowers on the rocky trail along Scott's Run include star chickweed (*Stellaria pubera*), early saxifrage (*Saxifraga virginiensis*), trailing arbutus (*Epigaea repens*), bluets (*Houstonia caerulea*), and solitary pussy-

Jeffersonia diphylla —
Twinleaf
(height: 6″–8″)

toes (*Antennaria solitaria*). In the upland woods are spring beauty (*Claytonia virginica*), round-lobed hepatica (*Hepatica americana*), bloodroot (*Sanguinaria canadensis*), cut-leaved toothwort (*Dentaria laciniata*), and slender toothwort (*Dentaria heterophylla*).

The moist hillsides near the river are carpeted with both the maroon and green forms of sessile trillium (*Trillium sessile*), as well as trout-lily (*Erythronium americanum*), Dutchman's breeches (*Dicentra cucullaria*), and squirrel corn (*Dicentra canadensis*). Other flowers on the rich slopes include wild ginger (*Asarum canadense*), twinleaf (*Jeffersonia diphylla*), and blue cohosh (*Caulophyllum thalictroides*).

The floodplain here is not as wide as at Turkey Run or Riverbend, but you can find floodplain species such as white trout-lily (*Erythronium albidum*), Virginia bluebells (*Mertensia virginica*), and the early blooming harbinger-of-spring (*Erigenia bulbosa*).

In late April, Jack-in-the-pulpit (*Arisaema triphyllum*), sessile bellwort (*Uvularia sessilifolia*), early meadowrue (*Thalictrum dioicum*), rue-anemone (*Anemonella thalictroides*), and wild geranium (*Geranium maculatum*) are added to the upland slopes. One particularly moist area along a little stream is covered with dwarf ginseng (*Panax trifolius*) and also has a few plants of crested iris (*Iris cristata*), shooting star (*Dodecatheon meadia*), and erect trillium (*Trillium erectum*). Because these last three species are not common in the Piedmont and occur so close together, it is thought that they were planted here.

In early May, the upland trails flower with yellow stargrass (*Hypoxis hirsuta*), spiderwort (*Tradescantia virginiana*), hispid buttercup (*Ranunculus hispidus*), golden Alexanders (*Zizia aurea*), clustered snakeroot (*Sanicula gregaria*), lyre-leaved sage (*Salvia lyrata*), one-flowered cancer-root (*Orobanche uniflora*), and rattlesnake-weed (*Hieracium venosum*). Several orchids grow in these rich woods, including pink lady's-slipper (*Cypripedium acaule*), yellow lady's-slipper (*Cypripedium calceolus*), showy orchis (*Orchis spectabilis*), puttyroot (*Aplectrum hyemale*), and large whorled pogonia (*Isotria verticillata*). Wood anemone (*Anemone quinquefolia*) and wild sarsaparilla (*Aralia nudicaulis*), species of the mountains, occur here on cool, north-facing slopes.

As the tree canopy closes over in June, fewer plants flower in the woods, but you may find lily-leaved twayblade (*Liparis lilifolia*), black cohosh (*Cimicifuga racemosa*), bowman's-root (*Porteranthus trifoliatus*), round-leaved pyrola (*Pyrola rotundifolia*), Indian pipe (*Monotropa uniflora*), and pinesap (*Monotropa hypopithys*). Late summer bloomers in the dry upland woods include cranefly orchid (*Tipularia discolor*) and downy rattlesnake-plantain (*Goodyera pubescens*).

In early fall, the woodland goldenrods and asters flower, including blue-stemmed goldenrod (*Solidago caesia*), silverrod (*Solidago bicolor*), elm-leaved goldenrod (*Solidago ulmifolia*), white wood aster (*Aster divaricatus*), calico aster (*Aster lateriflorus*), and heart-leaved aster (*Aster cordifolius*). Great lobelia (*Lobelia siphilitica*) and white turtlehead (*Chelone glabra*) bloom in a low wet seep along Scott's Run.

Scott's Run Nature Preserve is managed by the Fairfax County Park Authority and administered through Riverbend Park. There are no visitor facilities at Scott's Run at present, although there are plans for some "improvements." For more information or for a pamphlet on the spring wildflowers of Scott's Run Nature Preserve, call the Riverbend Nature Center at (703)759-3211.

Directions: From the Capital Beltway (I-495), take Georgetown Pike (VA-193) west. The park appears very quickly on the right. The upper parking lot gives access to trails through the upland woods and the lower parking lot leads to the trails along Scott's Run.

Great Falls Park

Great Falls Park, located on the Potomac River in northern Fairfax County, offers fine views of the powerful 60-foot waterfall and the rocky bluffs of Mather Gorge. The park contains almost 800 acres and stretches for three miles along the Virginia shore of the river. The areas near the visitor center are usually filled with picnickers and sightseers, but you can escape the crowds by walking in the woods, along the ruins of the old Patowmack Canal, or along the high bedrock terrace above the gorge.

Great Falls Park contains many diverse habitats such as bottomland woods on the floodplain above the falls, small marshes along the river, a pond, a swamp, rich moist woodlands, dry uplands, rocky bluffs, open bedrock terraces, terrace woodlands, and the deep ravine of Difficult Run at the south end of the park. Because of these varied habitats and the introduction of seeds and plants when the river floods, the park contains a rich and diverse flora despite heavy visitor use.

As early as February, you can find skunk cabbage (*Symplocarpus foetidus*) emerging in the swamp. In late March, the little harbinger-of-spring (*Erigenia bulbosa*) flowers on the floodplain. In early April, the moist woodlands bloom with spring beauty (*Claytonia virginica*), Dutchman's breeches (*Dicentra cucullaria*), squirrel corn (*Dicentra canadensis*), bloodroot (*Sanguinaria canadensis*), and cut-leaved toothwort (*Dentaria laciniata*). The hillside above the Swamp Trail is a veritable rock garden of round-lobed hepatica (*Hepatica americana*), rue-anemone (*Anemonella thalictroides*), and early saxifrage (*Saxifraga virginiensis*).

By mid-April, the terrace woodlands show a fine display of flowering plants. Moss phlox (*Phlox subulata*), wild pink (*Silene caroliniana*), and the dainty lyre-leaved rockcress (*Arabis lyrata*) bloom on the open rocks. Sessile trillium (*Trillium sessile*), trout-lily (*Erythronium americanum*), wild ginger (*Asarum canadense*), golden ragwort (*Senecio aureus*), and wild blue phlox (*Phlox divaricata*) flower in the moist woods.

Several plants typical of dry woodlands are found on the trail along Difficult Run. Mid-April flowers on the south-facing slope include hispid buttercup (*Ranunculus hispidus*), wood vetch (*Vicia caroliniana*), ovate-leaved violet (*Viola fimbriatula*), and trailing arbutus (*Epigaea repens*). In early May, this dry hillside blooms with yellow stargrass (*Hypoxis hirsuta*), spiderwort (*Tradescantia virginiana*), heart-leaved Alexanders (*Zizia aptera*), yellow pimpernel (*Taenidia integerrima*), violet wood-sorrel (*Oxalis violacea*), rattlesnake-weed (*Hieracium venosum*), and robin's plantain (*Erigeron pulchellus*).

Early May is a prime time to visit Great Falls Park as the woods are full of migrating songbirds, including several warblers that nest here. Flowers blooming in the upland woods include field chickweed (*Cerastium arvense*), lyre-leaved sage (*Salvia lyrata*), and chrysogonum (*Chrysogonum virginianum*). On the floodplain are starry false Solomons-seal (*Smilacina stellata*) and few-flowered valerian (*Valeriana pauciflora*).

In early summer, the open bedrock terrace comes into bloom, with nodding onion (*Allium cernuum*), leatherflower (*Clematis viorna*), tassel-rue (*Trautvetteria caroliniensis*), veiny pea (*Lathyrus venosus*), blue false indigo (*Baptisia australis*), smooth beardtongue (*Penstemon laevigatus*), and narrow-leaved white-topped aster (*Sericocarpus linifolius*). Late summer species flowering on the bedrock terrace include purple gerardia (*Agalinis purpurea*), Culver's-root (*Veronicastrum virginicum*), tall coreopsis (*Coreopsis tripteris*), and spiked blazing-star (*Liatris spicata*).

In August, marshy areas along the river north of the visitor center are brightened with halberd-leaved rose mallow (*Hibiscus laevis*), swamp milkweed (*Asclepias incarnata*), square-stemmed monkey-flower (*Mimulus ringens*), cardinal flower (*Lobelia cardinalis*), and thin-leaved sunflower (*Helianthus decapetalus*).

The woodlands bloom again in September with calico aster (*Aster lateriflorus*), white wood aster (*Aster divaricatus*), heart-leaved aster (*Aster cordifolius*), elm-leaved goldenrod (*Solidago ulmifolia*), zigzag goldenrod (*Solidago flexicaulis*), and silverrod (*Solidago bicolor*).

Even in October, you can find plants in flower on the open bedrock terrace. Look for late purple aster (*Aster patens*), stiff aster (*Aster linariifolius*), and riverbank goldenrod (*Solidago racemosa*). Riverbank goldenrod, rare in Virginia and Maryland, is found in both states only along the Potomac River gorge near Great Falls.

Great Falls Park is managed by the National Park Service. It is located at 9200 Old Dominion Drive, Great Falls, Virginia 22066; telephone (703) 285-2966. The visitor center has a snack bar and bookshop as well as rest rooms and picnic areas. There is plenty of parking. However, there may be a long line of cars waiting to get into the park on sunny weekend days. Wildflower walks led by knowledgeable volunteers are offered throughout the year. Call the park for more information.

Directions: From the Capital Beltway (I-495), take Georgetown Pike (VA-193) west for about four miles to Old Dominion Drive. Turn right at the park entrance.

Riverbend Park

Riverbend Park, a woodland oasis of over 400 acres, is located just north of Great Falls Park, and a trail along the river connects the two parks. Riverbend is a quieter park, without the great crowds of visitors often found at Great Falls.

In contrast to the dramatic landscape at Great Falls, Riverbend has gentle, rolling hills with broad stream valleys, and the river is wide and tranquil here above the falls. There are only a few rock outcrops, and the moderate slopes allow the buildup of rich soil and a mature forest. In the upland woods, oaks, beech, and tuliptree are dominant, with American holly and mountain laurel (*Kalmia latifolia*) in the understory. In the bottomlands, huge old sycamore and silver maple trees grow with pawpaw and spicebush below them.

The moist alluvial soil and undisturbed woodlands at Riverbend Park make a fine habitat for early spring wildflowers. At the end of March, the little harbinger-of-spring (*Erigenia bulbosa*) pokes up in low areas along the floodplain. Round-lobed hepatica (*Hepatica americana*) flowers on south-facing rocks in the open woods. Early April bloomers include spring beauty (*Claytonia virginica*), cut-leaved toothwort (*Dentaria laciniata*), bloodroot (*Sanguinaria canadensis*), twinleaf (*Jeffersonia diphylla*), Dutchman's breeches (*Dicentra cucullaria*), squirrel corn (*Dicentra canadensis*), and early saxifrage (*Saxifraga virginiensis*).

By mid-April, the bottomlands are covered with Virginia bluebells (*Mertensia virginica*), including several plants with white flowers. Trout-lily (*Erythronium americanum*) and its rarer cousin, white trout-lily (*Erythronium albidum*), bloom together among the bluebells. Clusters of sessile trillium (*Trillium sessile*) and wild ginger (*Asarum canadense*) flower along the riverside trail, and leaves of the strong-tasting ramps (*Allium tricoccum*) are scattered in the woods.

In May, upland plants in bloom include Indian cucumber-root (*Medeola virginiana*), perfoliate bellwort (*Uvularia perfoliata*), showy orchis (*Orchis spectabilis*), puttyroot orchid (*Aplectrum hyemale*), large whorled pogonia (*Isotria verticillata*), wild geranium (*Geranium maculatum*), and one-flowered cancer-root (*Orobanche uniflora*). The bottomlands are filled with dwarf ginseng (*Panax trifolius*), wild blue phlox (*Phlox divaricata*), golden ragwort (*Senecio aureus*), and few-flowered valerian (*Valeriana pauciflora*), a rare species found on both sides of the Potomac River in our area.

In summer, the open sunny fields come into flower with Deptford pink (*Dianthus armeria*), butterflyweed (*Asclepias tuberosa*), ox-eye daisy (*Chrysanthemum leucanthemum*), and black-eyed Susan (*Rudbeckia hirta*). In the shaded woodlands, a few species bloom, including Indian pipe (*Monotropa uniflora*), spotted wintergreen (*Chimaphila maculata*), and beechdrops (*Epifagus virginiana*). Late summer flowers on the floodplain are fringed loosestrife (*Lysimachia ciliata*), American germander (*Teucrium canadense*), and sweet-scented Indian plantain (*Cacalia suaveolens*), a rare species known from only a few locations in the state.

Riverbend Park is managed by the Fairfax County Park Authority and is located at 8814 Jeffery Road, Great Falls, VA 22066; telephone (703) 759-3211. A rustic log cabin serves as an attractive nature center and knowledgeable staff naturalists are usually available. Be sure to check the journals for wildflower sightings by the naturalists over the last few years. Wildflower walks are offered each spring at Riverbend and other Fairfax County parks. Call the park for more information.

Directions: From the Capital Beltway (I-495), take Georgetown Pike (VA-193) west for almost five miles, going past the entrance to Great Falls Park. Turn right on Riverbend Road for almost one mile, then right on Jeffery Road for three miles to the parking area for the nature center. Follow the signs to the nature center. Do not turn on Potomac Hills Street; this leads to the boat ramp.

Fraser Preserve

Fraser Preserve, a 220-acre undeveloped area owned by the Virginia Chapter of The Nature Conservancy, is tucked away in the suburbs about four miles above Great Falls.

The habitats at Fraser Preserve include open fields, young woodlands, wet meadows, bottomlands along the river, and a swampy area on the floodplain. The terrain slopes gently to the river and the trails are easy to follow. Several interesting areas occur where tree cutting above a sewer line and nearby gas pipeline has made open swaths in the woods.

Fraser Preserve has many of the same early spring wildflowers that occur at Riverbend and other nearby parks, including trout-lily (*Erythronium americanum*), sessile trillium (*Trillium sessile*), wild ginger (*Asarum canadense*), spring beauty (*Claytonia virginica*), star chickweed (*Stellaria pubera*), round-lobed hepatica (*Hepatica americana*), rue-anemone (*Anemonella thalictroides*), bloodroot (*Sanguinaria canadensis*), cut-leaved toothwort (*Dentaria laciniata*), and Virginia bluebells (*Mertensia virginica*).

Two spring flowers unusual for our area are found at the preserve. Purple cress (*Cardamine douglassii*), which resembles spring cress (*Cardamine rhomboidea*) but has pale purple petals, blooms in late March in the swampy area. Marsh marigold (*Caltha palustris*), which usually occurs in cold mountain seeps, flowers in late April in a remote area of the preserve.

In late summer, the wet meadows along the gas pipeline bloom with halberd-leaved rose mallow (*Hibiscus laevis*), cardinal flower (*Lobelia cardinalis*), swamp milkweed (*Asclepias incarnata*), seedbox (*Ludwigia alternifolia*), blue vervain (*Verbena hastata*), square-stemmed monkey-flower (*Mimulus ringens*), and winged monkey-flower (*Mimulus alatus*). In the swamp are masses of lizard's-tail (*Saururus cernuus*) and a small colony of purple fringeless orchid (*Habenaria peramoena*).

Fraser Preserve is managed by the Virginia Field Office of The Nature Conservancy and is open to the public for walking and nature study. The Nature Conservancy asks that visitors stay on the established trails, keep dogs on a leash, and avoid damage to all plants and animals. In keeping with the purpose of the preserve, there are no visitor facilities, picnic areas, or other amenities.

The one-mile entrance road is shared with a church camp and is usually locked unless a Nature Conservancy or church representative is present at the site. If you park outside the gate, please do not block the entrance or private driveways.

For more information about Fraser Preserve, contact The Nature Conservancy, Virginia Field Office, 1110 Rose Hill Drive, Charlottesville, VA 22901; telephone (804)295-6106.

Directions: From the Capital Beltway, take Georgetown Pike (VA-193) for almost eight miles, going through the village of Great Falls. Turn right

Lobelia cardinalis —
Cardinal flower
(height: 2′−4′)

on Springvale Road (VA-674) for two miles, turning left at the Chez Francois Restaurant and immediately right again, and continue on Springvale Road another half-mile to the preserve entrance.

CENTRAL AND WESTERN FAIRFAX COUNTY

Fairfax County, a highly developed suburban county just to the west of Washington, has several county and regional parks where natural areas have been preserved. Places in the Piedmont are included in this section, and other parks in Fairfax County, such as Huntley Meadows and Dyke Marsh, are discussed in Chapter 9, the Coastal Plain section of this book.

Deciduous forests once covered most of Fairfax County, but centuries of farming and the recent explosion of shopping malls and housing developments have changed the landscape. The old towns of Alexandria, Falls Church, and Fairfax are rich in historical interest, and newer areas such as Springfield and Reston also are major suburban centers.

Fairfax County parks are found in all parts of the county and lie along several different highways radiating from Washington. Extensive woodlands and outstanding displays of wildflowers occur mainly along the Potomac River and in a few stream valleys.

Places in the northern part of the county can be reached via VA-7 or VA-267 (Dulles Toll Road). Parks in the central area are reached from I-66, US-50, or US-29. A few places in southern Fairfax County also are accessed from I-395 and I-95.

Green Spring Gardens Park

Green Spring Gardens Park is the horticultural park for Fairfax County. Located on a lovely old eighteenth-century farm, the park contains cultivated areas, greenhouses, display gardens, and the new Virginia Native Plant Trail. This trail, developed as a cooperative project between the park and the Potowmack Chapter of the Virginia Native Plant Society, displays plants native to Virginia in both naturalistic and more formal settings.

The trail overlooks Turkeycock Run and contains different habitats such as clearings, wooded hillsides, and bottomlands along the creek. The woodland has been planted with numerous species native to the eastern United States. The short distance of the trail and the signs along the way make it possible for you to see many different native plants at one time.

April bloomers in the bottomland woods include wild ginger (*Asarum canadense*), spring beauty (*Claytonia virginica*), Virginia bluebells (*Mertensia virginica*), and wild blue phlox (*Phlox divaricata*). In the upland woods are bloodroot (*Sanguinaria canadensis*), and Virginia heartleaf (*Asarum virginicum*). The heartleaf is not found growing wild in Fairfax County, but has naturalized here very well.

In May, look in the pine woods for pink lady's-slipper (*Cypripedium acaule*) and in the upland woods for wild geranium (*Geranium maculatum*). On the rock wall grow moss phlox (*Phlox subulata*) and alumroot (*Heuchera americana*).

Summer flowers in the open field include wild bergamot (*Monarda fistulosa*) and fall phlox (*Phlox paniculata*).

Green Spring Gardens Park is managed by the Fairfax County Park Authority and is located at 4603 Green Spring Road, Alexandria, VA 22312; telephone (703)642-5173.

Directions: From Alexandria, take Duke Street (VA-236) west. Continue one mile past Shirley Highway (I-395) and turn right on Green Spring Road. From the Capital Beltway (I-495), take Little River Turnpike (VA-236) east for about three miles. Just past Braddock Road, turn left on Green Spring Road to the park. From the parking lot, the native plant trail is across the open lawn.

Clark's Crossing Park

Clark's Crossing Park is one of the few places in the Washington area where you can find the meadow habitat favored by late summer flowers. The small county park near the town of Vienna is contained within the 45-mile-long W&OD Railroad Regional Park. Along the old railroad right-of-way and under massive power lines, the open sunny habitat has been maintained for many years, and species of both dry and wet meadows have become established.

In mid-July, over 50 species may be in flower at Clark's Crossing. In dry areas along the horse trail and the bike trail are butterflyweed (*Asclepias tuberosa*), rose pink (*Sabatia angularis*), partridge-pea (*Cassia fasciculata*), pencil flower (*Stylosanthes biflora*), pink wild bean (*Strophostyles umbellata*), whorled coreopsis (*Coreopsis vertillicata*), black-eyed Susan (*Rudbeckia hirta*), and whorled rosinweed (*Silphium trifoliatum*). In low, wet areas beneath the power line pylons, you can find plants of wet meadows

Asclepias tuberosa —
Butterflyweed
(height: 1′–2′)

and marshes such as swamp milkweed (*Asclepias incarnata*), virgin's bower (*Clematis virginiana*), seedbox (*Ludwigia alternifolia*), square-stemmed monkey-flower (*Mimulus ringens*), New York ironweed (*Vernonia noveboracensis*), and hollow Joe-Pye-weed (*Eupatorium fistulosum*).

In mid-August, search the dry meadows for the tiny orchid, slender ladies'-tresses (*Spiranthes gracilis*). Early asters are in bloom, including cornel-leaved aster (*Aster infirmus*) and wavy-leaved aster (*Aster undulatus*), as well as tall coreopsis (*Coreopsis tripteris*), tall blue lettuce (*Lactuca biennis*), and the uncommon hairy sunflower (*Helianthus mollis*).

September brings an explosion of flowers of the composite family to these open fields. Asters are plentiful and include bushy aster (*Aster dumosus*), panicled aster (*Aster lanceolatus*), crooked-stem aster (*Aster prenanthoides*), and purple-stemmed aster (*Aster puniceus*). Several goldenrods are in bloom, such as early goldenrod (*Solidago juncea*), late goldenrod (*Solidago gigantea*), and lance-leaved goldenrod (*Solidago graminifolia*). Maryland golden-aster (*Chrysopsis mariana*) flowers in dry soil along the bike path and tickseed-sunflower (*Bidens polylepis*) brightens the wet meadows.

Clark's Crossing Park is managed by the Fairfax County Park Authority. There is a very small parking lot and there are no visitor facilities. For more information, contact the park authority office at 3701 Pender Drive, Fairfax, VA 22030; telephone (703)246-5680.

Directions: From the Capital Beltway (I-495), take VA-123 west for almost three miles to Vienna. Turn right on Beulah Road for one and one-half miles and then left on Clark's Crossing Road. Continue for one mile to the end of the road.

Reston Wildflower Trail

In the planned community of Reston in western Fairfax County, over 1,000 acres of open space have been preserved, and many areas have pleasant nature trails through woodlands and open fields.

In April, the woods have spring wildflowers typical of the region, such as spring beauty (*Claytonia virginica*), bloodroot (*Sanguinaria canadensis*), cut-leaved toothwort (*Dentaria laciniata*), and early saxifrage (*Saxifraga virginiensis*). May bloomers include smooth Solomon's-seal (*Polygonatum biflorum*), Jack-in-the-pulpit (*Arisaema triphyllum*), and Mayapple (*Podophyllum peltatum*).

At the 70-acre Vernon J. Walker Nature Area, a wildflower trail has been established with both naturally growing and planted native species. In April, you can find sessile trillium (*Trillium sessile*), trout-lily (*Erythronium americanum*), wild ginger (*Asarum canadense*), round-lobed hepatica (*Hepatica americana*), rue-anemone (*Anemonella thalictroides*), twinleaf (*Jeffersonia diphylla*), Dutchman's breeches (*Dicentra cucullaria*), Virginia bluebells (*Mertensia virginica*), and wild blue phlox (*Phlox divaricata*).

Early summer flowers in the open fields include Deptford pink (*Dianthus armeria*), black-eyed Susan (*Rudbeckia hirta*), and whorled coreopsis (*Coreopsis verticillata*). Late summer bloomers in wet meadows are New England aster (*Aster novae-angliae*), New York ironweed (*Vernonia noveboracensis*), hollow Joe-Pye-weed (*Eupatorium fistulosum*), and tickseed-sunflower (*Bidens polylepis*).

A small nature center building is located near the wildflower trail. For more information, contact the Reston Association, 1930 Isaac Newton Square, Reston, VA 22090; telephone (703)437-9580.

Directions: From the Capital Beltway (I-495), take the Dulles Toll Road (VA-267) for about seven miles to Wiehle Avenue. Turn left on Wiehle, then right on Sunrise Valley Drive, left on Soapstone Drive for about two miles. After crossing Glade Drive, look for the wildflower trail on the left.

Hidden Pond Park

Situated in a suburban area southwest of Alexandria, Hidden Pond Park has a nature center, a small pond with wetlands, and 25 acres of open fields and woods. It is adjacent to the 200-acre Pohick Valley Stream Park, and there are many interesting natural areas along the stream.

In late winter, skunk cabbage (*Symplocarpus foetidus*) can be found in wet swampy places. Early spring flowers in the moist woodlands include trout-lily (*Erythronium americanum*), spring beauty (*Claytonia virginica*), cut-leaved toothwort (*Dentaria laciniata*), bloodroot (*Sanguinaria canadensis*), and golden ragwort (*Senecio aureus*).

In May, look along the edges of upland woods for flowers of drier habitats such as spiderwort (*Tradescantia virginiana*), lyre-leaved sage (*Salvia lyrata*), large-leaved houstonia (*Houstonia purpurea*), and rattlesnake-weed (*Hieracium venosum*).

By June and July, the open fields come into bloom with Deptford pink (*Dianthus armeria*), Venus's looking-glass (*Triodanis perfoliata*), ox-eye daisy (*Chrysanthemum leucanthemum*), lance-leaved coreopsis (*Coreopsis lanceolata*), and black-eyed Susan (*Rudbeckia hirta*).

August is the month to visit Hidden Pond to see the flowering of wetland plants, including swamp milkweed (*Asclepias incarnata*), square-stemmed monkey-flower (*Mimulus ringens*), cardinal flower (*Lobelia cardinalis*), mad-dog skullcap (*Scutellaria lateriflora*), purple-headed sneeze-weed (*Helenium flexuosum*), and New York ironweed (*Vernonia noveboracensis*).

Even in September, you can find plants in bloom in the fields and open woods. On the dry barren hillsides, look for wild sensitive plant (*Cassia nictitans*), smooth small-leaved tick-trefoil (*Desmodium marilandicum*), Maryland golden-aster (*Chrysopsis mariana*), hyssop-leaved boneset (*Eupatorium hyssopifolium*), white heath aster (*Aster pilosus*), gray goldenrod (*Solidago nemoralis*), and lance-leaved goldenrod (*Solidago graminifolia*). In the woods, search for Indian tobacco (*Lobelia inflata*), horse-balm (*Collinsonia canadensis*), fall phlox (*Phlox paniculata*), and blue-stemmed goldenrod (*Solidago caesia*).

Managed by the Fairfax County Park Authority, Hidden Pond Park is located at 8511 Greeley Boulevard, Springfield, VA 22152; telephone (703) 451-9588. The nature center has exhibits, live animals, and programs for all ages.

Directions: From the Capital Beltway (I-495), take I-95 south for one mile. Take VA-644 (Old Keene Mill Road), west toward Springfield for about three and one-half miles. After the intersection with Rolling Road, look for the park sign at Greeley Boulevard. Turn left to the end of the road.

South Run District Park

South Run District Park is a small recreational park in the southwestern part of Fairfax County. Although there are houses nearby and the park is heavily used, the open fields under the power line provide habitat for some late-blooming meadow species.

September is a good time to visit this little park. In dry areas near the power line, look for slender gerardia (*Agalinis tenuifolia*), downy lobelia (*Lobelia puberula*), pineweed (*Hypericum gentianoides*), lion's-foot (*Prenanthes serpentaria*), Maryland golden-aster (*Chrysopsis mariana*), white heath aster (*Aster pilosus*), calico aster (*Aster lateriflorus*), lance-leaved goldenrod (*Solidago graminifolia*), and rough-stemmed goldenrod (*Solidago rugosa*).

South Run District Park, managed by the Fairfax County Park Authority, has ballfields, tennis courts, and a new recreational building. It is located at 9501 Pohick Road, Springfield, VA 22153; telephone (703)866-0566.

Directions: From the Capital Beltway (I-495), take I-95 south for one mile. Take VA-644 (Old Keene Mill Road) west for about six miles. Turn left on Pohick Road and go a mile and a half to the park entrance on the right.

Hidden Oaks Nature Center

Nestled within the 50-acre Annandale Community Park, Hidden Oaks Nature Center is located in the heart of Fairfax County. The trails wind through oak-pine woods typical of the area where the Piedmont province abuts the Coastal Plain.

Hidden Oaks is known for a grand display of pink lady's-slipper (*Cypripedium acaule*) in early May. The oaks and pines contribute to the acidic soil preferred by this spectacular orchid.

Other May-blooming flowers in the deciduous woodlands include smooth Solomon's-seal (*Polygonatum biflorum*), perfoliate bellwort (*Uvularia perfoliata*), Indian cucumber-root (*Medeola virginiana*), star chickweed (*Stellaria pubera*), and cut-leaved toothwort (*Dentaria laciniata*).

Hidden Oaks Nature Center is managed by the Fairfax County Park Authority. The center has interesting exhibits and regular programs for the public. It is located at 4020 Hummer Road, Annandale, VA 22003; telephone (703)941-1065.

Directions: From the Capital Beltway (I-495), take Little River Turnpike (VA-236) east. Make the first left turn on Hummer Road and continue to the park entrance.

Ellanor C. Lawrence Park

In the western part of Fairfax County, near the town of Centreville, is Ellanor C. Lawrence Park. Maintained primarily as a historical area, the park has 640 acres of nineteenth-century tobacco and dairy farms, as well as old fields, mature oak woodlands, steep-sided stream valleys, and a large pond.

April wildflowers along the streams include trout-lily (*Erythronium americanum*), wild ginger (*Asarum canadense*), spring beauty (*Claytonia virginica*), round-lobed hepatica (*Hepatica americana*), Virginia bluebells (*Mertensia virginica*), and wild blue phlox (*Phlox divaricata*). Some upland species in the woods are star chickweed (*Stellaria pubera*), rue-anemone (*Anemonella thalictroides*), bloodroot (*Sanguinaria canadensis*), cut-leaved toothwort (*Dentaria laciniata*), and yellow corydalis (*Corydalis flavula*).

The wooded hillsides continue flowering in May with the blooming of wild geranium (*Geranium maculatum*), wild pink (*Silene caroliniana*), wild stonecrop (*Sedum ternatum*), violet wood-sorrel (*Oxalis violacea*), spring forget-me-not (*Myosotis verna*), bluets (*Houstonia caerulea*), and rattlesnake-weed (*Hieracium venosum*). Large-flowered trillium (*Trillium grandiflorum*) was planted here and has naturalized in the woods.

By June, the flower show moves to the open fields. In Cabell's meadow grow Deptford pink (*Dianthus armeria*), spring vetch (*Vicia sativa*), pencil flower (*Stylosanthes biflora*), yellow goatsbeard (*Tragopogon pratensis*),

Sedum ternatum —
Wild stonecrop
(height: 4″–8″)

lance-leaved coreopsis (*Coreopsis lanceolata*), and black-eyed Susan (*Rudbeckia hirta*).

Ellanor C. Lawrence Park is located at 5040 Walney Road, Chantilly, VA 22021; telephone (703)631-0013. The Walney Visitor Center, a 200-year-old stone farmhouse, has exhibits on the human and natural history of the area.

Directions: From the Capital beltway (I-495), take I-66 west to Centreville. Go north on VA-28 for one-tenth mile and then right on Walney Road to the park.

Bull Run Regional Park

Bull Run Regional Park, a 1,000-acre stream-valley park, is located near Centreville on the western edge of Fairfax County. The meandering stream, Bull Run, famous in Civil War history, divides Fairfax County from neighboring Prince William County.

The park is known for a grand display of Virginia bluebells (*Mertensia virginica*) along the stream in mid-April. Other flowers found in the low-lying bottomlands are trout-lily (*Erythronium americanum*), spring beauty (*Claytonia virginica*), swamp buttercup (*Ranunculus septentrionalis*), spring cress (*Cardamine rhomboidea*), false mermaid (*Floerkea proserpinacoides*),

Mertensia virginica —
Virginia bluebells
(height: 1′–2′)

common blue violet (*Viola papilionacea*), and smooth yellow violet (*Viola pensylvanica*).

In the drier upland woods, April bloomers include yellow corydalis (*Corydalis flavula*), early saxifrage (*Saxifraga virginiensis*), bluets (*Houstonia caerulea*), dwarf dandelion (*Krigia virginica*), and plantain-leaved pussytoes (*Antennaria plantaginifolia*).

By mid-May, the carpet of bluebells is gone and the bottomlands are covered with Jack-in-the-pulpit (*Arisaema triphyllum*), Mayapple (*Podophyllum peltatum*), and the very invasive garlic mustard (*Alliaria petiolata*).

The Northern Virginia Regional Park Authority manages Bull Run Regional Park. There are many recreational facilities, picnic areas, and campgrounds. For more information, contact the park office at 7700 Bull Run Road, Centreville, VA 22020; telephone (703)631-0550.

Directions: From the Capital Beltway (I-495), take I-66 west past Centreville. Take US-29 west for two miles to Bull Run Post Office Road and turn left to the park entrance. The streamside trail begins near the visitor center.

Hemlock Overlook Regional Park

Hemlock Overlook Regional Park is located near the historic village of Clifton in western Fairfax County and is situated on the banks of Bull Run.

The park is true to its name, for a large stand of eastern hemlock trees grows on the hillside above the creek. The steep eroded hillsides create a habitat very different from the flat alluvial floodplain at Bull Run Regional Park a few miles upstream.

April flowers in the woodlands include wild ginger (*Asarum canadense*), spring beauty (*Claytonia virginica*), bloodroot (*Sanguinaria canadensis*), Dutchman's breeches (*Dicentra cucullaria*), and smooth yellow violet (*Viola pensylvanica*). In May, look for Jack-in-the-pulpit (*Arisaema triphyllum*), false Solomon's-seal (*Smilacina racemosa*), star chickweed (*Stellaria pubera*), wood anemone (*Anemone quinquefolia*), Mayapple (*Podophyllum peltatum*), and wild geranium (*Geranium maculatum*).

Interesting summer bloomers in the dry upland woods are downy rattlesnake-plantain (*Goodyera pubescens*) and pinesap (*Monotropa hypopithys*). In wet areas along the creek and around the pond grow tall meadowrue (*Thalictrum pubescens*), fringed loosestrife (*Lysimachia ciliata*), cardinal flower (*Lobelia cardinalis*), yellow sneezeweed (*Helenium autumnale*), and hollow Joe-Pye-weed (*Eupatorium fistulosum*).

Hemlock Overlook Regional Park is managed by the Northern Virginia Regional Park Authority. It is located at 13220 Yates Ford Road, Clifton, VA 22024; telephone (703)830-9252.

Directions: From the Capital Beltway (I-495), take I-66 west to Centreville. Take VA-28 south for about one-half mile and US-29 east for almost two miles. Turn right on Clifton Road for about four miles (through the village of Clifton), then turn right at Yates Ford Road and continue until the road ends at Hemlock Overlook.

WESTERN PRINCE WILLIAM COUNTY

A long, narrow county to the west of Fairfax County, Prince William County encompasses both Piedmont and Coastal Plain regions. Two national parks preserve thousands of acres of open land in this rapidly developing county: Manassas National Battlefield Park in the northern part and Prince William Forest Park in the south.

Sleepy villages and picturesque farms can still be found in far reaches of the county, but housing developments and shopping centers are encroaching even there. The city of Manassas, near the Civil War battlefield, is the largest municipality and the center of suburban sprawl.

I-66 and US-29 traverse the county in the north. VA-28 and VA-234 criss-cross the county, and I-95 and US-1 run along the eastern edge.

Manassas National Battlefield Park

Commemorating the Civil War battles of First Manassas and Second Manassas, this historical park is located along Bull Run just north of the city of Manassas. Over 4,500 acres are preserved much as they looked in the 1860s, and several old buildings are still standing. The wooded hillsides, bottomland forests, and open fields offer such a peaceful rural atmosphere that it is hard to imagine the violence that occurred here.

In mid-April, the Stone Bridge Trail along Bull Run has a grand display of Virginia bluebells (*Mertensia virginica*). The carpet of bluebells on the floodplain here is similar to that at Bull Run Regional Park a few miles downstream. Other wildflowers along the stream are trout-lily (*Erythronium americanum*), spring beauty (*Claytonia virginica*), Dutchman's breeches (*Dicentra cucullaria*), pale violet (*Viola striata*), smooth yellow violet (*Viola pensylvanica*), and false mermaid (*Floerkea proserpinacoides*). Look upstream for harbinger-of-spring (*Erigenia bulbosa*) and green violet (*Hybanthus concolor*).

In May, the moist woodlands along the creek harbor Jack-in-the-pulpit (*Arisaema triphyllum*), smooth Solomon's-seal (*Polygonatum biflorum*), and golden ragwort (*Senecio aureus*). In the oak-pine woods behind the visitor center, look for pink lady's-slipper (*Cypripedium acaule*), spotted wintergreen (*Chimaphila maculata*), and pipsissewa (*Chimaphila umbellata*).

Manassas Battlefield Park has many acres of grasslands and meadows that have been maintained for historical reasons and also provide fine habitat for summer-blooming species.

In July, visit Deep Cut Meadow, a beautiful meadow filled with native grasses such as little bluestem (*Andropogon scoparius*) and Indian grass (*Sorghastrum nutans*). In the dry, open meadow, you may find slender ladies'-tresses (*Spiranthes gracilis*), pencil flower (*Stylosanthes biflora*), wild yellow flax (*Linum virginianum*), purple milkwort (*Polygala sanguinea*), whorled milkweed (*Asclepias verticillata*), green milkweed (*Asclepias viridiflora*), hyssop skullcap (*Scutellaria integrifolia*), hairy ruellia (*Ruellia carolinensis*), and narrow-leaved white-topped aster (*Sericocarpus linifolius*).

In moist areas of the meadow, look for ragged fringed orchid (*Habenaria lacera*) and swamp milkweed (*Asclepias incarnata*). Back at the Stone Bridge Trail, look along the creek for the brilliant red cardinal flower (*Lobelia cardinalis*).

Late August and September bring new blooms to Deep Cut Meadow, including scaly blazing-star (*Liatris squarrosa*), New York ironweed (*Vernonia noveboracensis*), yellow sneezeweed (*Helenium autumnale*), orange coneflower (*Rudbeckia fulgida*), and lance-leaved goldenrod (*Solidago graminifolia*). In dry barren areas of the meadow, look for slender knotweed (*Polygonum tenue*), pink wild bean (*Strophostyles umbellata*), pinweed (*Lechea racemulosa*), blue curls (*Trichostema dichotomum*), buttonweed (*Diodia teres*), and gray goldenrod (*Solidago nemoralis*).

Manassas National Battlefield Park is managed by the National Park Service. A visitor center contains Civil War exhibits, a slide show, maps, and publications. An attractive brochure and many road signs describe the battles and the different areas of the park. For more information, contact the park headquarters at P.O. Box 1830, Manassas, VA 22110; telephone (703)754-7107.

Directions: From the Capital Beltway (I-495), take I-66 west to Manassas. Take VA-234 north to the visitor center on the right. For the Stone Bridge Trail, take VA-234 for about a mile from I-66, turn right on US-29, go a little over a mile and look for the sign on the left. For Deep Cut Meadow, turn left on US-29 from VA-234, go about a mile, and turn right on VA-622 (Featherbed Lane). The meadow is one-half mile on the left.

NVCC-Manassas Campus Nature Trail

At the Manassas campus of Northern Virginia Community College (NVCC), a one-mile nature trail has been developed through the high upland woods overlooking the college.

In early April, wildflowers such as spring beauty (*Claytonia virginica*), round-lobed hepatica (*Hepatica americana*), and cut-leaved toothwort (*Dentaria laciniata*) can be found on the moist hillsides. In mid-April, the trail passes by rue-anemone (*Anemonella thalictroides*) and golden Alexanders (*Zizia aurea*) on the slopes and early saxifrage (*Saxifraga virginiensis*) and common bluets (*Houstonia caerulea*) on the heights. A good display of trout-lily (*Erythronium americanum*) occurs on the floodplain along the stream.

The dry upland woods continue to bloom in May with the flowering of yellow stargrass (*Hypoxis hirsuta*), wild pink (*Silene caroliniana*), pinxter flower (*Rhododendron periclymenoides*), partridgeberry (*Mitchella repens*), and rattlesnake-weed (*Hieracium venosum*).

There are fewer woodland plants in flower in summer but some can be found. In June, look for lily-leaved twayblade (*Liparis lilifolia*) and four-leaved milkweed (*Asclepias quadrifolia*). In August, search for cranefly orchid (*Tipularia discolor*), downy rattlesnake-plantain (*Goodyera pubescens*), starry campion (*Silene stellata*), and smooth false-foxglove (*Aureolaria flava*).

Behind the main classroom building is the small Jack Finzel Memorial Garden, where native wildflowers have been planted in a natural woodland setting. Spring-bloomers here include bloodroot (*Sanguinaria canadensis*), Virginia bluebells (*Mertensia virginica*), and wild blue phlox (*Phlox divaricata*). Among the summer flowers are butterflyweed (*Asclepias tuberosa*) and orange coneflower (*Rudbeckia fulgida*).

Both the nature trail and the wildflower garden are maintained by the biology faculty of NVCC-Manassas Campus, located at 6901 Sudley Road, Manassas, VA 22110; telephone (703)257-6605.

Directions: From the Capital Beltway (I-495), take I-66 west to Manassas. Take VA-234 north for two-tenths of a mile and turn right at the college. Park in the commuter lot beyond the student parking lot. The trail begins between these parking lots. A visit to the NVCC-Manassas Campus Nature Trail can be combined with a visit to the nearby Manassas National Battlefield Park.

James Long Park

James Long Park is a county recreational park near Haymarket. Tennis courts, ballfields, and a library have been built on the open upland area, but the stream valley and wooded hillside above it have been preserved as natural areas. Beaver activity along the stream has created a marsh-like wet meadow.

Summer-flowering species in the wet meadow include seedbox (*Ludwigia alternifolia*), common hedge-nettle (*Stachys tenuifolia*), swamp milkweed (*Asclepias incarnata*), square-stemmed monkey-flower (*Mimulus ringens*), cardinal flower (*Lobelia cardinalis*), and boneset (*Eupatorium perfoliatum*). In drier parts of the meadow are biennial gaura (*Gaura biennis*), scarlet pimpernel (*Anagallis arvensis*), rose pink (*Sabatia angularis*), hyssop skullcap (*Scutellaria integrifolia*), and early goldenrod (*Solidago juncea*).

In late fall, the wet meadow produces an October surprise with the flowering of several groups of closed gentian (*Gentiana clausa*). Although not rare, this gentian is not commonly seen in our area. Other fall bloomers in the meadow include clammy cuphea (*Cuphea viscosissima*), yellow sneezeweed (*Helenium autumnale*), New York ironweed (*Vernonia noveboracensis*), and purple-stemmed aster (*Aster puniceus*).

On the dry hillside leading down to the creek, look for curlyheads (*Clematis ochroleuca*), blue curls (*Trichostema dichotomum*), hyssop skullcap (*Scutellaria integrifolia*), hairy ruellia (*Ruellia caroliniensis*), and stiff aster (*Aster linariifolius*).

James Long Park is managed by the Prince William County Park Authority and is located at 4603 James Madison Highway north of Haymarket. For more information, contact the park authority at 12249 Bristow Road, Bristow, VA 22013; telephone (703)361-7871. In 1993, the Prince William County Park Authority and the Virginia Native Plant Society signed an agreement to protect the natural area of this park.

Gentiana clausa —
Closed gentian
(height: 12″–18″)

Directions: From the Capital Beltway (I-495), take I-66 west to Haymarket. Take US-15 (James Madison Highway) north for about one and one-half miles. Look for a sign for the library and the park. Turn right into the park and continue up the hill, turning left past the library and the playground. The trail to the natural area begins at the far end of the parking lot.

Conway Robinson State Forest

Conway Robinson State Forest near Gainesville is a 400-acre oak woodland with relatively flat terrain. There are many trails through the woods and a picnic pavilion near the road.

In moist areas of the forest, look for April wildflowers such as spring beauty (*Claytonia virginica*), round-lobed hepatica (*Hepatica americana*), hispid buttercup (*Ranunculus hispidus*), and bloodroot (*Sanguinaria canadensis*).

May bloomers in the drier woods include both yellow lady's-slipper (*Cypripedium calceolus*) and pink lady's-slipper (*Cypripedium acaule*), puttyroot (*Aplectrum hyemale*), rue-anemone (*Anemonella thalictroides*), wild columbine (*Aquilegia canadensis*), and pennywort (*Obolaria virginica*). A small colony of large-flowered trillium (*Trillium grandiflorum*) found here has probably naturalized from old plantings.

In late summer and early fall, walk through the open fields along the pipeline. In dry areas, look for orange coneflower (*Rudbeckia fulgida*) and scaly blazing-star (*Liatris squarrosa*). In moist meadows, search for closed gentian (*Gentiana clausa*), cardinal flower (*Lobelia cardinalis*), and giant sunflower (*Helianthus giganteus*).

Conway Robinson State Forest is managed by the Virginia Department of Forestry. For more information, contact the Regional Forester, 9267 Corporate Circle, Manassas, VA 22110; telephone (703)368-3741.

Directions: From the Capital Beltway (I-495), take I-66 to Gainesville. Go east on US-29 for about one-half mile and look for the parking area on the left. Or you could come from Manassas Battlefield at the intersection of VA-234 and US-29 by continuing west on US-29 for three and one-half miles and parking on the right.

LOUDOUN COUNTY

Fenced horse farms and lovely old towns define Loudoun County to the west of Fairfax County. Leesburg, on the eastern edge of the county, is the only large town, and suburbia is spreading fast in this area. But farther away from Washington, open farmland alternates with forested hills and valleys. Still mostly rural, with many large estates, the land rolls westward to the foothills and the high Blue Ridge beyond.

US-50 traverses the southern edge of the county; VA-7 runs through the central section; and US-15 extends north and south.

Red Rock Wilderness Overlook Regional Park

Red Rock Wilderness Overlook Park is located on the Potomac River in eastern Loudoun County near Leesburg. It is just a few miles downriver from Ball's Bluff. In 1978, the 64-acre property was given to the Northern Virginia Regional Park Authority by Mrs. Frances Speke, who stipulated that the land be preserved in a natural state.

The park consists of a beautiful old farm with mature forests, rolling hills, and several rocky overlooks high above the river. These red siltstone bluffs provide fine views across the Potomac to the Maryland countryside, with Sugarloaf Mountain and the Catoctin Mountains in the distance.

Over three miles of well-maintained trails (all named for trees) wander through the woods, crossing streams and climbing hills. Because the bluffs rise so steeply from the river, there is very little floodplain in the park. However, the rich woodlands and rocky cliffs are excellent habitats for many spring wildflowers.

In mid-April, the hillsides are carpeted with Dutchman's breeches (*Dicentra cucullaria*) and squirrel corn (*Dicentra canadensis*), as well as spring beauty (*Claytonia virginica*), star chickweed (*Stellaria pubera*), rue-anemone (*Anemonella thalictroides*), cut-leaved toothwort (*Dentaria laciniata*), and slender toothwort (*Dentaria heterophylla*). On the bottom-lands at the north end of the park are trout-lily (*Erythronium americanum*), Virginia bluebells (*Mertensia virginica*), and wild blue phlox (*Phlox divaricata*).

In late April, bluets (*Houstonia caerulea*) and smooth rockcress (*Arabis laevigata*) bloom along the high trail to the overlooks. In the oak woods are bastard toadflax (*Comandra umbellata*), wild pink (*Silene caroliniana*), hispid buttercup (*Ranunculus hispidus*), yellow corydalis (*Corydalis flavula*), rattlesnake-weed (*Hieracium venosum*), and plantain-leaved pussytoes (*Antennaria plantaginifolia*).

At the main overlook, you can look down the steep bluffs to see masses of wild columbine (*Aquilegia canadensis*), lyre-leaved rockcress (*Arabis lyrata*), and early saxifrage (*Saxifraga virginiensis*). Other plants growing on the bluffs include live-forever (*Sedum telephioides*) and shale-barren goldenrod (*Solidago harrisii*).

Red Rock Wilderness Overlook Regional Park is managed by the Northern Virginia Regional Park Authority. The park authority plans no development of the property except for restoration of some of the old stone farm buildings. For more information, contact the park authority at 5400 Ox Road, Fairfax Station, VA 22039; telephone (703)352-5900.

Directions: From the Capital Beltway (I-495), take VA-7 west to Leesburg. Take US-15 north (Leesburg by-pass) for almost one mile, and turn right on Edward's Ferry Road. Continue for about one and one-half miles until you see on your left a high stone wall and then the sign for the park.

Ball's Bluff Regional Park

Ball's Bluff Regional Park, the site of a Civil War battle in October 1861, lies on a high ridge above the Potomac River just north of Leesburg. This quiet place, where Union and Confederate soldiers once fought and died, is now a favorite spot for botanists and birders in early spring.

Ball's Bluff has long been known as a rich area for early spring flowers. In 1987, the Northern Virginia Regional Park Authority obtained 170 acres to preserve as parkland in this developing area. The trails to the river are quite steep and rough and have no trail markers. Other trails go beside the river and along the high bluffs. The well-marked Interpretive Trail helps visitors understand the action during the Battle of Ball's Bluff.

The habitats at Ball's Bluff include dry oak woods on top of the siltstone bluffs, moist rich woodlands on the steep hillsides, and a wide alluvial floodplain along the river. The presence of plants such as twinleaf (*Jeffersonia diphylla*), green violet (*Hybanthus concolor*), and shooting star (*Dodecatheon meadia*) indicates calcareous soil at Ball's Bluff.

Flowering begins in March with early bloomers such as spring beauty (*Claytonia virginica*), twinleaf, bloodroot (*Sanguinaria canadensis*), and harbinger-of-spring (*Erigenia bulbosa*).

In mid-April, the rocky hillsides are filled with a wide variety of wildflowers including both maroon and green forms of sessile trillium (*Trillium sessile*), sessile bellwort (*Uvularia sessilifolia*), wild ginger (*Asarum canadense*), star chickweed (*Stellaria pubera*), blue cohosh (*Caulophyllum thalictroides*), Dutchman's breeches (*Dicentra cucullaria*), squirrel corn (*Dicentra canadensis*), and yellow corydalis (*Corydalis flavula*).

Along the river bottomland are masses of Virginia bluebells (*Mertensia virginica*), as well as trout-lily (*Erythronium americanum*) and its midwestern cousin, white trout-lily (*Erythronium albidum*). The maple-like leaves of broad-leaved waterleaf (*Hydrophyllum canadense*) carpet the bottomland.

Late April is the time to explore the high trails for flowers of drier habitats such as bastard toadflax (*Comandra umbellata*), rue-anemone (*Anemonella thalictroides*), birdfoot violet (*Viola pedata*), bluets (*Houstonia caerulea*), and rattlesnake-weed (*Hieracium venosum*). On one bluff is a small population of shooting star, an uncommon species in the Piedmont. On rock outcrops, look for lyre-leaved rockcress (*Arabis lyrata*), smooth rockcress (*Arabis laevigata*), early saxifrage (*Saxifraga virginiensis*), and green violet.

There is a large parking lot but there are no visitor facilities at Ball's Bluff. For more information, contact the Northern Virginia Regional Park Authority headquarters at 5400 Ox Road, Fairfax Station, VA 22039; telephone (703)352-5900.

Directions: From the Capital Beltway (I-495), take VA-7 west to Leesburg. Take US-15 north (Leesburg by-pass) for about one and one-half miles. At a large housing development, turn right on Battlefield Parkway and then left on Ball's Bluff Road for one mile to the parking lot. Walk down the road to a small walled cemetery, and take the trail straight ahead, which leads downhill to the river. For a fine spring outing, a visit to Ball's Bluff can be combined with a visit to Red Rock Wilderness Overlook Regional Park a few miles downriver.

9

Virginia Coastal Plain

SOUTHEASTERN FAIRFAX COUNTY

The Coastal Plain section of Fairfax County lies on the southeastern edge of the county south of Washington. A narrow corridor running between I-95 and the Potomac River, this part of the county has the flat terrain, oak–pine woodlands, and poor sandy soil typical of the Coastal Plain province. Many acres of freshwater tidal marshes occur along the river and its tributaries.

Some plants are well adapted to the light sterile soil and are more common in the Coastal Plain than in the Piedmont. Typical species of this region include partridge-pea (*Cassia fasciculata*), downy lobelia (*Lobelia puberula*), and buttonweed (*Diodia teres*).

As in other places near the city, much commercial and residential development has occurred in lower Fairfax County. However, the federal government owns most of the riverside property, including the George Washington Memorial Parkway, Fort Belvoir, and Mason Neck National Wildlife Refuge.

The historic city of Alexandria anchors the northern end of southeastern Fairfax County. Both I-95 and US-1 run north-south to the Lorton-Pohick Area, and the George Washington Memorial Parkway goes south along the river to Mount Vernon.

Winkler Botanical Preserve

Surrounded by a busy commercial area of Alexandria, the 40-acre Winkler Botanical Preserve is a quiet woodland sanctuary. A typical oak-

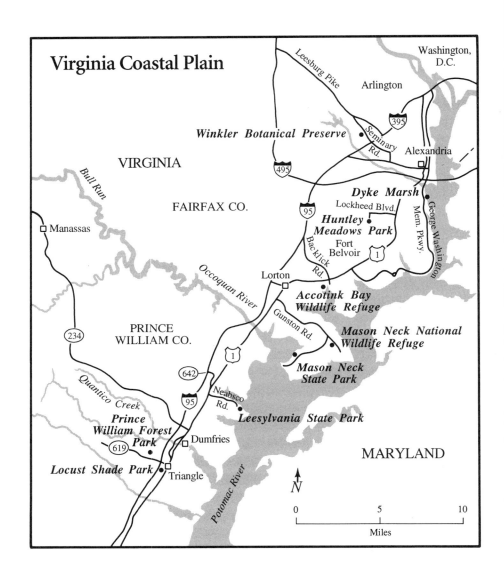

Virginia Coastal Plain

Washington, D.C.

Arlington

Leesburg Pike

Winkler Botanical Preserve

Seminary Rd.

395

Alexandria

VIRGINIA

Bull Run

495

FAIRFAX CO.

Manassas

95

Dyke Marsh

Lockheed Blvd.

Huntley Meadows Park

Fort Belvoir

1

Mem. Pkwy.

George Washington

Occoquan River

Lorton

Backlick Rd.

Accotink Bay Wildlife Refuge

234

PRINCE WILLIAM CO.

1

Gunston Rd.

Mason Neck National Wildlife Refuge

642

Mason Neck State Park

Quantico Creek

Neabsco Rd.

95

Leesylvania State Park

MARYLAND

Prince William Forest Park

619

Dumfries

Locust Shade Park

Triangle

Potomac River

N

0   5   10

Miles

hickory forest has been augmented with naturalized plantings illustrating different habitats and species of the Potomac River valley. The sanctuary is privately owned and the emphasis of the small staff is on research, design, and development. However, individuals and small groups are welcome to arrange a visit.

In May, the upland woods contain many wildflowers native to our area, such as pink lady's-slipper (*Cypripedium acaule*), yellow lady's-slipper (*Cypripedium calceolus*), large whorled pogonia (*Isotria verticillata*), wild geranium (*Geranium maculatum*), wild blue phlox (*Phlox divaricata*), and chrysogonum (*Chrysogonum virginianum*). Naturalized species of the southern Appalachians include crested iris (*Iris cristata*), Virginia heartleaf (*Asarum virginicum*), galax (*Galax aphylla*), and shortia (*Shortia galacifolia*).

A rock garden is habitat for wild pink (*Silene caroliniana*), alumroot (*Heuchera americana*), and wild bleeding-heart (*Dicentra eximia*).

In June, look for the southern "magnolia bog" with swamp magnolia (*Magnolia virginiana*), swamp azalea (*Rhododendron viscosum*), highbush blueberry (*Vaccinium corymbosum*), and several types of wetland ferns.

A small meadow has been developed at the Winkler Preserve, planted with native grasses and meadow wildflowers. In late July, many sun-loving species are in bloom, including cornel-leaved aster (*Aster infirmus*), woodland sunflower (*Helianthus divaricatus*), early goldenrod (*Solidago juncea*), grass-leaved blazing-star (*Liatris graminifolia*), and purple coneflower (*Echinacea purpurea*).

The Winkler Botanical Preserve office is located at 4900 Seminary Road, Alexandria, VA 22311, and the preserve is nearby. For more information or to arrange a visit, call (703)578-7888.

Directions: From Alexandria, take Seminary Road west. Go past I-395 about one mile and turn left. More exact directions will be given when you arrange a visit.

Dyke Marsh

Dyke Marsh is the largest tidal freshwater wetland on the Potomac River close to Washington. Only a mile south of Alexandria, it preserves over 300 acres of tidal marsh, bottomland forest, and floodplain along the river.

Dyke Marsh is home to many mammals, birds, and amphibians and has vegetation typical of freshwater marshes. Much of the wetland area is accessible only by boat, but a one-mile trail leads to the heart of the marsh and a few places are accessible from the George Washington Memorial Parkway.

The best time to see flowering plants in freshwater marshes is in July and August. At Dyke Marsh, the dominant species are broad-leaved cattail (*Typha latifolia*), broad-leaved arrowhead (*Sagittaria latifolia*), arrow arum (*Peltandra virginica*), and spatterdock (*Nuphar advena*). You may also find showy wetland species such as pickerelweed (*Pontederia cordata*), swamp rose mallow (*Hibiscus moscheutos*), swamp milkweed (*Asclepias incarnata*), cardinal flower (*Lobelia cardinalis*), and yellow sneezeweed (*Helenium autumnale*).

In the forest and thickets along the trail are groundnut (*Apios americana*), biennial gaura (*Gaura biennis*), common evening-primrose (*Oenothera biennis*), large-flowered leafcup (*Polymnia uvedalia*), and hollow Joe-Pye-weed (*Eupatorium fistulosum*).

September is a good time to visit Dyke Marsh. A large wetland area near the parkway is filled with the bright gold blooms of larger bur-marigold (*Bidens laevis*). Other species still in flower include marsh dayflower (*Murdannia keisak*), halberd-leaved tearthumb (*Polygonum arifolium*), arrow-leaved tearthumb (*Polygonum sagittatum*), spotted jewelweed (*Impatiens capensis*), and pale jewelweed (*Impatiens pallida*).

In the moist thickets are many yellow composites including green-headed coneflower (*Rudbeckia laciniata*), wingstem (*Verbesina alternifolia*), pale-leaved sunflower (*Helianthus strumosus*), and Jerusalem artichoke (*Helianthus tuberosus*).

A fall visit to Dyke Marsh could include a stop at adjacent Belle Haven Picnic Area to observe the many waterbirds that frequent this part of the river. You can see great blue heron, great egret, double-crested cormorant, Canada goose, and mallard. Also look for wintering ducks such as northern pintail, common merganser, bufflehead, and ruddy duck. Sometimes bald eagles are spotted in this area.

Dyke Marsh is managed by the National Park Service through the George Washington Memorial Parkway. The area has walking and bike trails, picnic tables, rest rooms, and a marina. For more information, contact the parkway headquarters at Turkey Run Park, McLean, VA 22101; telephone (703)285-2598.

Directions: From Washington or Alexandria, take the George Washington Parkway south. Go about one mile beyond the signs for the Capital

Pontederia cordata —
Pickerelweed
(height: 1′–3′)

Beltway (I-495) and look for the Belle Haven Picnic Area on the left. Park here and walk south for Dyke Marsh.

Huntley Meadows Park

Huntley Meadows Park, the largest park in Fairfax County, is located near a busy commercial strip south of Alexandria. The park contains over 1,000 acres of nontidal wetlands and Coastal Plain forests in the midst of heavy suburban development.

The many different habitats include freshwater marsh, shrub swamp, forested wetlands, oak-pine forest, and open fields. The Cedar Trail through the woods connects with the Heron Trail, which follows a boardwalk through the marsh.

Huntley Meadows provides fine wildlife habitat and is home to beaver, deer, otter, great blue heron, and the elusive king rail.

Summer and early fall are the best times to see wildflowers at Huntley Meadows. In June and July, in the open fields, you can find Deptford pink (*Dianthus armeria*), spotted St. Johnswort (*Hypericum punctatum*), whorled loosestrife (*Lysimachia quadrifolia*), narrow-leaved mountain-mint (*Pycnanthemum tenuifolium*), and ox-eye daisy (*Chrysanthemum leucanthemum*). In very dry, sandy soil grow bracted plantain (*Plantago aristata*), wild yellow flax (*Linum virginianum*), and dwarf dandelion (*Krigia virginica*). Flowering in the marsh are swamp rose (*Rosa palustris*) and buttonbush (*Cephalanthus occidentalis*).

In August, the wetlands are dominated by a large stand of lizard's-tail (*Saururus cernuus*). Other summer-flowering species are swamp rose mallow (*Hibiscus moscheutos*), seedbox (*Ludwigia alternifolia*), swamp milkweed (*Asclepias incarnata*), square-stemmed monkey-flower (*Mimulus ringens*), winged monkey-flower (*Mimulus alatus*), humped bladderwort (*Utricularia gibba*), and cardinal flower (*Lobelia cardinalis*).

In the open fields near the parking lot are partridge-pea (*Cassia fasciculata*), blue curls (*Trichostema dichotomum*), hyssop-leaved boneset (*Eupatorium hyssopifolium*), and early goldenrod (*Solidago juncea*).

September brings an abundance of bright gold to the open fields with the flowering of masses of tickseed-sunflower (*Bidens polylepis*), as well as tall goldenrod (*Solidago canadensis*), rough-stemmed goldenrod (*Solidago rugosa*), and lance-leaved goldenrod (*Solidago graminifolia*). Other fall-flowering species of dry areas are calico aster (*Aster lateriflorus*), white heath aster (*Aster pilosus*), and sweet everlasting (*Gnaphalium obtusifolium*).

The marsh still blooms in fall with white turtlehead (*Chelone glabra*), New York ironweed (*Vernonia noveboracensis*), flat-topped aster (*Aster umbellatus*), and climbing hempweed (*Mikania scandens*).

Even in mid-October, a visit to Huntley Meadows gives botanical pleasure with a small colony of closed gentian (*Gentiana clausa*) flowering in the forested wetland.

Huntley Meadows Park, managed by the Fairfax County Park Authority, is located at 3701 Lockheed Boulevard, Alexandria, VA 22306; telephone (703)768-2525. The trails are well marked, and there is an attractive visitor center with informative displays.

Directions: From the Capital Beltway (I-495), take US-1 south for three and one-half miles to Lockheed Boulevard. Turn right and go one-half mile to the park entrance on the left.

Accotink Bay Wildlife Refuge

Fort Belvoir, a large army base south of Mount Vernon, has preserved over 700 acres of tidal marshes and forested wetlands as the Accotink Bay Wildlife Refuge. Many trails wander through the different habitats of the refuge, and the Great Blue Heron Trail goes far out to the open marsh and tidal flats. Active beaver work has enlarged the broad marsh where Accotink Creek meets the Potomac River.

As with other freshwater wetlands, August is a good time to visit the Accotink Bay preserve. In the forested wetlands are many tidal creeks and beaver ponds where you may find arrow arum (*Peltandra virginica*), Virginia dayflower (*Commelina virginica*), false pimpernel (*Lindernia dubia*), cardinal flower (*Lobelia cardinalis*), and green-headed coneflower (*Rudbeckia laciniata*).

The open marsh is dominated by cattails, grasses, and sedges. Look for other freshwater-wetland species such as pickerelweed (*Pontederia cordata*), broad-leaved arrowhead (*Sagittaria latifolia*), swamp rose mallow (*Hibiscus moscheutos*), water hemlock (*Cicuta maculata*), groundnut (*Apios americana*), wild mint (*Mentha arvensis*), square-stemmed monkey-flower (*Mimulus ringens*), and climbing hempweed (*Mikania scandens*).

Accotink Bay Wildlife Refuge is managed by the Fort Belvoir Environmental and Natural Resource Office, Directorate of Engineering and Housing, Fort Belvoir, VA 22060. It is open to the public from dawn to dusk. There is ample parking, and a kiosk displays information and trail brochures. To arrange a group visit, call (703)806-4007.

Directions: From the Capital Beltway (I-495), take I-95 south for about four miles. Take the Fort Belvoir exit, turn right onto Backlick Road, and go about two miles to the intersection with US-1. Continue straight ahead through Tully Gate into Fort Belvoir. The refuge parking lot is three-fourths of a mile on the right. From Alexandria, take the George Washington Parkway south, go past Mount Vernon, continue to the intersection with US-1, turn left, and, at the third light, turn left again at Tully Gate.

Mason Neck National Wildlife Refuge and Mason Neck State Park

On the Potomac River almost 20 miles south of Washington lies a broad peninsula known as Mason Neck. The whole area was once part of the large plantation, Gunston Hall, owned by the Mason family. In 1969, the Mason Neck National Wildlife Refuge was established, containing over 2,000 acres of hardwood forest, river shoreline, and freshwater wetlands. Mason Neck State Park preserves another 1,800 acres on the northern side of the refuge along Belmont Bay.

The peninsula is well known as a nesting area for great blue herons and a wintering site for bald eagles. The refuge and park provide needed habitat for these large birds and protect the largest freshwater tidal wetlands in northern Virginia.

In the center of the refuge, the Woodmarsh Trail winds through hilly woodlands, finally coming to the open marsh. Short boardwalks in a few places make the wetlands accessible. The Great Marsh Trail leads from the east side of the refuge to an observation platform with a sweeping view of the broad marsh and the Maryland shore. In the state park, the Bay View Trail skirts the shore of Belmont Bay and crosses a small freshwater wetland.

Coastal Plain forests are not as rich in spring wildflowers as those in the Piedmont and mountains, but the mature woodlands at Mason Neck do have several April bloomers such as spring beauty (*Claytonia virginica*), bloodroot (*Sanguinaria canadensis*), cut-leaved toothwort (*Dentaria laciniata*), trailing arbutus (*Epigaea repens*), and bluets (*Houstonia caerulea*).

In May, the wetlands begin to flower with sweetflag (*Acorus calamus*), golden club (*Orontium aquaticum*), and yellow iris (*Iris pseudacorus*).

June bloomers in the marsh include arrow arum (*Peltandra virginica*), spatterdock (*Nuphar advena*), and swamp rose (*Rosa palustris*). And in the open fields are Deptford pink (*Dianthus armeria*), St. Andrew's cross (*Ascyrum hypericoides*), butterflyweed (*Asclepias tuberosa*), and ox-eye daisy (*Chrysanthemum leucanthemum*).

July and August are the best months to see the flowering of wetland plants, including broad-leaved arrowhead (*Sagittaria latifolia*), pickerelweed (*Pontederia cordata*), swamp rose mallow (*Hibiscus moscheutos*), cardinal flower (*Lobelia cardinalis*), and New York ironweed (*Vernonia noveboracensis*). A special treat at the boardwalk on the Woodmarsh Trail is a small colony of wild rice (*Zizania aquatica*).

Flowering in the wetlands continues into September and early October. Larger bur-marigold (*Bidens laevis*) turns the marsh bright gold, and marsh dayflower (*Murdannia keisak*), spotted jewelweed (*Impatiens capensis*), and New York aster (*Aster novi-belgii*) add to the colorful display.

Fall flowers in the upland areas include panicled aster (*Aster lanceolatus*), calico aster (*Aster lateriflorus*), lance-leaved goldenrod (*Solidago graminifolia*), and silverrod (*Solidago bicolor*).

Mason Neck National Wildlife Refuge is managed by the U.S. Fish and Wildlife Service and is located off Gunston Road just south of Lorton. For more information, contact the Refuge Manager at 14416 Jefferson Davis Highway, Suite 20A, Woodbridge, VA 22191; telephone (703)690-1297. Mason Neck State Park is managed by the Virginia Department of Conservation and Recreation, Division of State Parks, with an on-site office at 7301 High Point Road, Lorton, VA 22079; telephone (703)339-7265.

Directions: From the Capital Beltway (I-495), take I-95 south for about seven miles. Go east on Lorton Road to Lorton, and then turn right (south) on US-1 for about one mile. Turn left on Gunston Road (VA-242) and continue for about four miles to the signs for the refuge and the park.

SOUTHEASTERN PRINCE WILLIAM COUNTY

The southern part of Prince William County is dominated by the large federal holdings of Quantico Marine Corps Base and Prince William Forest Park. The fall line between the Piedmont and the Coastal Plain runs through the eastern side of these sites, close to highways I-95 and US-1.

Poor sandy soil, relatively flat terrain, and forests of pines, oaks, beech, and sweet gum characterize this part of the county. The broad, tidal Potomac River defines the eastern edge of southern Prince William County, and many coves and small bays dot the shoreline.

I-95 and US-1 run parallel to each other from Occoquan to Dumfries. VA-234 connects this southeastern section of the county to Manassas.

Leesylvania State Park

Opened in 1989, the 500-acre Leesylvania State Park is located at the lower end of Occoquan Bay where it joins the Potomac River. The park has historical areas, picnic areas, a marina, and nature trails.

Leesylvania contains a large freshwater tidal wetland, full of plants such as broad-leaved arrowhead (*Sagittaria latifolia*), arrow arum (*Peltandra virginica*), and spatterdock (*Nuphar advena*). In mid-May, sweetflag (*Acorus calamus*), yellow iris (*Iris pseudacorus*), and southern blue flag (*Iris virginica*) bloom in the marsh. Summer-flowering species include pickerelweed (*Pontederia cordata*), swamp rose mallow (*Hibiscus moscheutos*), cardinal flower (*Lobelia cardinalis*), yellow sneezeweed (*Helenium autumnale*), hollow Joe-Pye-weed (*Eupatorium fistulosum*), and New York ironweed (*Vernonia noveboracensis*).

In the upland woods, there are spring flowers such as star chickweed (*Stellaria pubera*), bloodroot (*Sanguinaria canadensis*), yellow corydalis (*Corydalis flavula*), and bluets (*Houstonia caerulea*). In August, look for cranefly orchid (*Tipularia discolor*), downy rattlesnake-plantain (*Goodyera pubescens*), naked-flowered tick-trefoil (*Desmodium nudiflorum*), Indian pipe (*Monotropa uniflora*), horse-balm (*Collinsonia canadensis*), and lopseed (*Phryma leptostachya*).

Leesylvania State Park is managed by the Virginia Department of Conservation and Recreation, Division of State Parks. For more information, contact the department at 1500 East Main Street, Richmond, VA 23219; telephone (804)786-1712.

Directions: From the Capital Beltway (I-495), take I-95 south for about 14 miles. Go east on VA-642 to the intersection with US-1. Go south on US-1 for about one-half mile and turn left on Neabsco Road. The park is on the right in one mile.

Houstonia caerulea —
Bluets
(height: 2″–8″)

Prince William Forest Park

Prince William Forest Park near Triangle was once a patchwork of cotton and tobacco farms. Now a second-growth forest of oaks, hickories, pines, and other trees covers the landscape. This large park has many campgrounds, two picnic areas, a nature center, and over 35 miles of well-marked trails.

The entrance to Prince William Forest Park is on the fall line between the hard, crystalline rocks of the Piedmont and the loose, unconsolidated soils of the Coastal Plain. Small waterfalls in the creeks and abrupt hillsides on the land mark this division between the two regions.

April wildflowers are found along the South Branch of Quantico Creek. The moist woodlands are habitat for spring beauty (*Claytonia virginica*), wood anemone (*Anemone quinquefolia*), rue-anemone (*Anemonella thalictroides*), hispid buttercup (*Ranunculus hispidus*), bloodroot (*Sanguinaria canadensis*), and slender toothwort (*Dentaria heterophylla*). The rocky upland woods have wild columbine (*Aquilegia canadensis*), early saxifrage (*Saxifraga virginiensis*), alumroot (*Heuchera americana*), and bluets (*Houstonia caerulea*).

*Chrysanthemum
leucanthemum* —
Ox-eye daisy
(height: 1′–3′)

In May, look in the pine woods for pink lady's-slipper (*Cypripedium acaule*) and in deciduous woods for violet wood-sorrel (*Oxalis violacea*) and one-flowered cancer-root (*Orobanche uniflora*). Open fields begin to bloom in June with wild indigo (*Baptisia tinctoria*), butterflyweed (*Asclepias tuberosa*), Venus's looking-glass (*Triodanis perfoliata*), and ox-eye daisy (*Chrysanthemum leucanthemum*).

Summer flowers in the fields and open areas include Deptford pink (*Dianthus armeria*), partridge-pea (*Cassia fasciculata*), pencil flower (*Stylosanthes biflora*), butter-and-eggs (*Linaria vulgaris*), and hairy ruellia (*Ruellia caroliniensis*). On the floodplain along the creek, look for cardinal flower (*Lobelia cardinalis*), flat-topped aster (*Aster umbellatus*), hollow Joe-Pye-weed (*Eupatorium fistulosum*), and New York ironweed (*Vernonia noveboracensis*).

Prince William Forest Park is managed by the National Park Service. For more information, contact Prince William Forest Park, Box 209, Triangle, VA 22172; telephone (703)221-7181 (park headquarters) or (703) 221-2104 (nature center).

Directions: From the Capital Beltway (I-495), take I-95 south about 20 miles to Triangle. Go west on VA-619 for only one-quarter mile to the park entrance on the right. Bear left at the fork for the stream valley trails and the loop road through the park.

Locust Shade Park

Locust Shade Park adjoins the south side of Prince William Forest Park. The park features many recreational facilities, including fishing, boating, tennis, ballfields, and picnic areas.

An August walk around the eight-acre lake produces a nice list of summer wildflowers. The open fields provide habitat for plants of dry soil, and beaver activity around the lake has created a little marsh with wetland plants.

On the high banks of the lake, look for partridge-pea (*Cassia fasciculata*), St. Andrew's cross (*Ascyrum hypericoides*), horse-balm (*Collinsonia canadensis*), buttonweed (*Diodia teres*), Indian tobacco (*Lobelia inflata*), hyssop-leaved boneset (*Eupatorium hyssopifolium*), and upland boneset (*Eupatorium sessilifolium*).

In the marshy area are groundnut (*Apios americana*), seedbox (*Ludwigia alternifolia*), water hemlock (*Cicuta maculata*), Virginia bugleweed (*Lycopus virginicus*), hollow Joe-Pye-weed (*Eupatorium fistulosum*), rough boneset (*Eupatorium pilosum*), and climbing hempweed (*Mikania scandens*).

In late summer and early fall, flowering plants can be seen even along the roadside. Look for butterfly pea (*Clitoria mariana*), wild kidney bean (*Phaseolus polystachios*), hoary tick-trefoil (*Desmodium canescens*), panicled tick-trefoil (*Desmodium paniculatum*), and early goldenrod (*Solidago juncea*).

Locust Shade Park is managed by the Prince William County Park Authority and is located at 4701 Locust Shade Drive, Triangle, VA 22172; telephone (703)221-2158 or (703)221-8579.

Directions: From the Capital Beltway (I-495), take I-95 south about 20 miles to Triangle. Go east on VA-619, then go south on US-1 and look for the park entrance on the right.

10

Virginia and West Virginia Mountains

THE BLUE RIDGE

The Blue Ridge Mountains of Virginia are more representative of the lofty southern Appalachians than are their counterparts in Maryland. Elevations reach over 4,000 feet; the topography is rugged, with peaks, cliffs, steep valleys, high waterfalls. Composed of erosion-resisting rocks such as greenstone, granite, or quartzite, the range rises dramatically from the flatter landscape to the east.

Fortunately for area residents, much of this beautiful mountain region is held as public land in Shenandoah National Park, the Blue Ridge Parkway, and George Washington National Forest. These thousands of acres protected from development provide excellent opportunities for quiet recreation such as hiking, camping, and nature study. The area covered by this book includes only the northern section of the Virginia Blue Ridge, but there are many excellent botanizing spots in the higher mountains to the south.

Because of the cooler climate of the Blue Ridge, some plants grow here that are not found in the warmer Piedmont and Coastal Plain provinces. Several species native to New England were pushed southward during the last glacial advance. Later, as the climate warmed, these species moved north again. However, in the cool forests of these high mountains, some relict colonies of northern plants remain.

Northern species found in Virginia's Blue Ridge include yellow clintonia (*Clintonia borealis*), large-flowered trillium (*Trillium grandiflorum*), nodding trillium (*Trillium cernuum*), swamp saxifrage (*Saxifraga pensylvanica*), and three-toothed cinquefoil (*Potentilla tridentata*).

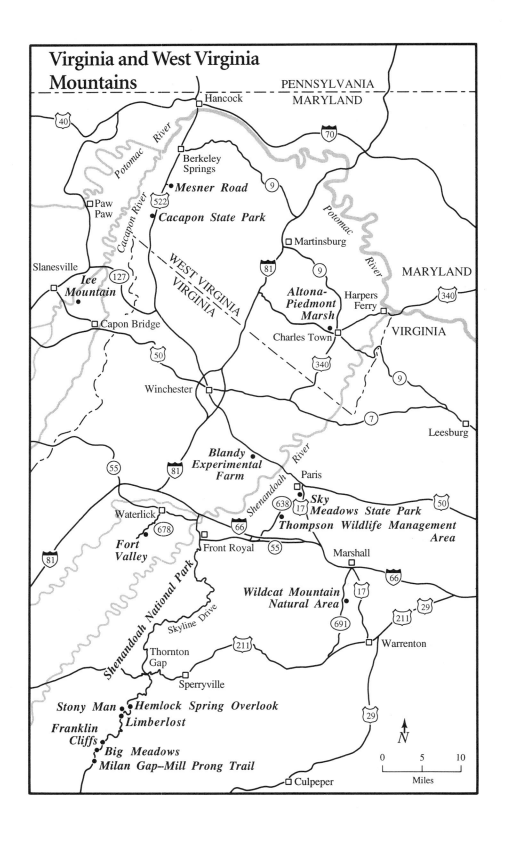

Virginia and West Virginia
Mountains

PENNSYLVANIA
MARYLAND

Hancock

40

70

Potomac River

Berkeley
Springs

9

Potomac

Mesner Road

522

Paw
Paw

Cacapon State Park

Cacapon River

Martinsburg

River

MARYLAND

81

9

Slanesville

127

Ice
Mountain

WEST VIRGINIA
VIRGINIA

Altona-
Piedmont
Marsh

Harpers
Ferry

340

Capon Bridge

Charles Town

VIRGINIA

50

340

9

Winchester

7

Leesburg

Blandy
Experimental
Farm

River

Paris

55

81

Shenandoah

Sky
Meadows State Park

638

17

50

Waterlick

Thompson Wildlife Management
Area

678

66

81

Fort
Valley

Front Royal

55

Marshall

66

Shenandoah National Park

Wildcat Mountain
Natural Area

17

29

691

211

Skyline Drive

Thornton
Gap

211

Warrenton

Sperryville

29

Stony Man

Hemlock Spring Overlook

Franklin
Cliffs

Limberlost

Big Meadows
Milan Gap–Mill Prong Trail

N

0   5   10

Miles

Culpeper

Several other plants found in the mountains are endemic to the southern and central Appalachians. Among these species are white clintonia (*Clintonia umbellulata*), tasselrue (*Trautvetteria caroliniensis*), Michaux's saxifrage (*Saxifraga michauxii*), and southern harebell (*Campanula divaricata*).

I-66 is the main highway going from Washington to Virginia's Blue Ridge Mountains. Other roads to the mountains are US-50 toward Winchester, VA-55 toward Front Royal, and US-211 toward Luray. US-29 skirts the eastern edge of the Blue Ridge, and Skyline Drive runs along the ridge of Shenandoah National Park.

Wildcat Mountain Natural Area

Wildcat Mountain is located in the foothills of the Blue Ridge Mountains near Warrenton. On the western slope is Wildcat Mountain Natural Area, a preserve of the Virginia Chapter of The Nature Conservancy. The preserve contains over 600 acres of second-growth forest and includes old farm sites, early successional woodlands, and mature oak-hickory forests. The topography is rugged, with elevations ranging from 500 feet to 1,200 feet near the top of the mountain. The steep, winding access trail is unmarked but easy to follow. Fire roads also run through the preserve.

Early May is a good time to visit Wildcat Mountain. In the upland woods, you can find several orchids, including showy orchis (*Orchis spectabilis*), puttyroot (*Aplectrum hyemale*), Wister's coralroot (*Corallorhiza wisteriana*), and lily-leaved twayblade (*Liparis lilifolia*). Other May-blooming species are perfoliate bellwort (*Uvularia perfoliata*), rue-anemone (*Anemonella thalictroides*), three-lobed violet (*Viola triloba*), yellow pimpernel (*Taenidia integerrima*), and pennywort (*Obolaria virginica*). On greenstone outcrops grow wild pink (*Silene caroliniana*), early saxifrage (*Saxifraga virginiensis*), and birdfoot violet (*Viola pedata*).

June flowers in the woods include devil's-bit (*Chamaelirium luteum*), black cohosh (*Cimicifuga racemosa*), bowman's-root (*Porteranthus trifoliatus*), four-leaved milkweed (*Asclepias quadrifolia*), and hairy skullcap (*Scutellaria elliptica*).

Open greenstone barrens on Wildcat Mountain produce a dry, somewhat calcareous habitat that harbors several species not common in the Blue Ridge. Look on these barrens for curlyheads (*Clematis ochroleuca*), pale corydalis (*Corydalis sempervirens*), spring forget-me-not (*Myosotis verna*), narrow-leaved horse-gentian (*Triosteum angustifolium*), and fame-flower (*Talinum teretifolium*).

Wildcat Mountain Natural Area is managed by the Virginia Field Office of The Nature Conservancy. It is open to the public by permission only. Contact Virginia Field Office, The Nature Conservancy, 1110 Rose Hill Drive, Charlottesville, VA 22901; (804)295-6106. The staff there can give you directions and information about visiting the preserve.

Directions: Take I-66 west from Washington to Marshall. Take US-17 south and very soon pick up VA-691 south. Exact directions will be given when you arrange your visit.

Thompson Wildlife Management Area

One of the richest botanical areas of Virginia's Blue Ridge Mountains is a state-owned game reserve, the G. Richard Thompson Wildlife Management Area, near Linden. The 4,000-acre management area occupies the eastern slopes of the Blue Ridge a few miles northeast of Shenandoah National Park.

The elevation ranges from 1,000 feet at the base to almost 2,200 feet at the top. Within the management area are several different habitats, including second-growth deciduous forest, open grassy clearings, and cool seepage swamps at the headwaters of mountain streams.

The Thompson Area is noted primarily for a magnificent display of large-flowered trillium (*Trillium grandiflorum*) in early May. Trillium expert Dr. Richard Lighty of the Mt. Cuba Center for the Study of Piedmont Flora has called it "the most dense and extensive trillium stand I have ever walked in and also one which shows the most variation." There are literally millions of trilliums here, growing not only along the woodland trails but also in roadside clearings and the front yards of nearby homes. The showy white flowers of this trillium are known to change to pink as they age, but in this population even newly opened flowers come in many shades from palest rose to almost crimson. The blossoms also show a great variety of petal size and shape.

Other species blooming in these rich woods in early May include several stands of yellow lady's-slipper (*Cypripedium calceolus*), many showy orchis (*Orchis spectabilis*), wild ginger (*Asarum canadense*), leatherleaf meadowrue (*Thalictrum coriaceum*), yellow corydalis (*Corydalis flavula*), slender toothwort (*Dentaria heterophylla*), green violet (*Hybanthus concolor*), pennywort

Trillium grandiflorum —
Large-flowered trillium
(height: 6″–20″)

(*Obolaria virginica*), and squawroot (*Conopholis americana*). Rue-anemone (*Anemonella thalictroides*), wild geranium (*Geranium maculatum*), heart-leaved Alexanders (*Zizia aptera*), three-lobed violet (*Viola triloba*), louse-wort (*Pedicularis canadensis*), and round-leaved ragwort (*Senecio obovatus*) flower in clearings and along the fire roads.

In the seepage swamps grow several species that are usually associated with more northern regions or higher elevations in the Appalachians. The cooler microclimate created here supports plants such as Canada Mayflower (*Maianthemum canadense*), false hellebore (*Veratrum viride*), marsh mari-gold (*Caltha palustris*), wood anemone (*Anemone quinquefolia*), golden saxifrage (*Chrysosplenium americanum*), miterwort (*Mitella diphylla*), and wild sarsaparilla (*Aralia nudicaulis*). Found here are both swamp saxifrage (*Saxifraga pensylvanica*), a northern species, and lettuce saxifrage (*Saxifraga micranthidifolia*), a southern Appalachian species.

By June, the trilliums are gone, but other flowers bloom in this undisturbed woodland. Look for Canada lily (*Lilium canadense*), goatsbeard (*Aruncus dioicus*), Virginia waterleaf (*Hydrophyllum virginianum*), showy skullcap (*Scutellaria serrata*), and four-leaved milkweed (*Asclepias quadrifolia*).

At the Thompson Area, the flower display continues into summer and fall. Late-blooming woodland species include starry campion (*Silene stellata*), fall phlox (*Phlox paniculata*), pale jewelweed (*Impatiens pallida*), woodland sunflower (*Helianthus divaricatus*), Schreber's aster (*Aster schreberi*), heart-leaved aster (*Aster cordifolius*), slender goldenrod (*Solidago erecta*), and blue-stemmed goldenrod (*Solidago caesia*).

The grand display of trilliums and other wildflowers at the Thompson Area has been enjoyed by many people over the years. Recent damage to the oak trees by gypsy moths and by subsequent logging along the trails has had some detrimental effects on the forest. In an effort to preserve the best botanical communities in the management area, an agreement to protect these areas of special value was signed in 1990 between the Virginia Department of Game and Inland Fisheries and the Virginia Native Plant Society.

The G. Richard Thompson Wildlife Management Area is managed by the Virginia Department of Game and Inland Fisheries, 4010 West Broad St., Box 11104, Richmond, VA 23230; telephone (804)257-1000. There are no visitor facilities at the site. The best areas for wildflowers are the Ted Lake Trail at parking lot #4 and the fire road at parking lot #6. Visitors should be aware that hunters also frequent the management area.

Directions: Go west on I-66 to the exit for Linden/Front Royal. Turn left over the highway and then left again onto VA-55. Go for about one and one-half miles to the hamlet of Linden and turn left on Freezeland Road (county road 638). After about one mile of climbing, bear right toward Blue Mountain Estates, continue for another three miles to parking lot #4 on the right and an additional mile up the mountain to parking lot #6 near the fire tower.

Sky Meadows State Park

On the eastern edge of the Blue Ridge, near the small town of Paris, is Sky Meadows State Park. Once a large estate and working farm, the 1,000-

acre park still maintains pastures, gardens, outbuildings, and the historic Mount Bleak mansion.

From the entrance road, a view of little ponds and open fields sweeps up to the 2,000-foot high ridge, and a long driveway leads to the visitor center in the old manor house. Several trails lead uphill from there, rising through the woods and joining the Appalachian Trail at the top.

In early May, the mountain blooms with large-flowered trillium (*Trillium grandiflorum*), false Solomon's-seal (*Smilacina racemosa*), yellow lady's-slipper (*Cypripedium calceolus*), pink lady's-slipper (*Cypripedium acaule*), wild columbine (*Aquilegia canadensis*), rue-anemone (*Anemonella thalictroides*), Dutchman's breeches (*Dicentra cucullaria*), and wild geranium (*Geranium maculatum*). In cool seeps grow skunk cabbage (*Symplocarpus foetidus*), swamp saxifrage (*Saxifraga pensylvanica*), and marsh blue violet (*Viola cucullata*).

Summer flowers in the woods include thimbleweed (*Anemone virginiana*), wild comfrey (*Cynoglossum virginianum*), and motherwort (*Leonurus cardiaca*). In the open fields are bouncing Bet (*Saponaria officinalis*), common milkweed (*Asclepias syriaca*), butterflyweed (*Asclepias tuberosa*), butter-and-eggs (*Linaria vulgaris*), spotted knapweed (*Centaurea maculosa*), ox-eye daisy (*Chrysanthemum leucanthemum*), and black-eyed Susan (*Rudbeckia hirta*). In wet areas, look for ragged fringed orchid (*Habenaria lacera*), tall meadowrue (*Thalictrum pubescens*), and cardinal flower (*Lobelia cardinalis*).

Sky Meadows State Park is managed by the Virginia Department of Conservation and Recreation, Division of State Parks. The park has historical exhibits, picnic areas, and a primitive campground. For more information, contact the park office at Route 1, Box 540, Delaplane, VA 22025; telephone (703)592-3556.

Directions: From the Capital Beltway (I-495), take US-50 west past Upperville to Paris and turn left on US-17. The park entrance is one mile south on the right. Alternatively, from I-495, you could take I-66 and go north on US-17 for five miles. Sky Meadows adjoins the Thompson Wildlife Management Area on the ridge, but there is no easy access between the two areas.

Shenandoah National Park

Shenandoah National Park, with almost 200,000 acres of protected forest, straddles the Blue Ridge between Front Royal and Charlottesville.

Mountain peaks, high meadows, steep valleys, bubbling streams, and sparkling waterfalls all add to the natural beauty of this popular park. Habitats particularly interesting to botanists include rich moist forests, cool seepage swamps, rocky mountaintops, and bedrock openings.

In Shenandoah National Park, the average temperatures are much cooler than in the Washington-Baltimore area, and many northern plants find favorable habitats in these mountains. On top of Stony Man and Hawksbill, the highest peaks in the park, climatic conditions are similar to the Canadian life zone, and growing here are trees of the far north, such as balsam fir and red spruce.

New England wildflowers found in the high elevations of the park include yellow clintonia (*Clintonia borealis*), rose twisted-stalk (*Streptopus roseus*), marsh marigold (*Caltha palustris*), and starflower (*Trientalis borealis*). Some northern species occurring in the park are rare in Virginia, including purple fringed orchid (*Habenaria fimbriata*), larger blue flag (*Iris versicolor*), Canadian burnet (*Sanguisorba canadensis*), and three-toothed cinquefoil (*Potentilla tridentata*).

The 100-mile-long Skyline Drive runs along the ridge, crossed in many places by the Appalachian Trail, side trails, and fire roads. There are numerous places to stop and search for wildflowers, and days could be spent making new discoveries in many different areas. Because of the limits of space in this book, only a few places in the central section of the park will be described, but you could explore with pleasure any woodland trail or mountain meadow.

Shenandoah National Park is managed by the National Park Service. For more information, contact Shenandoah National Park, Luray, VA 22835; telephone (703)999-2266. There are numerous picnic areas, several campgrounds, restaurants, and rest rooms along Skyline Drive. The road is very crowded on fine weekend days, particularly in June when the mountain laurel (*Kalmia latifolia*) is blooming and in October when the fall foliage is most colorful.

An annual wildflower festival is held in the park during mid-May, with special programs and naturalist-led walks.

Directions: From the Capital Beltway (I-495), take I-66 west. Take US-29 to Warrenton and there turn right on US-211. Go through the small town of Sperryville (passing numerous roadside stands) up to the entrance station at Thornton Gap. Turn south on Skyline Drive for the central section areas of Stony Man, Big Meadows, and Mill Prong Trail.

Skyline Drive

In early June, it is delightful to drive along Skyline Drive in Shenandoah National Park from Thornton Gap to Big Meadows. There are so many wildflowers along the road that it is tempting to stop every few yards to examine them all.

Even from the car, you can spot the bright white blooms of mountain laurel (*Kalmia latifolia*) and the deep pink blossoms of rose azalea (*Rhododendron prinophyllum*). Along the roadside are wild geranium (*Geranium maculatum*), goatsbeard (*Aruncus dioicus*), bowman's-root (*Porteranthus trifoliatus*), hairy-jointed meadow-parsnip (*Thaspium barbinode*), and four-leaved milkweed (*Asclepias quadrifolia*).

In dry rocky places grow wild pink (*Silene caroliniana*), bluets (*Houstonia caerulea*), gray beardtongue (*Penstemon canescens*), and field hawkweed (*Hieracium caespitosum*). Wild columbine (*Aquilegia canadensis*), a spring bloomer in other regions, here garlands rock outcrops and road banks all summer.

On a hillside near Hemlock Spring Overlook is a seepage swamp with false hellebore (*Veratrum viride*), lettuce saxifrage (*Saxifraga micranthidifolia*), marsh blue violet (*Viola cucullata*), and golden ragwort (*Senecio aureus*). Down the hill, in the cool, moist soil of the mature forest, grow yellow clintonia (*Clintonia borealis*), white monkshood (*Aconitum reclinatum*), and Canada violet (*Viola canadensis*).

A stop could be made at Limberlost, a dark forest of huge virgin hemlock trees. Not many flowers can thrive in the deep shade here, but you may find Canada Mayflower (*Maianthemum canadense*), rose twisted-stalk (*Streptopus roseus*), marsh marigold (*Caltha palustris*), and common wood-sorrel (*Oxalis montana*).

Just before Big Meadows is Franklin Cliffs, an area with wildflowers even in the parking lot. Here you might see wild blue phlox (*Phlox divaricata*), heart-leaved Alexanders (*Zizia aptera*), and lousewort (*Pedicularis canadensis*).

Late July is another good time to drive this section of Skyline Drive. While escaping the heat and humidity of the urban area, you can enjoy late summer wildflowers such as starry campion (*Silene stellata*), wild bergamot (*Monarda fistulosa*), hoary mountain-mint (*Pycnanthemum incanum*), tall bellflower (*Campanula americana*), woodland sunflower (*Helianthus divaricatus*), and whorled coreopsis (*Coreopsis verticillata*).

Aquilegia canadensis —
Wild columbine
(height: 1′–2′)

There are many places to pull over and take a short walk on the 20-mile drive from Thornton Gap to Big Meadows. Also in this section are the highest mountains in the park, Hawksbill and Stony Man, and the deep ravines of White Oak Canyon and Cedar Run. The short drive could take all day. For more information about Skyline Drive, contact Shenandoah National Park, Luray, VA 22835; telephone (703)999-2266.

Directions: From the entrance station at Thornton Gap (near mile 32), take Skyline Drive south. Hemlock Springs Overlook is near mile 40; Limberlost is near mile 43; and Franklin Cliffs are near mile 49.

Stony Man Nature Trail

The Stony Man Nature Trail is a climb up the southeast flank of 4,000-foot-high Stony Man, the second highest mountain in Shenandoah National Park. Since the trail begins at Skyland, at almost 3,700-foot elevation, the actual ascent is only about 300 feet and can easily be done by anyone in good health.

The forest on this high peak is quite different from forests in the valleys and in the Piedmont. In fact, many of the tree species are those of New England forests, including white pine, eastern hemlock, yellow birch, striped maple, and mountain-ash. Near the top of the mountain are red spruce and balsam fir, trees of the Canadian zone.

A hike up Stony Man is interesting at any time of year and the views across the Shenandoah Valley are spectacular. A fine time to explore this trail is in mid-June, when you can find common wildflowers blooming late on these cool heights, as well as some species unique to the high elevation.

Along the way you may see familiar spring flowers including wild columbine (*Aquilegia canadensis*), Virginia waterleaf (*Hydrophyllum virginianum*), rattlesnake-weed (*Hieracium venosum*), and golden ragwort (*Senecio aureus*). Other species are more common in the Blue Ridge than in the Piedmont, such as fly-poison (*Amianthium muscaetoxicum*), bowman's-root (*Porteranthus trifoliatus*), yellow pimpernel (*Taenidia integerrima*), hairy-jointed meadow-parsnip (*Thaspium barbinode*), heart-leaved Alexanders (*Zizia aptera*), and lousewort (*Pedicularis canadensis*).

As you climb higher, you'll find northern species such as yellow clintonia (*Clintonia borealis*), Canada Mayflower (*Maianthemum canadense*), rose twisted-stalk (*Streptopus roseus*), wild sarsaparilla (*Aralia nudicaulis*), and bush honeysuckle (*Diervilla lonicera*). These plants of cool climates are at home in the high mountains of the southern Appalachians.

At the top of the mountain, you will come to the bare rocky cliffs that make up the nose of the sleeping Stony Man. Composed of greenstone, a metamorphosed basalt, the peak is very hard and resistant to weathering. High winds, heavy rains, ice and snow in winter, and hot sun in summer make plant life on these open cliffs exceptionally difficult. Despite such harsh conditions, some species have adapted to this exposed habitat.

Look on the flatter parts of the cliffs for long-leaved houstonia (*Houstonia longifolia*) and gray beardtongue (*Penstemon canescens*) and in the rock crevices for live-forever (*Sedum telephioides*) and Rand's goldenrod (*Solidago randii*). Search the nooks and crannies of the cliffs for two high-altitude specialties, Michaux's saxifrage (*Saxifraga michauxii*), a southern Appalachian endemic, and three-toothed cinquefoil (*Potentilla tridentata*), a mountaintop species even in New England.

Stony Man Nature Trail begins at the north entrance to Skyland. The Skyland Lodge has rest rooms and a restaurant. For more information, contact Shenandoah National Park, Luray, VA 22835; telephone (703)999-2266.

Directions: From the entrance station at Thornton Gap, take Skyline Drive south. The Stony Man Trail begins at the north entrance to Skyland near mile 42.

Big Meadows and Big Meadows Swamp Trail

Big Meadows, a very popular area for visitors to Shenandoah National Park, is actually more of a low thicket than a meadow. The large clearing on the east side of Skyline Drive is covered with shrubs of the heath family such as lowbush blueberry (*Vaccinium vacillans*) and maleberry (*Lyonia ligustrina*). Trails lead down from the road through the meadows to a shrub swamp of meadowsweet (*Spiraea latifolia*) and gray dogwood (*Cornus racemosa*).

Mid-June is a good time to visit Big Meadows. Look for wild columbine (*Aquilegia canadensis*) still in flower here in the mountains, as well as wild sarsaparilla (*Aralia nudicaulis*), spreading dogbane (*Apocynum androsaemifolium*), and the bright orange butterflyweed (*Asclepias tuberosa*).

In early July, look in the upper meadows for wild indigo (*Baptisia tinctoria*), hare figwort (*Scrophularia lanceolata*), pale Indian-plantain (*Cacalia atriplicifolia*), black-eyed Susan (*Rudbeckia hirta*), and field hawkweed

Iris versicolor —
Larger blue flag
(height: 2′–3′)

(*Hieracium caespitosum*). And search the wet areas of the lower meadows for ragged fringed orchid (*Habenaria lacera*) and tasselrue (*Trautvetteria caroliniensis*).

On the west side of the road near the visitor center is the Big Meadows Swamp Trail. The trail begins in young woodlands, crosses several streams, then traverses a forest of gray birch—a northern tree rare in Virginia—and ends at the seepage swamp.

In late June, the open woods are habitat for fly-poison (*Amianthium muscaetoxicum*), yellow stargrass (*Hypoxis hirsuta*), white baneberry (*Actaea alba*), leatherleaf meadowrue (*Thalictrum coriaceum*), black cohosh (*Cimicifuga racemosa*), round-leaved pyrola (*Pyrola rotundifolia*), and poke milkweed (*Asclepias exaltata*).

In the seepage areas at stream crossings, look for species of this cool, wet habitat, such as false hellebore (*Veratrum viride*), swamp buttercup (*Ranunculus septentrionalis*), Pennsylvania bittercress (*Cardamine pensylvanica*), lettuce saxifrage (*Saxifraga micranthidifolia*), and marsh blue violet (*Viola cucullata*).

The Big Meadows Swamp is a good example of a high-elevation seepage swamp formed by the headwaters of small streams. The swamp is dominated by wetland shrubs such as meadowsweet (*Spiraea latifolia*) and maleberry (*Lyonia ligustrina*). In the openings, there is a progression of northern wetland species, from marsh marigold (*Caltha palustris*) in May, to pale green orchid (*Habenaria flava*) and larger blue flag (*Iris versicolor*) in June, to Canadian burnet (*Sanguisorba canadensis*) in July.

The Byrd Visitor Center is located at the Big Meadows area, and there is a lodge, a camp store, and a snack bar. The visitor center has a small natural history display and sells maps, books, and pamphlets. For more information, contact Shenandoah National Park, Luray, VA 22835; telephone (703)999-2266.

Directions: From the entrance station at Thornton Gap, take Skyline Drive south. Big Meadows is at mile 51.

Mill Prong Trail

The Mill Prong Trail, at Milam Gap in Shenandoah National Park, is a rocky trail downhill through second-growth woods into a hemlock forest along a stream.

Mid-May is a good time to take this walk to enjoy such special mountain wildflowers as large-flowered trillium (*Trillium grandiflorum*), yellow lady's-slipper (*Cypripedium calceolus*), and pink lady's-slipper (*Cypripedium acaule*). Look for the yellow lady's-slipper in the hardwood forest and the pink lady's-slipper in the hemlocks.

Other species blooming at this time are hispid buttercup (*Ranunculus hispidus*), blue cohosh (*Caulophyllum thalictroides*), miterwort (*Mitella diphylla*), heart-leaved Alexanders (*Zizia aptera*), and three-lobed violet (*Viola triloba*).

Come again in June to see fly-poison (*Amianthium muscaetoxicum*), Canada Mayflower (*Maianthemum canadense*), and round-leaved orchid (*Habenaria orbiculata*). At the bottom of the hill, along the stream, look for false hellebore (*Veratrum viride*), white monkshood (*Aconitum reclinatum*), and lettuce saxifrage (*Saxifraga micranthidifolia*).

There is a small parking area at Milam Gap and the Mill Prong Trail is across Skyline Drive. For more information, contact Shenandoah National Park, Luray, VA 22835; telephone (703)999-2266.

Directions: From the entrance station at Thorton Gap, take Skyline Drive south. Milam Gap is between mile 52 and mile 53, just south of Big Meadows.

THE SHENANDOAH VALLEY

The Great Valley stretches south from Maryland through West Virginia and Virginia, where it has long been known as the Shenandoah Valley. Because the underlying limestone is water soluble, the valley has many caves, caverns, sinkholes, and springs.

Sandwiched between the Blue Ridge and the Ridge and Valley regions, the Shenandoah Valley remains a peaceful rural area. It has rich calcareous soil, relatively flat terrain, and large productive farms. The Shenandoah River slowly loops its way to its rendezvous with the Potomac River at Harpers Ferry.

As most of this prime agricultural land is privately held, there are very few parks or places with public access along the Shenandoah River. If you were to go by canoe from the US-50 bridge, you would pass masses of Virginia bluebells (*Mertensia virginica*) carpeting the bottomlands and limestone-loving species such as twinleaf (*Jeffersonia diphylla*) and dwarf larkspur (*Delphinium tricorne*) on the uplands.

In the Shenandoah Valley are some very unusual inland wetlands.

Where marl marshes occur around limestone springs, calciphilic species such as marsh skullcap (*Scutellaria galericulata*) and spotted Joe-Pye-weed (*Eupatorium maculatum*) may occur.

In some areas, sinkhole ponds have formed in the soluble limestone. Where acidic rocks eroding from the nearby mountains have filled in the ponds, an acidic wetland may form, containing Coastal Plain species such as marsh St. Johnswort (*Hypericum virginicum*) and Maryland meadow beauty (*Rhexia mariana*).

Winchester is the largest town in the Shenandoah Valley, and many highways meet there. Access to the valley from Washington or Baltimore is via one of the westbound highways such as I-70, VA-7, US-50, or I-66. US-340 runs north and south on the east side of the valley, and US-11 and I-81 go down the west side.

Blandy Experimental Farm — The State Arboretum of Virginia

Blandy Farm, the home of the State Arboretum of Virginia, is located in the Shenandoah Valley a few miles east of Winchester. Over 600 acres of open fields and mountain views frame the 135-acre arboretum. A collection of mature trees and shrubs, representing over 1,000 species and varieties, is the focus of the arboretum, and natural vegetation and plantings of native species are expanding at Blandy.

In early May, flowering dogwood (*Cornus florida*) and redbud (*Cercis canadensis*) make a colorful display at Blandy. In the wooded areas are smooth Solomon's-seal (*Polygonatum biflorum*), false Solomon's-seal (*Smilacina racemosa*), wild ginger (*Asarum canadense*), spring beauty (*Claytonia virginica*), slender toothwort (*Dentaria heterophylla*), and plantain-leaved pussytoes (*Antennaria plantaginifolia*).

On the grassy lawns, look for species of this open habitat, such as bulbous buttercup (*Ranunculus bulbosus*), wild peppergrass (*Lepidium virginicum*), Carolina cranesbill (*Geranium carolinianum*), field pansy (*Viola rafinesquii*), yellow wood-sorrel (*Oxalis stricta*), and bluets (*Houstonia caerulea*).

In the pond grow sweetflag (*Acorus calamus*), yellow iris (*Iris pseudacorus*), and spatterdock (*Nuphar advena*).

In June, there is a grand display of prickly pear (*Opuntia humifusa*) on the rocks by the pond. Yellow bedstraw (*Galium verum*) covers the meadows along with field flowers such as Deptford pink (*Dianthus arme-ria*), common fleabane (*Erigeron philadelphicus*), and ox-eye daisy (*Chrysanthemum leucanthemum*).

In July, the old stone walls are carpeted with everlasting pea (*Lathyrus latifolius*), and the fields are brightened with wild bergamot (*Monarda fistulosa*), black-eyed Susan (*Rudbeckia hirta*), yellow goatsbeard (*Tragopogon pratensis*), and nodding thistle (*Carduus nutans*).

Blandy Experimental Farm is owned and managed by the University of Virginia. An old estate house provides offices and meeting rooms, and several walkways wind through the arboretum plantings. Visitors are welcome in the arboretum. For more information or to arrange a tour, contact Blandy Experimental Farm, P.O. Box 175, Boyce, VA 22620; telephone (703)837-1758.

Directions: From the Capital Beltway (I-495), take I-66 and US-17 to US-50 west. About four miles after crossing the Shenandoah River, look for the sign for the state arboretum and turn left into Blandy Experimental Farm.

Altona-Piedmont Marsh

Located near Charles Town in West Virginia's eastern panhandle, Altona-Piedmont Marsh encompasses 70 acres of a calcareous type of wetland known as a marl marsh. This unusual ecosystem is rare in the eastern United States, and Altona-Piedmont Marsh harbors several plant species that are rare in our area.

After many years of negotiation with surrounding landowners, the West Virginia Chapter of The Nature Conservancy dedicated the Altona-Piedmont Marsh in April 1990. The 90-acre preserve contains 20 acres of buffer area around the central wetlands.

A visit in late July will let you see the marsh at its peak. Flowering then are water parsnip (*Sium suave*), floating water-pennywort (*Hydrocotyle ranunculoides*), swamp milkweed (*Asclepias incarnata*), blue vervain (*Verbena hastata*), square-stemmed monkey-flower (*Mimulus ringens*), and spotted Joe-Pye-weed (*Eupatorium maculatum*). Adding to the interest and beauty of this community are marsh skullcap (*Scutellaria galericulata*), a northern species very rare in our area, and winged loosestrife (*Lythrum alatum*), a midwestern species rare in the east.

Altona-Piedmont Marsh is managed by the West Virginia Field Office of The Nature Conservancy. Although it is open to the public, it is not an easy place to explore. Anyone visiting must be aware that the marsh is bisected by an active railroad line, and a train comes by several times a day. There is no way to avoid the train except to plunge into the marsh, so if you do come, wear boots and be alert! For more information, contact The Nature Conservancy, West Virginia Field Office, 723 Kanawha Boulevard East, Suite 500, Charleston, WV 25337; telephone (304)345-4350.

Directions: From I-70 or VA-9, take US-340 south, or from VA-7, take US-340 north to Charles Town. From Charles Town, take US-9 to WV-51. Call (304)345-4350 for exact directions and parking and walking guidelines.

RIDGE AND VALLEY

Beyond the Shenandoah Valley lie the mountains of the Ridge and Valley province. With elevations ranging from 1,000 to over 3,000 feet, the topography varies from hilly to very steep.

Sandstone and shale, ancient sedimentary rocks, form the backbone of this roller-coaster region. Many mountaintops have dramatic rocky peaks made of hard, resistant sandstone. Also found in this region are shale barrens, extremely dry habitats sometimes occurring on steep, south-facing shale slopes.

In the Ridge and Valley province, the soil is thin, rocky, and not very productive, so there have never been large farms. The main occupations of this region are lumbering, quarrying, natural-gas drilling, and small-scale farming. Much of the land is held by the federal government in the George Washington National Forest.

Plants of the heath family, such as azaleas and blueberries, thrive in the poor acidic soil of these mountains and valleys. Showy wildflowers of this region include turkeybeard (*Xerophyllum asphodeloides*), vernal iris (*Iris verna*), and fringed polygala (*Polygala pauciflora*). Some notable shale-barren species are Kate's Mountain clover (*Trifolium virginicum*), shale-barren wild buckwheat (*Eriogonum allenii*), and shale-barren evening-primrose (*Oenothera argillicola*).

There are no large cities in this region, but Front Royal and Winchester are gateway cities to the Ridge and Valley province. From the Washington-Baltimore area, I-66, US-50, and I-70 give access to I-81 and US-11, which run north and south on the western side of the Shenandoah Valley.

Fort Valley

Fort Valley is a narrow canyon on the west side of Massanutten Mountain just a few miles west of Front Royal. County Road 678 follows Passage Creek south from Waterlick to Elizabeth Furnace and on down through the valley. Steep cliffs rise up on both sides of the road below the 2,200-foot-high Signal Knob. Elizabeth Furnace Recreation Area in the George Washington National Forest has campgrounds, picnic areas, and several trails to explore, including the long climb up the mountain.

Late April is a good time to visit this area to see spring wildflowers. In the low woodlands near Elizabeth Furnace are trout-lily (*Erythronium americanum*), spring beauty (*Claytonia virginica*), rue-anemone (*Anemonella thalictroides*), cut-leaved toothwort (*Dentaria laciniata*), Virginia bluebells (*Mertensia virginica*), and golden ragwort (*Senecio aureus*). Hike the fire roads and trails across from Elizabeth Furnace and look for vernal iris (*Iris verna*), rocktwist (*Draba ramosissima*), southern wood violet (*Viola hirsutula*), and trailing arbutus (*Epigaea repens*).

About eight miles into Fort Valley from Waterlick, the valley opens up into an area of farm fields and shale cliffs along the roadside. In this dry rocky habitat grow species such as moss phlox (*Phlox subulata*), wild pink (*Silene caroliniana*), prickly pear (*Opuntia humifusa*), and birdfoot violet (*Viola pedata*). On particularly steep, south-facing shale slopes, you should search for rare shale-barren species, including Kate's Mountain clover (*Trifolium virginicum*), mountain pimpernel (*Taenidia montana*), shale-barren pussytoes (*Antennaria virginica*), and pussytoes ragwort (*Senecio antennariifolius*).

In late May and early June, the roadsides near Elizabeth Furnace are lined with four-leaved milkweed (*Asclepias quadrifolia*), gray beardtongue (*Penstemon canescens*), rattlesnake-weed (*Hieracium venosum*), and chrysogonum (*Chrysogonum virginianum*). You also may see goat's-rue (*Tephrosia virginiana*), long-leaved houstonia (*Houstonia longifolia*), spiked lobelia (*Lobelia spicata*), and feverfew (*Parthenium integrifolium*).

Some July and August bloomers on the dry shale cliffs are live-forever (*Sedum telephioides*), pencil flower (*Stylosanthes biflora*), whorled coreopsis (*Coreopsis verticillata*), and woodland sunflower (*Helianthus divaricatus*). A brilliant gold blossom high on a crumbly shale bank may be the rare shale-barren evening-primrose (*Oenothera argillicola*). If you return to Fort Valley in September, look on the hillsides for stiff aster (*Aster linariifolius*) and Maryland golden-aster (*Chrysopsis mariana*).

The Elizabeth Furnace and Signal Knob areas in Fort Valley are managed by the U.S. Forest Service. Other areas along the road may be privately owned, so be careful where you park and walk. For more information, contact George Washington National Forest, Lee Ranger District, Federal Building, Harrisonburg, VA 22801; telephone (703)433-2491.

Directions: From Front Royal, take VA-55 west about five miles to the crossroads of Waterlick. Go left (south) on County Route 678 (Powell's Fort Road). Elizabeth Furnace is on the left in about four miles. The shale banks begin a few miles farther south on route 678.

Ice Mountain

Ice Mountain, often called "nature's refrigerator," is a very unusual ecosystem in which ice accumulates beneath the rocks and cools the surrounding habitat. Now protected as a preserve of West Virginia chapter of the Nature Conservancy, Ice Mountain is located near Capon Bridge in eastern West Virginia.

Usually the coldest place on a mountain is at the top, but at Ice Mountain it is at the bottom, where huge blocks of sandstone insulate a persistent layer of ice. Breezes of cold air can be felt coming from the talus slope as you walk along the trail. An experiment in August 1964 found the air temperature to be 88°F. and the temperature in the rock grottos to be 38°F.! Ice can be found under the boulders even on the hottest summer days.

This phenomenon creates a cold microhabitat at Ice Mountain that is comparable to the high mountains of West Virginia or the north country in Canada or even Alaska. Northern species are at home here, including trees such as white pine, eastern hemlock, yellow birch, and mountain maple. Even more remarkable is an assemblage of boreal wildflowers that includes prickly wild rose (*Rosa acicularis*), bunchberry (*Cornus canadensis*), starflower (*Trientalis borealis*), twinflower (*Linnaea borealis*), and northern bedstraw (*Galium boreale*).

Ice Mountain is managed by the West Virginia Field Office of The Nature Conservancy. Because of the fragile nature of the ecosystem, access to the site is limited to Nature Conservancy tours. For more information, contact The Nature Conservancy, West Virginia Field Office, 723 Kanawha Boulevard East, Suite 500, Charleston, WV 25337; telephone (304)345-4350.

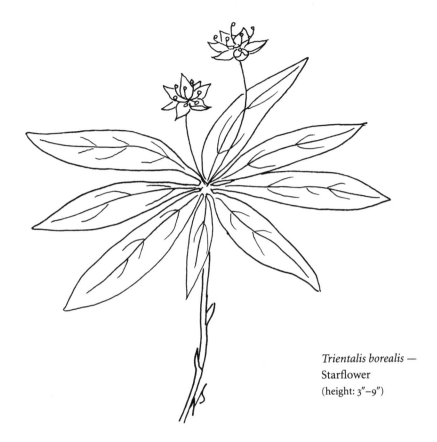

Trientalis borealis —
Starflower
(height: 3″–9″)

Directions: From Winchester, take US-50 west to Capon Bridge. Exact directions will be given when you sign up for a tour.

Cacapon State Park

Cacapon State Park is located near Berkeley Springs in West Virginia's eastern panhandle. The park covers over 6,000 acres in a long narrow band along the eastern side of Cacapon Mountain. Rising to a height of 2,300 feet, this ridge of Oriskany sandstone dominates the landscape. Many well-marked trails wander through the woodlands, wetlands, and open fields of the park.

In late April and early May, the mountain woods are filled with flowering dogwood (*Cornus florida*) and redbud (*Cercis canadensis*), as well as spring beauty (*Claytonia virginica*), round-lobed hepatica (*Hepatica americana*), early meadowrue (*Thalictrum dioicum*), rue-anemone (*Anemonella thalictroides*), and cut-leaved toothwort (*Dentaria laciniata*). Even the grassy lawns have early spring wildflowers such as whitlow-grass (*Draba verna*), field pansy (*Viola rafinesquii*), and bluets (*Houstonia caerulea*).

On rock outcrops, look for wild columbine (*Aquilegia canadensis*), early saxifrage (*Saxifraga virginiensis*), trailing arbutus (*Epigaea repens*), and birdfoot violet (*Viola pedata*).

May bloomers in the open fields include yellow pimpernel (*Taenidia integerrima*) and white beardtongue (*Penstemon digitalis*). Look in the moist deciduous woodlands for yellow lady's-slipper (*Cypripedium calceolus*) and in the pine woods for pink lady's-slipper (*Cypripedium acaule*).

In late June and July, you can find field flowers such as wild bergamot (*Monarda fistulosa*), Venus's looking-glass (*Triodanis perfoliata*), chicory (*Cichorium intybus*), and ox-eye daisy (*Chrysanthemum leucanthemum*).

Late summer bloomers along the roadsides are butter-and-eggs (*Linaria vulgaris*), yarrow (*Achillea millefolium*), and spotted knapweed (*Centaurea maculosa*).

Cacapon State Park is managed by the West Virginia Department of Natural Resources, Division of Parks and Recreation. There is a large lodge with a restaurant and many recreational facilities. For more information, contact Cacapon State Park, Berkeley Springs, WV 25411; telephone (304) 258-1022.

Directions: From Virginia, take VA-7 or US-50 west to Winchester. Take US-522 north toward Berkeley Springs. The park entrance is on the left about nine miles south of Berkeley Springs. From Maryland, take I-70 or I-270 to Frederick and take I-70 west past Hancock. Go south on US-522, cross into West Virginia, go through Berkeley Springs, and continue to the park.

Berkeley Springs — Mesner Road

Mesner Road is a delightful country road located between the town of Berkeley Springs and Cacapon State Park. The road winds for several miles along the edge of a small stream, past woodlands, fields, and rocky hillsides.

In late April and early May, look along the north side of the road for shale banks flowering with birdfoot violet (*Viola pedata*) and moss phlox (*Phlox subulata*). Redbud (*Cercis canadensis*) and flowering dogwood (*Cor-*

Rudbeckia hirta —
Black-eyed Susan
(height: 1′–3′)

nus florida) bloom in the dry oak woods, along with rue-anemone (*Anemonella thalictroides*), bloodroot (*Sanguinaria canadensis*), and cut-leaved toothwort (*Dentaria laciniata*). Wild blue phlox (*Phlox divaricata*) and golden ragwort (*Senecio aureus*) flower in moister areas.

About two miles along Mesner Road, take the left fork and cross over a stream. In the moist bottomlands along the stream, look for trout-lily (*Erythronium americanum*), spring beauty (*Claytonia virginica*), early meadowrue (*Thalictrum dioicum*), Dutchman's breeches (*Dicentra cucullaria*), and Virginia bluebells (*Mertensia virginica*). On the rocky hillsides, search for wild stonecrop (*Sedum ternatum*) and early saxifrage (*Saxifraga virginiensis*).

In July, the open roadsides are filled with summer flowers such as common milkweed (*Asclepias syriaca*), common St. Johnswort (*Hypericum perforatum*), wild bergamot (*Monarda fistulosa*), downy false-foxglove (*Aureolaria virginica*), black-eyed Susan (*Rudbeckia hirta*), and spotted knapweed (*Centaurea maculosa*).

August and September bloomers are biennial gaura (*Gaura biennis*), common evening-primrose (*Oenothera biennis*), tickseed-sunflower (*Bidens polylepis*), and early goldenrod (*Solidago juncea*).

Directions: From Virginia, take VA-7 or US-50 west to Winchester. Take US-522 north toward Berkeley Springs. After passing Cacapon State Park, go about five more miles and turn right on Mesner Road. From Maryland, take I-70 west from Frederick past Hancock, go south on US-522 and cross into West Virginia. Go through the town of Berkeley Springs, continue for about five miles, and turn left on Mesner Road.

THE SPECIES

This part of the book gives information on all wildflower species mentioned in chapters 2 through 10, plus some additional common species. More than 730 species are covered: over 90 species of monocotyledons in chapter 11 and over 640 species of dicotyledons in chapter 12. Not every flowering plant species growing in the area covered by this book is included. Species mentioned only by common name in the first two sections of the book are not included in this part. These species are trees such as oaks, hickories, and conifers, as well as ferns, clubmosses, and mosses.

This part is organized in a standardized format. Monocotyledons and dicotyledons are listed separately. Within these two categories, the families, genera, and species are arranged alphabetically.

As mentioned in the introduction to this book, the scientific names used are, for the most part, from Fernald, *Gray's Manual of Botany*, eighth edition. These scientific names are familiar to the users of Peterson and McKenny, *A Field Guide to Wildflowers of Northeastern and North-central North America*, and Newcomb, *Newcomb's Wildflower Guide*. In some cases, on the advice of expert taxonomists reviewing our manuscript, the nomenclatural and taxonomic changes found in the second edition of Gleason and Cronquist, *Manual of Vascular Plants of Northeastern United States and Adjacent Canada* have been used in this book. For readers unfamiliar with these nomenclatural changes, these names have been cross-referenced to those found in *Gray's Manual*. Where scientific names from Gleason and Cronquist are not used in chapters 2 through 10, they are given in parentheses in chapters 11 and 12. The scientific names used in this book are ones the authors think are appropriate. Plant taxonomy and nomenclature, like other areas of biology, are constantly undergoing change.

Common names follow the scientific names in this section. Common names of wildflowers vary in different references. In this book, the common names used are primarily those from Peterson's and Newcomb's wildflower guides.

The typical blooming period for each species is the next information given for each species. The blooming period may vary from one year to the next and from one locality to another. Plants will bloom later in more northern locations or at higher elevations. A species will bloom much earlier on a protected south-facing slope than on a north-facing slope. The beginning and ending blooming dates of flowers may vary by a month or longer. Also, some spring-flowering species such as violets (*Viola* spp.) may bloom again in the fall when the days are the same length as during spring flowering.

Each species is identified as native (i.e., naturally occurring in the United States) or introduced (i.e., not naturally occurring in the United States). Some native species that do not occur naturally in our area but are planted in arboreta or gardens are included in this section; such species are identified as "planted in our area." Species noted as "native and/or introduced" are thought to have both native and introduced varieties.

The typical habitats for each species are given next. The habitats listed for each species are representative of those observed by the authors for the area covered by the book. In general, these habitat terms follow those given in chapter 3.

The geographic range or distribution in the Washington-Baltimore area is indicated for each species as Coastal Plain, Piedmont, and/or mountains. If a species is found in all of these regions, the range is described as "throughout." The mountain distribution designation covers the Blue Ridge, Great Valley, Ridge and Valley, and Allegheny Plateau regions covered by this book. The ranges are based on information from Harville, et al., *Atlas of the Virginia Flora,* third edition; Brown and Brown, *Herbaceous Plants of Maryland;* Brown and Brown, *Woody Plants of Maryland;* and observations of the authors.

For each species the relative abundance in the area covered by the book is also provided. The categories used are "abundant," "common," "uncommon," "rare," and "very rare." These status designations are based on lists from the Virginia Division of Natural Heritage and the Maryland Natural Heritage Program, as well as the observations of the authors.

11

Monocotyledons

ALISMATACEAE (**ARROWHEAD/WATER-PLANTAIN FAMILY**)

Alisma subcordatum — **Small water-plantain.** June–Sept.; native; shallow water, freshwater marshes, streambanks; throughout; common.

Sagittaria falcata — see *S. lancifolia.*

Sagittaria lancifolia (*S. falcata*) — **Scythe-fruited arrowhead, lance-leaved arrowhead.** July–Oct.; native; shallow (often brackish) water, streambanks; Coastal Plain; uncommon.

Sagittaria latifolia — **Broad-leaved arrowhead, common arrowhead.** June–Sept.; native; shallow water, freshwater marshes, streambanks; throughout; common.

AMARYLLIDACEAE (**AMARYLLIS/DAFFODIL FAMILY**)

Hypoxis hirsuta — **Yellow stargrass.** Apr.–Sept.; native; open upland woods, meadows; throughout; common.

ARACEAE (**ARUM FAMILY**)

Acorus calamus — **Sweetflag.** May–July; native; freshwater marshes, shallow water, streambanks; throughout; uncommon to common.

Arisaema dracontium — **Green dragon.** May–June; native; wet woods, floodplains; throughout; uncommon.

Arisaema triphyllum — **Jack-in-the-pulpit.** Apr.–June; native; moist woods; throughout; common.

Calla palustris — **Wild calla, water-arum.** May–June; native; bogs; mountains; very rare (see Finzel Swamp).

Orontium aquaticum — **Golden club.** Apr.–May; native; freshwater marshes, shallow water; throughout; uncommon.

Peltandra virginica — **Arrow arum.** May–July; native; swamps, ponds, freshwater marshes; throughout (mainly Coastal Plain and Piedmont); common.

Symplocarpus foetidus — **Skunk cabbage.** Feb.–Mar.; native; swamps, stream edges, seeps; throughout; common (locally abundant).

COMMELINACEAE (**SPIDERWORT FAMILY**)

Aneilema keisak — see *Murdannia keisak.*

Commelina communis — **Asiatic dayflower.** June–Aug.; introduced; swales, moist disturbed sites; throughout; abundant.

Commelina virginica — **Virginia dayflower.** June–Oct.; native; moist to wet woods, streambanks; Coastal Plain and Piedmont; uncommon.

Murdannia keisak (*Aneilema keisak*) — **Marsh dayflower.** Sept.–Oct.; introduced; freshwater marshes, pond edges; Coastal Plain and Piedmont; uncommon to common.

Tradescantia virginiana — **Spiderwort.** Apr.–July; native; dry to moist upland woods, meadows; throughout; common.

ERIOCAULACEAE (**PIPEWORT FAMILY**)

Eriocaulon decangulare — **Ten-angled pipewort.** June–Oct.; native; moist acidic soils, bogs; Coastal Plain; rare.

GRAMINEAE — see POACEAE.

IRIDACEAE (**IRIS FAMILY**)

Belamcanda chinensis — **Blackberry-lily.** June–July; introduced; edges of dry woods, meadows, roadsides; throughout; uncommon.

Iris cristata — **Crested iris, dwarf crested iris.** Apr.–May; native; moist woods, streambanks; Piedmont and mountains; rare to uncommon.

Iris pseudacorus — **Yellow iris, yellow flag.** May–July; introduced; freshwater marshes, swamps, moist meadows; throughout; common.

Iris verna — **Vernal iris, dwarf iris.** Mar.–May; native; dry open woods, clearings; throughout (mainly mountains); rare to uncommon.

Iris versicolor — **Larger blue flag.** May–July; native; seeps, wet meadows; throughout (mainly mountains); rare to uncommon.

Iris virginica — **Southern blue flag.** May–July; native; freshwater marshes, stream edges; Coastal Plain; rare to uncommon.

Sisyrinchium angustifolium — **Stout blue-eyed grass.** May–July; native; open fields, meadows, lawns; throughout; common.

Sisyrinchium mucronatum — **Slender blue-eyed grass.** May–July; native; fields, meadows; throughout; common.

LILIACEAE (LILY FAMILY)

Allium cernuum — **Nodding onion.** July–Aug.; native; dry woods, fields, rock outcrops; Piedmont and mountains; common.

Allium tricoccum — **Ramps, wild leek.** June–Aug.; native; moist woods; Piedmont and mountains; uncommon.

Amianthium muscaetoxicum — **Fly-poison.** May–July; native; dry open woods, meadows; throughout (mainly mountains); uncommon to common.

Chamaelirium luteum — **Devil's-bit.** May–June; native; dry woods; throughout; uncommon.

Clintonia borealis — **Yellow clintonia.** May–June; native; cool moist woods, seeps; mountains; rare.

Clintonia umbellulata — **White clintonia.** May–June; native; moist woods, seeps; mountains; uncommon.

Erythronium albidum — **White trout-lily.** Mar.–May; native; floodplains; Piedmont; rare.

Erythronium americanum — **Trout-lily, fawn-lily, yellow adder's-tongue.** Mar.–May; native; moist woods, floodplains, bottomland woods; throughout; common.

Hemerocallis fulva — **Day-lily.** June–Aug.; introduced; roadsides, disturbed sites; throughout; common.

Lilium canadense — **Canada lily.** July–Aug.; native; wet woods, moist meadows; throughout (mainly Piedmont and mountains); uncommon.

Lilium superbum — **Turk's-cap lily.** July–Aug.; native; open woods, wet meadows, freshwater marshes; throughout; uncommon.

Maianthemum canadense — **Canada Mayflower, wild lily-of-the-valley.** May–July; native; cool moist woods; throughout (mainly mountains); common.

Medeola virginiana — **Indian cucumber-root.** May–June; native; dry to moist woods; throughout; common.

Melanthium virginicum — **Bunchflower.** June–July; native; wet woods, wet meadows, seeps; throughout; uncommon.

Muscari racemosum — **Grape hyacinth.** Apr.–June; introduced; fields, roadsides, lawns; throughout; common.

Ornithogalum nutans — **Nodding star-of-Bethlehem.** Apr.–June; introduced; edges of woods, floodplains; throughout; uncommon to common.

Ornithogalum umbellatum — **Star-of-Bethlehem.** Apr.–June; introduced; floodplains, moist clearings, lawns; throughout; common.

Polygonatum biflorum — **Smooth Solomon's-seal.** May–June; native; dry to moist woods; throughout; common.

Smilacina racemosa — **False Solomon's-seal, Solomon's plume, spikenard.** May–July; native; dry to moist woods; throughout; common.

Smilacina stellata — **Starry false Solomon's-seal.** May–July; native; floodplains; throughout; rare.

Streptopus roseus — **Rose twisted-stalk.** May–July; native; cool moist woods; mountains; rare.

Trillium cernuum — **Nodding trillium.** Apr.–June; native; moist woods; mountains; rare.

Trillium erectum — **Erect trillium, red trillium, wake-robin.** Apr.–June; native; moist woods; Piedmont and mountains; uncommon.

Trillium flexipes — **Drooping trillium.** Apr.–June; native to midwestern states; moist woods; very rare (see Susquehanna State Park).

Trillium grandiflorum — **Large-flowered trillium.** Apr.–June; native; cool moist woods; mainly mountains; uncommon to common (locally abundant).

Trillium luteum — **Yellow trillium.** Apr.–June; native to southern Appalachians (planted in our area).

Trillium sessile — **Sessile trillium, toadshade.** Apr.–May; native; moist woods; throughout; uncommon to common.

Trillium undulatum — **Painted trillium.** May–June; native; cool moist woods; mountains; rare to uncommon.

Uvularia perfoliata — **Perfoliate bellwort.** Apr.–June; native; dry to moist woods; throughout; common.

Uvularia sessilifolia — **Sessile bellwort, wild oats.** May–June; native; dry to moist woods; throughout; common.

Veratrum viride — **False hellebore.** May–July; native; seeps, slow-moving streams, seepage swamps; throughout (mainly Piedmont and mountains); uncommon to common.

Xerophyllum asphodeloides — **Turkeybeard.** May–July; native; dry woods; Coastal Plain and mountains; uncommon.

Yucca filamentosa — **Yucca, Spanish bayonet.** June–Sept.; native to southeastern states; dry woods, fields, roadsides; throughout; common.

ORCHIDACEAE (**ORCHID FAMILY**)

Aplectrum hyemale — **Puttyroot, Adam-and-Eve.** May–June; native; upland woods; throughout; uncommon to common.

Corallorhiza maculata — **Spotted coralroot.** July–Aug.; native; dry woods; Piedmont and mountains; uncommon.

Corallorhiza wisteriana — **Wister's coralroot.** Mar.–May; native; moist woods; throughout; rare.

Cypripedium acaule — **Pink lady's-slipper.** Apr.–June; native; upland acidic woods (especially pine woods); throughout; uncommon.

Cypripedium calceolus — **Yellow lady's-slipper.** Apr.–June; native; moist woods (often with alkaline soils); throughout; uncommon.

Epipactis helleborine — **Helleborine.** June–Sept.; introduced; moist woods, roadsides; Piedmont and mountains; uncommon.

Goodyera pubescens — **Downy rattlesnake-plantain.** July–Aug.; native; dry upland woods; throughout; uncommon to common.

Habenaria ciliaris — **Yellow fringed orchid.** July–Aug.; native; moist woods, bogs, swamps; throughout; rare.

Habenaria clavellata — **Green wood orchid.** July–Aug.; native; moist acidic woods, seeps; throughout; uncommon.

Habenaria fimbriata — **Purple fringed orchid, large purple fringed orchid.** June–Aug.; native; wet woods, seeps; mountains; rare.

Habenaria flava — **Pale green orchid.** June–Aug.; native; wet meadows, swales; throughout; rare to uncommon.

Habenaria lacera — **Ragged fringed orchid, green fringed orchid.** June–Aug.; native; wet woods, meadows; throughout; uncommon.

Habenaria orbiculata — **Round-leaved orchid.** July–Aug.; native; moist woods; mountains; rare.

Habenaria peramoena — **Purple fringeless orchid.** June–Aug.; native; wet open woods, wet meadows, ditches; Piedmont and mountains; rare.

Isotria verticillata — **Large whorled pogonia.** May–June; native; dry to moist acidic woods; throughout; uncommon.

Liparis lilifolia — **Lily-leaved twayblade, large twayblade.** June–Aug.; native; dry to moist woods; throughout; uncommon.

Orchis spectabilis — **Showy orchis.** Apr.–June; native; moist woods; throughout; uncommon.

Pogonia ophioglossoides — **Rose pogonia.** May–Aug.; native; bogs; throughout; rare.

Spiranthes cernua — **Nodding ladies'-tresses.** Aug.–Nov.; native; moist to wet woods, meadows; throughout; uncommon.

Spiranthes gracilis (*S. lacera*) — **Slender ladies'-tresses.** Aug.–Oct.; native; dry open woods, fields; throughout; uncommon to common.

Spiranthes lacera — see *S. gracilis.*

Tipularia discolor — **Cranefly orchid.** July–Aug.; native; moist woods; throughout; uncommon to common.

POACEAE (GRAMINEAE) (**GRASS FAMILY**)

Andropogon gerardi — **Big bluestem.** June–Sept.; native; dry meadows, fields, rock outcrops, serpentine barrens; throughout; common.

Andropogon scoparius (*Schizachyrium scoparium*) — **Little bluestem.** Aug.–Oct.; native; open woods, dry meadows; throughout; common.

Andropogon virginicus — **Broomsedge.** Aug.–Nov.; native; dry open woods, dry old fields (nutrient-depleted), roadsides; throughout; abundant.

Distichlis spicata — **Spikegrass.** Aug.–Oct.; native; salt marshes; Coastal Plain; common.

Phragmites australis (*P. communis*) — **Reedgrass.** July–Sept.; native and/or introduced; wet soils, ditches, freshwater marshes, brackish marshes; Coastal Plain and Piedmont; abundant.

Phragmites communis — see *P. australis.*

Schizachyrium scoparium — see *Andropogon scoparius.*

Sorghastrum nutans — **Indian grass.** Aug.–Sept.; native; dry to moist meadows, serpentine barrens; throughout; common.

Spartina alterniflora — **Salt-marsh cordgrass.** July–Sept.; native; salt marshes; Coastal Plain; common to abundant.

Spartina cynosuroides — **Big cordgrass.** Aug.–Oct.; native; brackish marshes, salt marshes; Coastal Plain; common.

Spartina patens — **Salt-meadow hay, salt-meadow grass.** June–Oct.; native; brackish marshes, salt marshes; Coastal Plain; common.

Zizania aquatica — **Wild rice.** June–Sept.; native; freshwater marshes; Coastal Plain; uncommon (locally common).

PONTEDERIACEAE (**PICKERELWEED FAMILY**)

Heteranthera dubia (*Zosterella dubia*) — **Water stargrass.** July–Oct.; native; shallow streams; Piedmont and mountains; common.

Pontederia cordata — **Pickerelweed.** June–Nov.; native; freshwater marshes, ponds; Coastal Plain and Piedmont; common.

Zosterella dubia — see *Heteranthera dubia.*

TYPHACEAE (CATTAIL FAMILY)

Typha angustifolia — **Narrow-leaved cattail.** May–June; native; freshwater marshes, brackish marshes, ditches; throughout (mainly Coastal Plain); common.

Typha latifolia — **Broad-leaved cattail.** June–July; native; freshwater marshes, ditches; throughout; common.

12

Dicotyledons

ACANTHACEAE (ACANTHUS FAMILY)

Justicia americana — **Water willow.** June–Aug.; native; shallow waters of rivers and streams, rocky shores; throughout; common (locally abundant).

Ruellia caroliniensis — **Hairy ruellia.** June–Aug.; native; dry to moist woods; throughout; uncommon.

Ruellia strepens — **Smooth ruellia.** May–Aug.; native; moist woods, floodplains; Piedmont and mountains; rare.

APIACEAE (UMBELLIFERAE) (CARROT/PARSLEY FAMILY)

Aegopodium podagraria — **Goutweed.** June–Aug.; introduced; road-sides, disturbed sites; throughout; uncommon.

Cicuta maculata — **Water hemlock.** June–Aug.; native; stream and pond banks, freshwater marshes, wet swales; throughout; common.

Conium maculatum — **Poison hemlock.** June–Aug.; introduced; moist to wet fields, floodplains, ditches; throughout; common.

Cryptotaenia canadensis — **Honewort.** May–July; native; moist woods; throughout; common.

Daucus carota — **Queen Anne's lace.** June–Sept.; introduced; dry fields, roadsides, disturbed sites; throughout; abundant.

Erigenia bulbosa — **Harbinger-of-spring, pepper-and-salt.** Feb.–Apr.; native; bottomland woods, floodplains; Piedmont and mountains; uncommon.

Eryngium aquaticum — **Rattlesnake-master.** July–Sept.; native; fresh-water to brackish marshes; Coastal Plain; uncommon.

Heracleum lanatum (*H. maximum*) — **Cow parsnip.** June–July; native;

moist woods, clearings, roadsides; throughout (mainly Piedmont and mountains); common.

Heracleum maximum — see *H. lanatum.*

Hydrocotyle ranunculoides — **Floating water-pennywort.** June–Sept.; native; shallow waters of ponds and stream edges; throughout; uncommon.

Hydrocotyle umbellata — **Water-pennywort.** June–Sept.; native; banks or shallow waters of ponds, streams, and freshwater marshes; mainly Coastal Plain; uncommon.

Hydrocotyle verticillata — **Whorled water-pennywort.** July–Aug.; native; banks or shallow waters of ponds, streams, and freshwater marshes; Coastal Plain; uncommon.

Osmorhiza claytoni — **Sweet Cicely.** Apr.–June; native; moist woods; throughout; abundant.

Osmorhiza longistylis — **Aniseroot, smooth sweet Cicely.** Apr.–June; native; moist woods; throughout; common.

Pseudotaenidia montana — see *Taenidia montana.*

Ptilimnium capillaceum — **Mock bishop's-weed.** July–Oct.; native; freshwater marshes, brackish marshes; Coastal Plain; uncommon.

Sanicula canadensis — **Short-styled snakeroot.** May–July; native; dry to moist woods; throughout; uncommon to common.

Sanicula gregaria — **Clustered snakeroot.** May–July; native; dry to moist woods, floodplains; throughout; common to abundant.

Sanicula marilandica — **Black snakeroot.** May–July; native; dry to moist open woods, meadows, thickets; throughout; uncommon.

Sanicula trifoliata — **Long-fruited snakeroot, long-beaked snakeroot.** May–June; native; dry to moist upland woods; Piedmont and mountains; rare.

Sium suave — **Water parsnip.** July–Sept.; native; streambanks, freshwater marshes, swamps; throughout; common.

Taenidia integerrima — **Yellow pimpernel.** May–July; native; upland woods; throughout; uncommon to common.

Taenidia montana (Pseudotaenidia montana) — **Mountain pimpernel.** Apr.–June; native; shale barrens, rock outcrops; mountains; rare.

Thaspium barbinode — **Hairy-jointed meadow-parsnip.** Apr.–June; native; moist woods; throughout; uncommon.

Thaspium trifoliatum — **Woodland meadow-parsnip.** June–July; native; moist woods; throughout; uncommon.

Zizia aptera — **Heart-leaved Alexanders.** Apr.–June; native; open upland woods; throughout (mainly mountains); uncommon.

Zizia aurea — **Golden Alexanders.** Apr.–June; native; moist woods, meadows; Piedmont and mountains; uncommon to common.

APOCYNACEAE (**DOGBANE FAMILY**)

Apocynum androsaemifolium — **Spreading dogbane.** June–July; native; upland woods, fields; throughout; uncommon.

Apocynum cannabinum — **Indian hemp.** May–Aug.; native; borders of woods, fields, open disturbed sites; throughout; common to abundant.

Vinca minor — **Common periwinkle.** Mar.–June; introduced; open woods, old abandoned home sites; throughout; common to abundant.

ARALIACEAE (**GINSENG FAMILY**)

Aralia nudicaulis — **Wild sarsaparilla.** May–June; native; cool moist woods; throughout; uncommon to common.

Panax quinquefolius — **Wild ginseng.** June–Aug.; native; cool moist woods; throughout; rare (from over-collecting for medicinal uses).

Panax trifolius — **Dwarf ginseng.** Apr.–May; native; moist woods, bottomland woods, floodplains; throughout (mainly Coastal Plain and Piedmont); uncommon to common.

ARISTOLOCHIACEAE (**BIRTHWORT FAMILY**)

Asarum canadense — **Wild ginger.** Apr.–June; native; moist upland woods, bottomland woods; throughout; common.

Asarum virginicum (*Hexastylis virginica*) — **Virginia heartleaf.** Apr.–May; native to southeastern states (mainly planted in our area).

Hexastylis virginica — see *Asarum virginicum.*

ASCLEPIADACEAE (**MILKWEED FAMILY**)

Ampelamus albidus — **Sandvine.** July–Sept.; native; riverbanks, floodplains, alluvial soils, thickets; throughout; uncommon.

Asclepias amplexicaulis — **Blunt-leaved milkweed.** May–July; native; dry fields; throughout (mainly Coastal Plain and Piedmont); uncommon.

Asclepias exaltata — **Poke milkweed.** June–July; native; moist woods, meadows, roadsides; Piedmont and mountains; uncommon to common.

Asclepias incarnata — **Swamp milkweed.** June–Aug.; native; freshwater marshes, wet meadows, pond edges; throughout; common.

Asclepias purpurascens — **Purple milkweed.** June–July; native; dry to moist fields; throughout; uncommon.

Asclepias quadrifolia — **Four-leaved milkweed.** May–July; native; upland woods; throughout (mainly Piedmont and mountains); uncommon.

Asclepias rubra — **Red milkweed.** June–Aug.; native; bogs, seeps; Coastal Plain and Piedmont; rare.

Asclepias syriaca — **Common milkweed.** June–Aug.; native; fields, meadows, roadsides, disturbed sites; throughout; abundant.

Asclepias tuberosa — **Butterflyweed.** June–Sept.; native; dry open woods, fields, roadsides; throughout; common.

Asclepias verticillata — **Whorled milkweed.** June–Sept.; native; dry woods, fields, meadows, rock outcrops, serpentine barrens; throughout; uncommon.

Asclepias viridiflora — **Green milkweed.** June–Aug.; native; dry fields; throughout; uncommon.

Gonolobus carolinensis — see *Matelea carolinensis*.

Matelea carolinensis (*Gonolobus carolinensis*) — **Angle-pod.** June–July; native; moist woods, thickets; throughout (mainly Coastal Plain); rare to uncommon.

ASTERACEAE (COMPOSITAE) (ASTER FAMILY)

Achillea millefolium — **Yarrow.** May–Nov.; native and/or introduced; fields, roadsides, disturbed sites; throughout; abundant.

Actinomeris alternifolia — see *Verbesina alternifolia*.

Anaphalis margaritacea — **Pearly everlasting.** July–Sept.; native; dry fields; mountains; rare.

Antennaria neglecta — **Field pussytoes.** Apr.–May; native; dry woods, fields; throughout; common.

Antennaria plantaginifolia — **Plantain-leaved pussytoes.** Apr.–June; native; dry upland woods, fields, roadsides; throughout; common.

Antennaria solitaria — **Solitary pussytoes.** Apr.–May; native; moist open woods; Coastal Plain and Piedmont; uncommon.

Antennaria virginica — **Shale-barren pussytoes.** Apr.–May; native; shale barrens, rock outcrops; Piedmont and mountains; rare.

Anthemis arvensis — **Field chamomile.** May–Aug.; introduced; fields, disturbed sites; throughout; common.

Anthemis cotula — **Mayweed.** June–Aug.; introduced; fields, disturbed sites; throughout; common.

Arctium minus — **Common burdock.** July–Oct.; introduced; fields, roadsides, disturbed sites; throughout; abundant.

Aster cordifolius — **Heart-leaved aster.** Aug.–Nov.; native; dry to moist woods, clearings; throughout; common.

Aster depauperatus — **Serpentine aster.** July–Oct.; native; serpentine barrens; Piedmont; rare.

Aster divaricatus — **White wood aster.** July–Oct.; native; dry to moist woods; throughout; common.

Aster dumosus — **Bushy aster.** Aug.–Nov.; native; dry to moist fields, clearings, open areas; throughout; common.

Aster infirmus — **Cornel-leaved aster.** July–Sept.; native; open woods; throughout; uncommon.

Aster laevis — **Smooth aster.** Aug.–Nov.; native; dry open woods, fields; throughout; common.

Aster lanceolatus (A. simplex) — **Panicled aster.** Aug.–Oct.; native; moist meadows, shores of streams and ponds; throughout; common.

Aster lateriflorus — **Calico aster.** Aug.–Oct.; native; dry to moist open woods, fields; throughout; common.

Aster linariifolius — **Stiff aster.** July–Oct.; native; dry open woods, rock outcrops; throughout; uncommon.

Aster macrophyllus — **Large-leaved aster.** Aug.–Sept.; native; dry woods, clearings; Piedmont and mountains; uncommon.

Aster novae-angliae — **New England aster.** Aug.–Oct.; native; moist woods and meadows; throughout; common.

Aster novi-belgii — **New York aster.** Aug.–Oct.; native; wet meadows, freshwater marshes; Coastal Plain and Piedmont; uncommon.

Aster oblongifolius — **Aromatic aster, shale-barren aster.** Aug.–Oct.; native; shale cliffs, rock outcrops; Piedmont and mountains; uncommon.

Aster patens — **Late purple aster.** Aug.–Nov.; native; dry open woods, rock outcrops; throughout; common.

Aster paternus — see *Sericocarpus asteroides.*

Aster pilosus — **White heath aster.** Aug.–Oct.; native; dry fields; throughout; abundant.

Aster prenanthoides — **Crooked-stem aster.** Aug.–Oct.; native; moist woods, wet meadows, freshwater marshes, streambanks; throughout (mainly Piedmont and mountains); common.

Aster puniceus — **Purple-stemmed aster.** Aug.–Nov.; native; moist to wet meadows, freshwater marshes, swamps; throughout; common.

Aster schreberi — **Schreber's aster.** July–Oct.; native; moist woods; Piedmont and mountains; uncommon.

Aster simplex — see *A. lanceolatus.*

Aster solidagineus — see *Sericocarpus linifolius.*

Aster tenuifolius — **Large salt-marsh aster.** Aug.–Oct.; native; brackish marshes, salt marshes; Coastal Plain; common.

Aster umbellatus — **Flat-topped aster.** Aug.–Nov.; native; wet woods, clearings; throughout; uncommon.

Aster undulatus — **Wavy-leaved aster.** Aug.–Nov.; native; dry woods, open clearings; throughout; common.

Baccharis halimifolia — **Groundsel-tree.** Aug.–Nov.; native; old fields, edges of brackish or salt marshes; Coastal Plain; common.

Bidens aristosa — **Tickseed-sunflower.** Aug.–Oct.; native; dry to moist fields, roadsides; throughout; uncommon to common.

Bidens bipinnata — **Spanish needles.** Aug.–Oct.; native; dry to moist fields, roadsides, disturbed sites; throughout; common.

Bidens cernua — **Nodding bur-marigold.** Aug.–Oct.; native; riverbanks, freshwater marshes, wet meadows; throughout; common.

Bidens connata — **Swamp beggar-ticks.** Aug.–Oct.; native; riverbanks, freshwater marshes; throughout; common.

Bidens frondosa — **Beggar-ticks, sticktight.** Aug.–Oct.; native; moist fields, meadows, roadsides, disturbed sites; throughout; abundant.

Bidens laevis — **Larger bur-marigold.** Aug.–Oct.; native; freshwater marshes, pond edges, riverbanks; throughout; common.

Bidens polylepis — **Tickseed-sunflower.** Aug.–Oct.; native; dry to moist fields and meadows, roadsides; throughout; abundant.

Cacalia atriplicifolia — **Pale Indian plantain.** July–Sept.; native; dry to moist woods, fields, meadows; throughout; uncommon to common.

Cacalia suaveolens — **Sweet-scented Indian plantain.** July–Sept.; native; bottomland woods, floodplains, alluvial soils; Piedmont and mountains; rare.

Carduus nutans — **Nodding thistle.** June–Oct.; introduced; fields, roadsides, disturbed sites; throughout; common.

Centaurea jacea — **Brown knapweed.** June–Sept.; introduced; fields, roadsides, disturbed sites; mountains; uncommon.

Centaurea maculosa — **Spotted knapweed.** June–Aug.; introduced; fields, roadsides, disturbed sites; throughout; common to abundant.

Chrysanthemum leucanthemum — **Ox-eye daisy.** May–Nov.; introduced; fields, meadows, roadsides; throughout; abundant.

Chrysogonum virginianum — **Chrysogonum, golden star, green and gold.** Mar.–June; native; moist open woods; throughout; common.

Chrysopsis mariana — **Maryland golden-aster.** Aug.–Oct.; native; sandy soils of dry woods, fields; throughout; common.

Cichorium intybus — **Chicory.** May–Oct.; introduced; fields, roadsides, disturbed sites; throughout; abundant.

Cirsium arvense — **Canada thistle.** June–Oct.; introduced; fields, roadsides, disturbed sites; throughout; common.

Cirsium discolor — **Field thistle.** July–Oct.; native; fields, roadsides; throughout; common.

Cirsium muticum — **Swamp thistle.** July–Sept.; native; moist fields, wet meadows, seeps; throughout (mainly Piedmont and mountains); uncommon.

Cirsium pumilum — **Pasture thistle.** June–Sept.; native; dry fields, meadows, disturbed sites; throughout (mainly Piedmont and mountains); uncommon.

Cirsium vulgare — **Bull thistle.** June–Sept.; introduced; fields, roadsides, disturbed sites; throughout; abundant.

Conyza canadensis — see *Erigeron canadensis.*

Coreopsis lanceolata — **Lance-leaved coreopsis.** May–Aug.; native to midwestern states; dry sandy fields, roadsides; throughout; common.

Coreopsis tripteris — **Tall coreopsis.** Aug.–Sept.; native; dry to moist meadows, clearings; throughout; uncommon.

Coreopsis verticillata — **Whorled coreopsis.** June–July; native; dry open clearings, rock outcrops; throughout; uncommon.

Echinacea purpurea — **Purple coneflower.** June–Oct.; native to midwestern states (planted in our area).

Eclipta alba — see *E. prostrata.*

Eclipta prostrata (E. alba) — **Eclipta, Yerba-de-tajo.** July–Oct.; introduced; disturbed sites; throughout; common.

Elephantopus carolinianus — **Elephant's-foot.** July–Oct.; native; edges of woods, clearings; throughout; common.

Erechtites hieracifolia — **Pilewort.** July–Oct.; native; dry fields, roadsides, disturbed sites; throughout; abundant.

Erigeron annuus — **Daisy fleabane.** May–Nov.; native; open woods, fields; throughout; abundant.

Erigeron canadensis (*Conyza canadensis*) — **Horseweed.** July–Nov.; native; dry fields, roadsides, disturbed sites; throughout; abundant.

Erigeron philadelphicus — **Common fleabane.** Apr.–Oct.; native; open woods, fields, roadsides, thickets; throughout; abundant.

Erigeron pulchellus — **Robin's plantain.** Apr.–July; native; open woods, roadsides, fields; throughout; common.

Erigeron strigosus — **Lesser daisy fleabane, white-top.** May–Sept.; native; fields, roadsides, disturbed sites; throughout; common.

Eupatorium altissimum — **Tall boneset, tall thoroughwort.** Aug.–Oct.; native; dry fields, clearings; throughout; uncommon.

Eupatorium coelestinum — **Mistflower.** July–Oct.; native; moist woods, old fields, clearings; throughout; common.

Eupatorium fistulosum — **Hollow Joe-Pye-weed.** July–Sept.; native; moist woods (often bottomlands), wet meadows, freshwater marshes, ditches; throughout; common to abundant.

Eupatorium hyssopifolium — **Hyssop-leaved boneset, hyssop-leaved thoroughwort.** Aug.–Oct.; native; dry to moist fields, meadows; Coastal Plain and Piedmont; common.

Eupatorium maculatum — **Spotted Joe-Pye-weed.** July–Oct.; native; wet meadows, freshwater marshes; Piedmont and mountains; rare to uncommon.

Eupatorium perfoliatum — **Boneset.** July–Oct.; native; moist to wet woods, fields, meadows, thickets; throughout; common to abundant.

Eupatorium pilosum — **Rough boneset.** July–Sept.; native; bogs, moist clearings; throughout (mainly Coastal Plain and Piedmont); uncommon to common.

Eupatorium pubescens — see *E. rotundifolium.*

Eupatorium purpureum — **Sweet Joe-Pye-weed.** July–Sept.; native; moist woods, bottomland woods, floodplains; throughout; common.

Eupatorium rotundifolium (*E. pubescens*) — **Round-leaved boneset.** July–Sept.; native; dry fields, clearings; throughout; common.

Eupatorium rugosum — **White snakeroot.** Aug.–Oct.; native; moist upland woods, clearings, thickets; throughout; abundant.

Eupatorium serotinum — **Late-flowering boneset, late-flowering thoroughwort.** Aug.–Oct.; native; dry old fields, disturbed sites; Coastal Plain and Piedmont; uncommon.

Eupatorium sessilifolium — **Upland boneset.** Aug.–Sept.; native; dry to moist woods; throughout (mainly Piedmont and mountains); common.

Euthamia graminifolia — see *Solidago graminifolia.*

Galinsoga ciliata — see *G. quadriradiata.*

Galinsoga quadriradiata (*G. ciliata*) — **Galinsoga.** May–Nov.; introduced; fields, roadsides, disturbed sites; throughout; abundant.

Gnaphalium obtusifolium — **Sweet everlasting, rabbit tobacco.** Aug.–Nov.; native; dry fields, dry meadows, roadsides, disturbed sites; throughout; common.

Helenium autumnale — **Yellow sneezeweed.** Aug.–Nov.; native; wet meadows, freshwater marshes, riverbanks; throughout; common.

Helenium flexuosum (*H. nudiflorum*) — **Purple-headed sneezeweed.** June–Aug.; native; fields, moist meadows, freshwater marshes; throughout; uncommon.

Helenium nudiflorum — see *H. flexuosum.*

Helianthus decapetalus — **Thin-leaved sunflower.** Aug.–Oct.; native; moist woods, thickets; throughout; common.

Helianthus divaricatus — **Woodland sunflower.** June–Oct.; native; dry open woods, roadsides; throughout; common.

Helianthus giganteus — **Giant sunflower, tall sunflower.** Aug.–Oct.; native; moist woods, clearings; throughout; uncommon to common.

Helianthus mollis — **Hairy sunflower.** Aug.–Oct.; native to midwestern states; fields, meadows; Piedmont; uncommon.

Helianthus occidentalis — **Western sunflower.** July–Aug.; native; rock outcrops, rocky riverbanks; Piedmont; rare.

Helianthus strumosus — **Pale-leaved sunflower.** July–Sept.; native; moist woods, thickets, streambanks; throughout; common.

Helianthus tuberosus — **Jerusalem artichoke.** Aug.–Oct.; native; borders of woods, thickets, ditches; throughout; common.

Heliopsis helianthoides — **Ox-eye.** June–Sept.; native; dry to moist woods, clearings, thickets; throughout; common.

Heterotheca subaxillaris — **Camphorweed.** July–Sept.; native; dry fields, sandy clearings; Coastal Plain; common.

Hieracium caespitosum (*H. pratense*) — **Field hawkweed, king devil.** May–Sept.; introduced; fields, clearings, roadsides, disturbed sites; throughout; abundant.

Hieracium paniculatum — **Panicled hawkweed.** July–Sept.; native; dry to moist woods, fields; Piedmont and mountains; common.

Hieracium pratense — see *Hieracium caespitosum.*

Hieracium venosum — **Rattlesnake-weed.** May–June; native; dry upland woods, clearings; throughout; common.

Hypochoeris radicata — **Cat's-ear.** May–Aug.; introduced; fields, roadsides, disturbed sites; throughout (mainly Coastal Plain and Piedmont); common.

Krigia virginica — **Dwarf dandelion.** May–June; native; fields, clearings; throughout; common.

Lactuca biennis — **Tall blue lettuce.** Aug.–Oct.; native; moist woods, fields, thickets, disturbed sites; Piedmont and mountains; common.

Lactuca canadensis — **Wild lettuce.** July–Sept.; native; dry woods, fields, disturbed sites; throughout; abundant.

Lactuca floridana — **Florida lettuce.** July–Oct.; native; moist woods, clearings, thickets; throughout; common.

Liatris graminifolia — **Grass-leaved blazing-star.** Sept.–Oct.; native; dry fields, clearings; throughout; uncommon.

Liatris spicata — **Spiked blazing-star.** Aug.–Oct.; native; dry fields, rock outcrops; throughout; rare.

Liatris squarrosa — **Scaly blazing-star.** July–Sept.; native; dry fields, clearings; Coastal Plain and Piedmont; uncommon.

Matricaria matricarioides — **Pineapple-weed.** June–Sept.; introduced; fields, roadsides; mainly Piedmont and mountains; common.

Mikania scandens — **Climbing hempweed.** Aug.–Oct.; native; moist fields, freshwater marshes, thickets; Coastal Plain and Piedmont; common.

Parthenium integrifolium — **Feverfew, wild quinine.** June–Sept.; native; dry open woods, fields, roadsides; throughout; uncommon.

Pluchea odorata (*P. purpurascens*) — **Salt-marsh fleabane.** Aug.–Sept.; native; brackish marshes, salt marshes; Coastal Plain; common.

Pluchea purpurascens — see *P. odorata.*

Polymnia canadensis — **Small-flowered leafcup.** July–Sept.; native; moist woods, rock outcrops; Piedmont and mountains; uncommon to common.

Polymnia uvedalia — **Large-flowered leafcup.** July–Sept.; native; open fields, clearings, thickets; throughout; common.

Prenanthes alba — **White lettuce.** Aug.–Oct.; native; dry to moist open woods, fields; throughout; uncommon.

Prenanthes serpentaria — **Lion's-foot, gall-of-the-earth.** Aug.–Oct.; native; open woods, dry fields, dry meadows, roadsides; throughout; common.

Rudbeckia fulgida — **Orange coneflower.** Aug.–Oct.; native; dry to moist woods, fields; Piedmont and mountains; uncommon to common.

Rudbeckia hirta — **Black-eyed Susan.** June–Oct.; native; dry fields, meadows, clearings, roadsides; throughout; abundant.

Rudbeckia laciniata — **Green-headed coneflower.** July–Sept.; native; moist open woods, floodplains, clearings, thickets; throughout; common.

Senecio antennariifolius — **Pussytoes ragwort.** May–June; native; shale barrens, dry shaly soils; mountains; rare.

Senecio aureus — **Golden ragwort.** Mar.–June; native; wet woods, floodplains, seeps; throughout; common to abundant.

Senecio obovatus — **Round-leaved ragwort.** Apr.–June; native; dry to moist woods, clearings; mainly Piedmont and mountains; uncommon.

Senecio pauperculus — **Balsam ragwort.** June–Aug.; native; dry fields, meadows (often on nutrient-poor soils); Piedmont and mountains; uncommon.

Sericocarpus asteroides (*Aster paternus*) — **Toothed white-topped aster.** June–Sept.; native; dry woods, fields, thickets; throughout; common.

Sericocarpus linifolius (*Aster solidagineus*) — **Narrow-leaved white-topped aster.** June–Sept.; native; dry woods, fields, thickets; throughout; uncommon.

Silphium trifoliatum — **Whorled rosinweed.** July–Sept.; native; dry open woods, fields, thickets; throughout; common.

Solidago altissima — see *S. canadensis.*

Solidago arguta var. *harrisii* — see *S. harrisii.*

Solidago bicolor — **Silverrod.** Aug.–Oct.; native; dry woods, rock outcrops, roadsides; throughout; common.

Solidago caesia — **Blue-stemmed goldenrod, wreath goldenrod.** July–Oct.; native; dry to moist woods; throughout; common.

Solidago canadensis (including *S. altissima* by Gleason and Cronquist) — **Tall goldenrod.** Aug.–Nov.; native; dry to moist fields, meadows, thickets, roadsides; throughout; abundant.

Solidago erecta — **Slender goldenrod.** Aug.–Oct.; native; dry woods, fields; throughout; common.

Solidago flexicaulis — **Zigzag goldenrod.** Aug.–Oct.; native; moist woods, streambanks, bottomland woods; throughout (mainly Piedmont and mountains); common.

Solidago gigantea — **Late goldenrod.** Aug.–Oct.; native; dry to moist fields, clearings; throughout; common.

Solidago graminifolia (*Euthamia graminifolia*) — **Lance-leaved goldenrod, grass-leaved goldenrod.** Aug.–Oct.; native; dry to moist fields and meadows, clearings, freshwater marshes; throughout; common.

Solidago harrisii (*S. arguta* var. *harrisii*) — **Shale-barren goldenrod.** June–Sept.; native; shale barrens, limestone and greenstone cliffs and barrens; mountains; uncommon.

Solidago juncea — **Early goldenrod.** July–Oct.; native; open woods, fields, clearings, roadsides; throughout; abundant.

Solidago nemoralis — **Gray goldenrod.** Aug.–Nov.; native; dry fields, clearings; throughout; common.

Solidago racemosa (*S. simplex* var. *racemosa*) — **Riverbank goldenrod.** July–Nov.; native; rock outcrops and bluffs along rivers; Piedmont; rare.

Solidago randii (*S. simplex* var. *randii*) — **Rand's goldenrod.** July–Sept.; native; greenstone cliffs and barrens; mountains; rare.

Solidago rugosa — **Rough-stemmed goldenrod.** Aug.–Oct.; native; dry to moist fields, clearings; throughout; common.

Solidago sempervirens — **Seaside goldenrod.** July–Nov.; native sandy soils; Coastal Plain; common.

Solidago simplex var. *racemosa* — see *S. racemosa*.

Solidago simplex var. *randii* — see *S. randii*.

Solidago ulmifolia — **Elm-leaved goldenrod.** Aug.–Sept.; native; dry to moist open woods, fields, streambanks, thickets; throughout (mainly Piedmont and mountains); common.

Sonchus oleraceus — **Common sow-thistle.** July–Oct.; introduced; fields, roadsides, disturbed sites; throughout; abundant.

Taraxacum officinale — **Common dandelion.** Jan.–Dec.; introduced; lawns, fields, disturbed sites; throughout; abundant.

Tragopogon pratensis — **Yellow goatsbeard.** June–July; introduced; fields, roadsides, disturbed sites; mountains; common.

Tussilago farfara — **Coltsfoot.** Mar.–Apr.; introduced; roadsides, disturbed sites; throughout; common.

Verbesina alternifolia (*Actinomeris alternifolia*) — **Wingstem.** July–Oct.; native; moist woods, fields, thickets, disturbed sites, ditches; throughout; abundant.

Verbesina occidentalis — **Crownbeard.** July–Oct.; native; damp woods, fields, clearings; throughout; common.

Vernonia glauca — **Broad-leaved ironweed.** July–Oct.; native; dry to moist woods, fields; throughout; uncommon.

Vernonia noveboracensis — **New York ironweed.** Aug.–Oct.; native; wet meadows, swales, freshwater marshes, streambanks, riverbanks, ditches; throughout; common.

BALSAMINACEAE (IMPATIENS FAMILY)

Impatiens capensis — **Spotted jewelweed, spotted touch-me-not.** June–Sept.; native; moist woods, streambanks, swales, ditches, freshwater marshes; throughout; abundant.

Impatiens pallida — **Pale jewelweed, pale touch-me-not.** June–Sept.; native; moist woods, streambanks, swales, freshwater marshes; Piedmont and mountains; common.

BERBERIDACEAE (BARBERRY FAMILY)

Caulophyllum thalictroides — **Blue cohosh.** Apr.–May; native; moist woods (often in calcareous soils); Piedmont and mountains; uncommon.

Jeffersonia diphylla — **Twinleaf.** Apr.–May; native; moist woods, bluffs (often in calcareous soils); Piedmont and mountains; uncommon.

Podophyllum peltatum — **Mayapple.** Apr.–May; native; moist woods, shaded roadsides; throughout; abundant.

BORAGINACEAE (BORAGE/FORGET-ME-NOT FAMILY)

Cynoglossum virginianum — **Wild comfrey.** May–June; native; upland woods; throughout; uncommon.

Echium vulgare — **Viper's bugloss.** June–Sept.; introduced; dry fields, roadsides, disturbed sites; throughout; common.

Lithospermum arvense — **Corn gromwell.** Apr.–July; introduced; fields, meadows, disturbed sites; Piedmont and mountains; uncommon to common.

Lithospermum canescens — **Hoary puccoon.** Apr.–June; native; dry woods, fields, shale cliffs, rock outcrops; Piedmont and mountains; uncommon.

Mertensia virginica — **Virginia bluebells.** Apr.–May; native; alluvial soils, wooded floodplains, bottomland woods; throughout; common (locally abundant).

Myosotis laxa — **Smaller forget-me-not.** May–July; native; wet meadows, streambanks; throughout; uncommon.

Myosotis scorpioides — **True forget-me-not.** May–Sept.; introduced; wet fields and meadows, seeps, streambanks; throughout; uncommon.

Myosotis verna — **Spring forget-me-not.** Apr.–May; native; dry rocky woods, fields, clearings; Coastal Plain and Piedmont; uncommon.

Onosmodium virginianum — **False gromwell.** May–Aug.; native; open woods, dry soils; Coastal Plain and Piedmont; rare.

BRASSICACEAE (CRUCIFERAE) (**MUSTARD FAMILY**)

Alliaria officinalis — see *A. petiolata.*

Alliaria petiolata (*A. officinalis*) — **Garlic mustard.** Apr.–June; introduced; moist woods, floodplains, roadsides, disturbed sites; throughout; abundant.

Arabidopsis thaliana — **Mouse-ear cress.** Apr.–May; introduced; fields, roadsides, lawns, disturbed sites; throughout; uncommon to common.

Arabis laevigata — **Smooth rockcress.** Mar.–June; native; rocky woods, rock outcrops; throughout; common.

Arabis lyrata — **Lyre-leaved rockcress.** Apr.–June; native; dry woods, rock ledges, rocky bluffs, sandy clearings; throughout; uncommon to common.

Arabis patens — **Spreading rockcress.** Apr.–June; native; rock outcrops, rock ledges; Piedmont and mountains; uncommon.

Barbarea verna — **Early winter cress.** Mar.–May; introduced; cultivated fields, disturbed sites; throughout; abundant.

Barbarea vulgaris — **Common winter cress, yellow rocket.** Mar.–June; introduced; cultivated fields, disturbed sites; throughout; abundant.

Brassica rapa — **Field mustard.** May–Oct.; introduced; fields, disturbed sites; throughout; common.

Capsella bursa-pastoris — **Shepherd's purse.** Mar.–Oct.; introduced; roadsides, lawns, disturbed sites; throughout; common.

Cardamine angustata — see *Dentaria heterophylla.*

Cardamine bulbosa — see *C. rhomboidea.*

Cardamine concatenata — see *Dentaria laciniata.*

Cardamine douglassii — **Purple cress.** Mar.–Apr.; native; wet bottom-land woods, seeps; throughout; rare to uncommon.

Cardamine hirsuta — **Hairy bittercress.** Jan.–Apr.; introduced; fields, roadsides, lawns, disturbed sites; throughout; abundant.

Cardamine pensylvanica — **Pennsylvania bittercress.** Apr.–May; native; wet woods, seeps; throughout; common.

Cardamine rhomboidea (*C. bulbosa*) — **Spring cress.** Apr.–May; native; moist to wet woods, bottomland woods, wet fields; throughout; common.

Dentaria heterophylla (*Cardamine angustata*) — **Slender toothwort.** Apr.–May; native; moist woods; throughout; uncommon to common.

Dentaria laciniata (*Cardamine concatenata*) — **Cut-leaved toothwort.** Mar.–May; native; moist woods; throughout; common.

Draba ramosissima — **Rocktwist.** Apr.–June; native; rock outcrops; mountains; uncommon.

Draba verna — **Whitlow grass.** Mar.–June; introduced; fields, lawns, disturbed sites; throughout; common.

Hesperis matronalis — **Dame's rocket.** May–July; introduced; open woods, roadsides, thickets; throughout; common.

Lepidium campestre — **Field peppergrass.** Apr.–Sept.; introduced; fields, disturbed sites; throughout; common.

Lepidium virginicum — **Wild peppergrass, poor-man's pepper.** Apr.–Nov.; native; fields, lawns, roadsides, disturbed sites; throughout; common.

Nasturtium officinale (*Rorippa nasturtium-aquaticum*) — **Watercress.** Apr.–Oct.; introduced; streams, springs, ponds; throughout; common.

Rorippa nasturtium-aquaticum — see *Nasturtium officinale*.

Thlaspi arvense — **Field pennycress.** Apr.–Aug.; introduced; fields, lawns, disturbed sites; throughout; common.

CACTACEAE (**CACTUS FAMILY**)

Opuntia humifusa — **Prickly pear.** June–July; native; rocks, shale cliffs, sandy clearings; throughout; uncommon to common.

CAMPANULACEAE (**BLUEBELL FAMILY**)

Campanula americana — **Tall bellflower.** June–Sept.; native; moist open woods, borders of woods; Piedmont and mountains; uncommon.

Campanula divaricata — **Southern harebell.** July–Sept.; native dry woods, rock outcrops; mountains; uncommon.

Campanula rotundifolia — **Harebell.** June–Sept.; native; rock outcrops, cliffs, dry open areas; mountains; rare.

Lobelia cardinalis — **Cardinal flower.** July–Sept.; native; streambanks, riverbanks, freshwater marshes, pond edges, wet meadows; throughout; common.

Lobelia inflata — **Indian tobacco.** July–Oct.; native; dry open woods, borders of woods, fields; throughout; common.

Lobelia puberula — **Downy lobelia.** Aug.–Oct.; native; dry to moist woods, meadows, clearings; Coastal Plain and Piedmont; uncommon.

Lobelia siphilitica — **Great lobelia.** Aug.–Sept.; native; streambanks, riverbanks, pond edges; throughout; common.

Lobelia spicata — **Spiked lobelia.** June–Aug.; native; dry to moist meadows, fields; throughout (mainly Piedmont and mountains); uncommon to common.

Specularia perfoliata — see *Triodanis perfoliata.*

Triodanis perfoliata (*Specularia perfoliata*) — **Venus's looking-glass.** May–June; native; old fields, rock outcrops, disturbed sites; throughout; common.

CAPRIFOLIACEAE (**HONEYSUCKLE FAMILY**)

Diervilla lonicera — **Bush honeysuckle.** June–Aug.; native; cool dry woods, rock outcrops, clearings; mountains; uncommon.

Linnaea borealis — **Twinflower.** June–Aug.; native; cool moist woods; mountains; rare.

Triosteum angustifolium — **Narrow-leaved horse-gentian.** May–June; native; dry to moist woods, fields; Piedmont and mountains; uncommon.

Triosteum perfoliatum — **Horse-gentian, tinker's-weed, wild coffee.** Aug.–Oct.; native; woods, thin rocky soils; throughout; uncommon to common.

Viburnum acerifolium — **Maple-leaved viburnum.** May–June; native; dry to moist woods; throughout; common.

Viburnum dentatum — **Arrowwood, southern arrowwood.** May–June; native; moist woods, swamps; throughout; common.

Viburnum nudum — **Possum-haw.** May–June; native; wet woods, swamps; throughout (mainly Coastal Plain and Piedmont; uncommon.

CARYOPHYLLACEAE (PINK FAMILY)

Arenaria serpyllifolia — **Thyme-leaved sandwort.** Apr.–Aug.; introduced; sandy fields, disturbed sites; throughout; common.

Cerastium arvense — **Field chickweed.** Apr.–July; native; open rocky woods, fields, meadows; mainly Piedmont; uncommon to common.

Dianthus armeria — **Deptford pink.** May–Oct.; introduced; dry fields, lawns, roadsides; throughout; common.

Lychnis alba (*Silene latifolia*) — **Evening lychnis, white campion.** May–Sept.; introduced; fields, roadsides, disturbed sites; throughout; common.

Saponaria officinalis — **Bouncing Bet, soapwort.** July–Oct.; introduced; fields, roadsides, disturbed sites; throughout; common to abundant.

Silene caroliniana — **Wild pink.** Apr.–June; native; dry woods, rock outcrops and bluffs; throughout; common.

Silene cucubalus — see *S. vulgaris.*

Silene latifolia — see *Lychnis alba.*

Silene stellata — **Starry campion.** June–Oct.; native; dry to moist open woods, clearings; throughout; common.

Silene vulgaris (*S. cucubalus*) — **Bladder campion.** May–Aug.; introduced; fields, borders of dry woods, roadsides; throughout; common.

Stellaria longifolia — **Long-leaved stitchwort.** May–July; native; moist meadows; throughout; common.

Stellaria media — **Common chickweed.** Jan.–Dec.; introduced; fields, lawns, disturbed sites; throughout; abundant.

Stellaria pubera — **Star chickweed, giant chickweed.** Apr.–May; native; dry to moist woods, rock outcrops; throughout; common.

CISTACEAE (ROCKROSE FAMILY)

Helianthemum canadense — **Frostweed.** May–June; native; sandy clearings; throughout (mainly Coastal Plain); uncommon.

Lechea racemulosa — **Pinweed.** July–Aug.; native; edges of woods, fields, meadows; throughout; uncommon to common.

CLETHRACEAE (PEPPERBUSH FAMILY)

Clethra alnifolia — **Sweet pepperbush.** July–Sept.; native; swamps, bogs; Coastal Plain; common.

COMPOSITAE — see ASTERACEAE.

CONVOLVULACEAE (**MORNING GLORY FAMILY**)

Calystegia sepium — see *Convolvulus sepium.*

Convolvulus arvensis — **Field bindweed.** June–Oct.; introduced; fields, roadsides, disturbed sites; throughout; abundant.

Convolvulus sepium (*Calystegia sepium*) — **Hedge bindweed.** June–Oct.; native and/or introduced; fields, roadsides, disturbed sites; throughout; common.

Ipomoea coccinae — **Small red morning glory.** Aug.–Oct.; introduced; fields, roadsides, disturbed sites; throughout; uncommon.

Ipomoea hederacea — **Ivy-leaved morning glory.** July–Oct.; introduced; fields, roadsides, disturbed sites; throughout; common.

Ipomoea lacunosa — **Small white morning glory.** July–Oct.; native; fields, roadsides, disturbed sites; throughout; common.

Ipomoea pandurata — **Wild potato vine.** June–Oct.; native; dry woods, fields, roadsides; disturbed sites; throughout; common.

Ipomoea purpurea — **Common morning glory.** July–Oct.; introduced; borders of fields, roadsides, disturbed sites; throughout; abundant.

CORNACEAE (**DOGWOOD FAMILY**)

Cornus amomum — **Silky dogwood.** May–June; native; swamps, seeps, riverbanks; throughout; common.

Cornus canadensis — **Bunchberry, dwarf dogwood, dwarf cornel.** June–July; native; cool moist woods; mountains; very rare.

Cornus florida — **Flowering dogwood.** Apr.–May; native; dry to moist woods; throughout; common.

Cornus racemosa — **Gray dogwood.** May–July; native; moist woods, streambanks; mountains; uncommon.

CRASSULACEAE (**SEDUM FAMILY**)

Sedum telephioides — **Live-forever.** July–Sept.; native; rock outcrops, cliffs; Piedmont and mountains; uncommon.

Sedum ternatum — **Wild stonecrop.** Apr.–May; native; moist rocky woods, streambanks, rock outcrops; Piedmont and mountains; common.

CRUCIFERAE — see BRASSICACEAE.

DIAPENSIACEAE (**DIAPENSIA FAMILY**)

Galax aphylla — **Galax.** May–June; native to southern Appalachians (planted in our area).

Shortia galacifolia — **Shortia, Oconee bells.** Mar.–Apr.; native to southern Appalachians (planted in our area).

DIPSACACEAE (TEASEL FAMILY)

Dipsacus laciniatus — **Teasel.** July–Sept.; introduced; old fields, roadsides, disturbed sites; throughout; common.

Dipsacus sylvestris — **Teasel.** July–Sept.; introduced; old fields, roadsides, disturbed sites; throughout; common.

DROSERACEAE (SUNDEW FAMILY)

Drosera filiformis — **Thread-leaved sundew.** June–Sept.; native; bogs, sandy wetlands; Coastal Plain; rare.

Drosera intermedia — **Spatulate-leaved sundew.** June–Aug.; native; bogs, sandy wetlands; Coastal Plain; rare.

Drosera rotundifolia — **Round-leaved sundew.** June–Aug.; native; bogs, peatlands; Coastal Plain and mountains; rare.

ERICACEAE (HEATH FAMILY)

Epigaea repens — **Trailing arbutus.** Mar.–Apr.; native; rocky or sandy slopes (usually nutrient-poor acidic soils); throughout; uncommon to common.

Eubotrys racemosa — see *Leucothoe racemosa*.

Gaultheria hispidula — **Creeping snowberry.** May; native; bogs; mountains; very rare.

Gaultheria procumbens — **Wintergreen.** June–Aug.; native; dry woods, clearings; throughout; uncommon.

Kalmia angustifolia — **Sheep laurel.** May–July; native; bogs, cool acidic wetlands; Coastal Plain and mountains; rare.

Kalmia latifolia — **Mountain laurel.** May–June; native; dry acidic woods; throughout; common.

Leucothoe racemosa (*Eubotrys racemosa*) — **Fetterbush.** May–June; native; moist acidic woods; throughout (mainly Coastal Plain and Piedmont); uncommon to common.

Lyonia ligustrina — **Maleberry.** May–July; native; wet woods, swamps, bogs; throughout; uncommon.

Lyonia mariana — **Staggerbush.** Apr.–May; native; dry to moist sandy woods; Coastal Plain; uncommon.

Rhododendron maximum — **Rosebay, great laurel.** May–July; native; moist acidic woods; Piedmont and mountains; uncommon to common.

Rhododendron nudiflorum — see *R. periclymenoides*.

Rhododendron periclymenoides (*R. nudiflorum*) — **Pinxter flower, pink**

azalea. Apr.–May; native; dry to moist acidic woods, streambanks; throughout; common.

Rhododendron prinophyllum (R. roseum) — **Rose azalea, hoary azalea.** May–June; native; cool moist woods; Piedmont and mountains; uncommon.

Rhododendron roseum — see *R. prinophyllum.*

Rhododendron viscosum — **Swamp azalea.** May–June; native; swamps, bogs, streambanks; throughout; uncommon.

Vaccinium corymbosum — **Highbush blueberry.** Apr.–June; native; moist acidic woods, old fields, bogs, swamps; throughout; common.

Vaccinium macrocarpon — **Large cranberry.** June–Aug.; native; bogs; Coastal Plain and mountains; rare.

Vaccinium oxycoccos — **Small cranberry.** Aug.–Oct.; native; bogs; mountains; very rare.

Vaccinium pallidum — see also *V. vacillans.*

Vaccinium stamineum — **Deerberry.** Apr.–June; native; dry acidic woods; throughout; common.

Vaccinium vacillans (included in *V. pallidum* by Gleason and Cronquist) — **Lowbush blueberry, late lowbush blueberry.** Apr.– June; native; dry acidic woods; throughout; common.

EUPHORBIACEAE (SPURGE FAMILY)

Euphorbia corollata — **Flowering spurge.** July–Oct.; native; dry open woods, fields; throughout; common.

Euphorbia cyparissias — **Cypress spurge.** Apr.–Aug.; introduced; dry fields, roadsides, disturbed sites; throughout; common.

FABACEAE (LEGUMINOSAE) (PEA FAMILY)

Amphicarpa bracteata — see *Amphicarpaea bracteata.*

Amphicarpaea bracteata (Amphicarpa bracteata) — **Hog peanut.** Aug.– Sept.; native; moist woods, thickets; throughout; common.

Apios americana — **Groundnut, wild bean.** July–Sept.; native; moist woods, thickets; throughout; common.

Astragalus distortus — **Bent milk-vetch.** Apr.–June; native; shale barrens; mountains; rare.

Baptisia australis — **Blue false indigo.** May–June; native; open rocky riverbanks; Piedmont and mountains; rare.

Baptisia tinctoria — **Wild indigo.** June–Sept.; native; dry open woods, fields, clearings; throughout; common.

Cassia fasciculata (*Chamaecrista fasciculata*) — **Partridge-pea.** July–Sept.; native; borders of dry woods, fields, roadsides; throughout; common.

Cassia marilandica (*Senna marilandica*) — **Wild senna.** July–Aug.; native; dry open woods, borders of woods, fields; throughout; uncommon.

Cassia nictitans (*Chamaecrista nictitans*) — **Wild sensitive plant.** July–Oct.; native; dry sandy fields, roadsides, disturbed sites; throughout; common.

Cercis canadensis — **Redbud.** Apr.–May; native; moist woods; throughout; common.

Chamaecrista fasciculata — see *Cassia fasciculata*.

Chamaecrista nictitans — see *Cassia nictitans*.

Clitoria mariana — **Butterfly pea.** June–Aug.; native; dry woods, clearings, rocky banks; throughout; uncommon.

Coronilla varia — **Crown vetch.** June–Oct.; introduced; roadsides, disturbed sites; throughout; common.

Desmodium canadense — **Showy tick-trefoil.** July–Sept.; native; thickets, clearings; mainly mountains; rare.

Desmodium canescens — **Hoary tick-trefoil.** July–Sept.; native; woods, dry fields; throughout; common.

Desmodium marilandicum — **Smooth small-leaved tick-trefoil.** July–Sept.; native; dry sandy clearings; throughout; uncommon.

Desmodium nudiflorum — **Naked-flowered tick-trefoil.** July–Sept.; native; dry to moist woods; throughout; common.

Desmodium paniculatum — **Panicled tick-trefoil.** July–Sept.; native; dry open woods, fields; throughout; common.

Desmodium pauciflorum — **Few-flowered tick-trefoil.** July–Aug.; native; moist woods; Coastal Plain and Piedmont; uncommon.

Desmodium rigidum — **Rigid tick-trefoil, stiff tick-trefoil.** July–Sept.; native; dry sandy woods; throughout; rare.

Desmodium rotundifolium — **Prostrate tick-trefoil.** July–Sept.; native; dry woods, rocky banks; throughout; uncommon.

Desmodium viridiflorum — **Velvety tick-trefoil.** Aug.–Sept.; native; sandy soils, clearings; Coastal Plain and Piedmont; rare.

Dolichos lablab — **Hyacinth bean.** Aug.–Oct.; introduced; fields, meadows, disturbed sites; Coastal Plain; uncommon.

Lathyrus latifolius — **Everlasting pea.** June–Sept.; introduced; fields, roadsides, thickets; throughout; common.

Lathyrus venosus — **Veiny pea.** May–July; native; open rocky areas; Piedmont and mountains; uncommon.

Lespedeza capitata — **Round-headed bushclover.** July–Oct.; native; meadows, clearings; Coastal Plain and Piedmont; common.

Lespedeza intermedia — **Wandlike bushclover.** Aug.–Sept.; native; open woods, dry fields, thickets; throughout; common.

Lespedeza procumbens — **Trailing bushclover.** Aug.–Sept.; native; dry sandy woods, fields, roadsides; throughout; common.

Lespedeza repens — **Creeping bushclover.** Aug.–Sept.; native; dry fields, roadsides; throughout; common.

Lespedeza stipulacea — **Korean bushclover.** July–Sept.; introduced; fields, roadsides, disturbed sites; throughout; abundant.

Lespedeza virginica — **Slender bushclover.** July–Sept.; native; dry open woods, fields, roadsides; throughout; common.

Medicago lupulina — **Black medick.** May–Oct., introduced; fields, roadsides, disturbed sites; throughout; common.

Medicago sativa — **Alfalfa.** May–Oct.; introduced; fields, roadsides, disturbed sites; throughout; common.

Melilotus alba — **White sweet clover.** May–Oct.; introduced; fields, roadsides, disturbed sites; throughout; abundant.

Melilotus officinalis — **Yellow sweet clover.** May–Oct.; introduced; fields, roadsides, disturbed sites; throughout; abundant.

Phaseolus polystachios — **Wild kidney bean.** July–Sept.; native; dry woods, thickets; throughout; uncommon.

Senna marilandica — see *Cassia marilandica*.

Strophostyles helvola — **Trailing wild bean.** July–Oct.; native; moist sandy woods, clearings; throughout (mainly Coastal Plain and Piedmont); uncommon.

Strophostyles umbellata — **Pink wild bean.** July–Oct.; native; dry woods, fields, clearings; throughout (mainly Coastal Plain and Piedmont); uncommon to common.

Stylosanthes biflora — **Pencil flower.** June–Aug.; native; dry fields, borders of open woods; throughout; common.

Tephrosia virginiana — **Goat's-rue.** May–Aug.; native; dry woods, clearings, open rocky areas; throughout; uncommon.

Trifolium agrarium — see *T. aureum.*

Trifolium arvense — **Rabbit-foot clover.** May–Oct.; introduced; fields, lawns, disturbed sites; throughout; rare.

Trifolium aureum (*T. agrarium*) — **Yellow hop clover.** June–Sept.; introduced; fields, lawns; throughout; common.

Trifolium hybridum — **Alsike clover.** June–Oct.; introduced; fields, disturbed sites; throughout; common.

Trifolium pratense — **Red clover.** May–Nov.; introduced; fields, roadsides, lawns, disturbed sites; throughout; abundant.

Trifolium repens — **White clover.** May–Oct.; introduced; fields, roadsides, lawns, disturbed sites; throughout; abundant.

Trifolium virginicum — **Kate's Mountain clover.** Apr.–May; native; shale barrens; mountains; rare.

Vicia angustifolia — **Narrow-leaved vetch.** May–Oct.; introduced; fields, roadsides, disturbed sites; throughout; common.

Vicia caroliniana — **Wood vetch, Carolina vetch.** Apr.–July; native; dry to moist woods, thickets; throughout; uncommon.

Vicia sativa — **Spring vetch.** May–July; introduced; open fields, roadsides; throughout; uncommon.

FUMARIACEAE (included in PAPAVERACEAE in *Gray's Manual*)
(BLEEDING-HEART FAMILY)

Corydalis flavula — **Yellow corydalis.** Apr.–May; native; dry to moist open woods, disturbed sites; throughout; common.

Corydalis sempervirens — **Pale corydalis, pink corydalis.** May–Sept.; native; rock outcrops, cliffs; Piedmont and mountains; uncommon.

Dicentra canadensis — **Squirrel corn.** Apr.–May; native; moist woods, floodplains, moist rocky slopes; throughout; common.

Dicentra cucullaria — **Dutchman's breeches.** Apr.–May; native; moist woods, floodplains, moist rocky slopes; throughout; common.

Dicentra eximia — **Wild bleeding-heart.** Apr.–Sept.; native; rocky woods, rock outcrops; Piedmont and mountains; uncommon.

GENTIANACEAE (GENTIAN FAMILY)

Gentiana andrewsii — **Fringe-tip closed gentian.** Aug.–Oct.; native; wet meadows; Piedmont; very rare.

Gentiana clausa — **Closed gentian, bottle gentian.** Sept.–Oct.; native; wet meadows; Piedmont and mountains; uncommon.

Gentiana crinita (Gentianopsis crinita) — **Fringed gentian.** Aug.–Nov.; native; streambanks; very rare (see Soldiers Delight).

Gentiana villosa — **Striped gentian.** Aug.–Oct.; native; dry to moist open woods, clearings; throughout; rare.

Gentianopsis crinita — see *Gentiana crinita.*

Obolaria virginica — **Pennywort.** Apr.–May; native; moist woods; throughout; uncommon to common.

Sabatia angularis — **Rose pink.** July–Sept.; native; open woods, fields, clearings; throughout; uncommon.

GERANIACEAE (**GERANIUM FAMILY**)

Geranium carolinianum — **Carolina cranesbill.** May–July; native; fields, roadsides; throughout; common.

Geranium maculatum — **Wild geranium.** Apr.–June; native; dry to moist open woods, meadows, roadsides; throughout; common.

Geranium molle — **Dove's-foot cranesbill.** May–Aug.; introduced; fields, roadsides, lawns, disturbed sites; throughout; common.

Geranium pusillum — **Small-flowered cranesbill.** June–Sept.; introduced; fields, roadsides, disturbed sites; Piedmont and mountains; uncommon to common.

GUTTIFERAE — see HYPERICACEAE.

HYDROPHYLLACEAE (**WATERLEAF FAMILY**)

Ellisia nyctelea — **Ellisia.** Apr.–July; native; moist woods, floodplains; Piedmont and mountains; uncommon.

Hydrophyllum canadense — **Broad-leaved waterleaf.** May–June; native; moist woods, bottomland woods, floodplains; throughout; common (locally abundant).

Hydrophyllum virginianum — **Virginia waterleaf.** May–June; native; dry to moist woods; throughout; common.

Nemophila microcalyx — see *N. triloba.*

Nemophila triloba (N. microcalyx) — **Nemophila.** Apr.–May; native; moist woods; Coastal Plain; uncommon.

Phacelia dubia — **Small-flowered phacelia.** Apr.–May; native; rocky woods, rock outcrops; throughout; uncommon to common.

Phacelia purshii — **Miami mist.** Apr.–May; native; moist woods; Piedmont; rare to uncommon.

Phacelia ranunculacea — **Coville's phacelia, buttercup phacelia.** Apr.–May; native; moist woods; Coastal Plain and Piedmont; rare.

HYPERICACEAE (GUTTIFERAE) (ST. JOHNSWORT FAMILY)

Ascyrum hypericoides (*Hypericum hypericoides*) — **St. Andrew's cross.**
June–Aug.; native; open woods, dry fields; throughout; uncommon
to common.

Hypericum gentianoides — **Pineweed, orange grass.** July–Aug.; native;
dry fields, rock outcrops, disturbed sites; throughout; uncommon.

Hypericum hypericoides — see *Ascyrum hypericoides.*

Hypericum mutilum — **Dwarf St. Johnswort.** July–Sept.; native; wet
meadows, bogs, freshwater marshes; throughout; common.

Hypericum perforatum — **Common St. Johnswort.** June–Sept.; introduced; dry fields, roadsides; throughout; common.

Hypericum prolificum (*H. spathulatum*) — **Shrubby St. Johnswort.** July–
Sept.; native; dry open woods, rock outcrops; throughout; common.

Hypericum punctatum — **Spotted St. Johnswort.** June–Sept.; native;
moist fields, roadsides; throughout; common.

Hypericum spathulatum — see *H. prolificum.*

Hypericum virginicum (*Triadenum virginicum*) — **Marsh St. Johnswort.**
July–Aug.; native; swamps, bogs; Coastal Plain and mountains; uncommon.

Triadenum virginicum — see *Hypericum virginicum.*

LABIATAE — see LAMIACEAE.

LAMIACEAE (LABIATAE) (MINT FAMILY)

Ajuga reptans — **Bugleweed, bugle.** Apr.–July; introduced; lawns,
ditches, moist disturbed sites; throughout; uncommon.

Collinsonia canadensis — **Horse-balm.** July–Sept.; native; moist woods;
throughout; common.

Cunila origanoides — **Dittany.** July–Sept.; native; dry woods; throughout; common.

Glechoma hederacea — **Gill-over-the-ground, ground ivy.** Mar.–July; introduced; roadsides, lawns, disturbed sites; throughout; abundant.

Hedeoma pulegioides — **American pennyroyal.** July–Sept.; native; upland woods, clearings; throughout; common.

Lamium amplexicaule — **Henbit.** Mar.–Nov.; introduced; fields, lawns,
disturbed sites; throughout; abundant.

Lamium purpureum — **Purple dead-nettle.** Mar.–Oct.; introduced;
fields, roadsides, lawns, disturbed sites; throughout; abundant.

Leonurus cardiaca — **Motherwort.** June–Aug.; introduced; open woods, fields, roadsides, disturbed sites; mainly Piedmont and mountains; common.

Lycopus americanus — **Water horehound.** June–Sept.; native; freshwater marshes, pond shores; throughout; common.

Lycopus virginicus — **Virginia bugleweed.** July–Oct.; native; freshwater marshes, pond shores, riverbanks; throughout; common.

Mentha arvensis — **Wild mint.** July–Sept.; native; wet meadows, freshwater marshes; throughout; common.

Mentha piperita — **Peppermint.** June–Oct.; introduced; wet meadows, abandoned homesites; throughout; uncommon.

Mentha spicata — **Spearmint.** June–Aug.; introduced; streambanks, ditches, disturbed sites; throughout; uncommon.

Monarda clinopodia — **Basil balm.** June–Sept.; native; bottomland woods, floodplains, clearings; Piedmont and mountains; uncommon to common.

Monarda didyma — **Bee balm, Oswego tea.** July–Sept.; native; moist woods; mainly Piedmont and mountains; uncommon.

Monarda fistulosa — **Wild bergamot.** July–Aug.; native; borders of dry woods, dry fields, dry meadows; throughout (mainly Piedmont and mountains); common.

Monarda punctata — **Horsemint.** July–Oct.; native; dry woods, sandy fields; Coastal Plain and Piedmont; uncommon.

Nepeta cataria — **Catnip.** June–Sept.; introduced; fields, roadsides, disturbed sites; throughout; common.

Perilla frutescens — **Beefsteak plant.** Aug.–Oct.; introduced; borders of woods, fields, disturbed sites; throughout; abundant.

Prunella vulgaris — **Heal-all, selfheal.** May–Nov.; native and/or introduced; dry woods, fields, roadsides, lawns, disturbed sites; throughout; abundant.

Pycnanthemum incanum — **Hoary mountain-mint.** July–Sept.; native; dry woods, fields; throughout; uncommon to common.

Pycnanthemum tenuifolium — **Narrow-leaved mountain-mint.** July–Sept.; native; dry to moist fields; throughout; common.

Salvia lyrata — **Lyre-leaved sage.** Apr.–June; native; open woods, fields, meadows; throughout; common.

Satureja vulgaris — **Wild basil.** July–Sept.; native; dry open woods, edges of woods, fields; throughout; common.

Scutellaria elliptica — **Hairy skullcap.** May–June; native; dry upland woods; throughout; common.

Scutellaria epilobiifolia — see *S. galericulata*.

Scutellaria galericulata (*S. epilobiifolia*) — **Marsh skullcap.** June–Aug.; native; wet calcareous soils, marl marshes; mountains; very rare.

Scutellaria integrifolia — **Hyssop skullcap.** May–July; native; dry to wet woods, open fields; throughout; common.

Scutellaria lateriflora — **Mad-dog skullcap.** June–Sept.; native; moist woods, wet meadows, riverbanks; throughout; uncommon to common.

Scutellaria nervosa — **Veined skullcap.** May–June; native; moist woods; Piedmont and mountains; rare.

Scutellaria ovata — **Heart-leaved skullcap.** May–July; native; dry woods; Piedmont and mountains; uncommon.

Scutellaria saxatilis — **Rock skullcap.** June–Sept.; native; rocky woods; Piedmont and mountains; rare.

Scutellaria serrata — **Showy skullcap.** May–June; native; moist woods; Piedmont and mountains; uncommon.

Stachys hyssopifolia — **Hyssop-leaved hedge-nettle.** June–Aug.; native; moist sandy soils; throughout; rare.

Stachys tenuifolia — **Common hedge-nettle.** June–Sept.; native; wet meadows, freshwater marshes, streambanks; throughout; uncommon.

Teucrium canadense — **American germander, wood sage.** July–Sept.; native; wet woods, bottomlands, freshwater marshes, riverbanks; throughout; common.

Trichostema dichotomum — **Blue curls.** Aug.–Oct.; native; dry upland sandy fields; throughout; uncommon to common.

LEGUMINOSAE — see FABACEAE.

LENTIBULARIACEAE (**BLADDERWORT FAMILY**)

Utricularia gibba — **Humped bladderwort.** June–Sept.; native; ponds, freshwater marshes, shallow streams; Coastal Plain and Piedmont; uncommon.

Utricularia vulgaris — **Common bladderwort.** May–Sept.; native; ponds, ditches; mainly Coastal Plain; common.

LIMNANTHACEAE (**FALSE MERMAID FAMILY**)

Floerkea proserpinacoides — **False mermaid.** Apr.–June; native; floodplains, bottomlands; Piedmont; uncommon to common.

LINACEAE (FLAX FAMILY)

Linum sulcatum — **Grooved yellow flax.** July–Sept.; native; dry sandy fields, serpentine sites; Piedmont; rare.

Linum virginianum — **Wild yellow flax.** June–Sept.; native; dry fields; throughout; common.

LYTHRACEAE (LOOSESTRIFE FAMILY)

Cuphea petiolata — see *C. viscosissima*.

Cuphea viscosissima (*C. petiolata*) — **Clammy cuphea.** July–Oct.; native; fields, roadsides; throughout (mainly Piedmont and mountains); common.

Decodon verticillatus — **Swamp loosestrife, water willow.** July–Aug.; native; freshwater marshes, swamps; Coastal Plain; uncommon.

Lythrum alatum — **Winged loosestrife.** June–Sept.; native; wet calcareous soils; Piedmont and mountains; rare.

Lythrum salicaria — **Purple loosestrife.** June–Sept.; introduced; freshwater marshes, pond shores, ditches; throughout; common.

Rotala ramosior — **Toothcup.** June–Sept.; native; freshwater marshes, muddy banks, ditches, pond edges; throughout; uncommon.

MAGNOLIACEAE (MAGNOLIA FAMILY)

Magnolia virginiana — **Swamp magnolia, sweet bay.** May–July; native; swamps, bogs; Coastal Plain; common.

MALVACEAE (MALLOW FAMILY)

Abutilon theophrasti — **Indian mallow, velvetleaf.** July–Oct.; introduced; dry fields, disturbed sites; throughout; common.

Hibiscus laevis (*H. militaris*) — **Halberd-leaved rose mallow.** July–Sept.; native; freshwater marshes, riverbanks, streambanks, swamps; throughout (mainly Piedmont); uncommon to common.

Hibiscus militaris — see *H. laevis*.

Hibiscus moscheutos (including *H. palustris* by Gleason and Cronquist) — **Swamp rose mallow.** July–Sept.; native; freshwater marshes, riverbanks; throughout; common.

Hibiscus palustris — see *H. moscheutos*.

Kosteletzkya virginica — **Seashore mallow.** July–Sept.; native; brackish marshes, salt marshes; Coastal Plain; common.

Sida spinosa — **Prickly mallow.** June–Oct.; introduced; fields, disturbed sites; throughout; common.

MELASTOMATACEAE (MEADOW BEAUTY FAMILY)

Rhexia mariana — **Maryland meadow beauty.** June–Sept.; native; freshwater marshes, sandy bogs, wet meadows; throughout (mainly Coastal Plain and Piedmont); uncommon.

Rhexia virginica — **Virginia meadow beauty.** June–Sept.; native; moist to wet meadows, freshwater marshes, bogs; throughout; common.

NYCTAGINACEAE (FOUR-O'CLOCK FAMILY)

Mirabilis nyctaginea — **Wild four-o'clock.** June–Oct.; introduced; fields, disturbed sites; throughout; uncommon.

NYMPHAEACEAE (WATER-LILY FAMILY)

Nuphar advena — **Spatterdock, yellow pond-lily.** May–Oct.; native; ponds, slow-moving streams, freshwater marshes; throughout; common.

Nymphaea odorata — **Fragrant water-lily.** June-Sept.; native; ponds, slow-moving streams; throughout; uncommon.

OLEACEAE (**OLIVE FAMILY**)

Chionanthus virginicus — **Fringetree.** May; native; dry woods, rock outcrops; throughout; common.

ONAGRACEAE (EVENING-PRIMROSE FAMILY)

Circaea lutetiana (*C. quadrisulcata*) — **Enchanter's nightshade.** June–Sept.; native; moist woods; throughout; common.

Circaea quadrisulcata — see *C. lutetiana*.

Epilobium coloratum — **Purple-leaved willow-herb.** July–Oct.; native; wet meadows, freshwater marshes; throughout; uncommon.

Epilobium glandulosum — **Northern willow-herb.** June–Sept.; native; wet meadows; Piedmont and mountains; rare to uncommon.

Gaura biennis — **Biennial gaura.** July–Oct.; native; dry to moist open woods, fields, disturbed sites; throughout; common.

Ludwigia alternifolia — **Seedbox.** June–Sept.; native; wet meadows, freshwater marshes, swales; throughout; common.

Ludwigia palustris — **Water purslane.** June–Sept.; introduced; freshwater marshes, shallow ponds, shallow streams; throughout; common.

Oenothera argillicola — **Shale-barren evening-primrose.** June–Oct.; native; shale barrens; mountains; rare.

Oenothera biennis — **Common evening-primrose.** June–Oct.; native; dry open woods, fields, roadsides; throughout; common.

Oenothera fruticosa — **Sundrops.** May–Sept.; native; borders of woods, fields, meadows; throughout; common.

Oenothera laciniata — **Cut-leaved evening-primrose.** May–Oct.; native; dry fields, nutrient-poor soils; throughout (mainly Coastal Plain and Piedmont); common.

Oenothera perennis — **Small sundrops.** May–Aug.; native; dry to moist open woods, fields, meadows; Piedmont and mountains; uncommon.

OROBANCHACEAE (**BROOMRAPE FAMILY**)

Conopholis americana — **Squawroot.** Apr.–June; native; moist oak woods; throughout; common.

Epifagus virginiana — **Beechdrops.** Aug.–Oct.; native; beech woods; throughout; common.

Orobanche uniflora — **One-flowered cancer-root.** Apr.–June; native; moist woods; throughout; uncommon.

OXALIDACEAE (**WOOD-SORREL FAMILY**)

Oxalis acetosella — see *O. montana.*

Oxalis montana (*O. acetosella*) — **Common wood-sorrel.** May–Aug.; native; cool moist woods, coniferous forests; mountains; uncommon.

Oxalis stricta — **Yellow wood-sorrel.** Apr.–Oct.; native; open woods, dry fields, lawns, roadsides; throughout; abundant.

Oxalis violacea — **Violet wood-sorrel.** Apr.–July; native; dry to moist upland woods; throughout; uncommon to common.

PAPAVERACEAE (see also FUMARIACEAE) (**POPPY FAMILY**)

Chelidonium majus — **Celandine.** Apr.–July; introduced; borders of moist woods, roadsides; Piedmont and mountains; uncommon to common.

Papaver dubium — **Orange poppy.** May–July; introduced; fields, roadsides; throughout; common.

Sanguinaria canadensis — **Bloodroot.** Mar.–Apr.; native; upland woods; throughout; common.

Stylophorum diphyllum — **Celandine poppy.** Apr.–May; native to midwestern states; moist woods; throughout; rare.

PASSIFLORACEAE (**PASSION FLOWER FAMILY**)

Passiflora incarnata — **Passion flower, Maypops.** June–Aug.; native; fields, thickets, sandy soils; Coastal Plain and Piedmont; rare.

Passiflora lutea — **Yellow passion flower.** June–Aug.; native; borders of woods, floodplains, thickets; throughout; uncommon.

PHRYMACAEAE (**LOPSEED FAMILY**)

Phryma leptostachya — **Lopseed.** July–Sept.; native; moist woods; throughout; uncommon.

PHYTOLACCACEAE (**POKEWEED FAMILY**)

Phytolacca americana — **Pokeweed.** July–Oct.; native; damp fields, damp roadsides, disturbed sites; throughout; abundant.

PLANTAGINACEAE (**PLANTAIN FAMILY**)

Plantago aristata — **Bracted plantain.** June–Nov.; native; dry clearings, disturbed sites (nutrient-poor soils); throughout; uncommon.

Plantago lanceolata — **English plantain.** Apr.–Oct.; introduced; lawns, roadsides, disturbed sites; throughout; abundant.

Plantago rugelii — **Broad-leaved plantain.** July–Oct.; native; lawns, fields, disturbed sites; throughout; abundant.

PLUMBAGINACEAE (**LEADWORT FAMILY**)

Limonium carolinianum — **Sea lavender.** Aug.–Oct.; native; brackish marshes, salt marshes; Coastal Plain; uncommon.

POLEMONIACEAE (**PHLOX FAMILY**)

Phlox divaricata — **Wild blue phlox.** Apr.–June; native; moist woods, floodplains, bottomland woods; throughout; common.

Phlox maculata — **Wild sweet William.** May–July; native; wet meadows, streambanks, seeps; throughout; uncommon.

Phlox paniculata — **Fall phlox, garden phlox.** July–Oct.; native; moist open woods, floodplains; throughout; common.

Phlox stolonifera — **Creeping phlox.** Apr.–June; native to southern and central Appalachians (planted in our area).

Phlox subulata — **Moss phlox, moss pink.** Mar.–Dec.; native; rock outcrops, cliffs, shale barrens; throughout; common.

Polemonium reptans — **Greek valerian.** Apr.–June; native; moist woods; Piedmont and mountains; uncommon.

POLYGALACEAE (**MILKWORT FAMILY**)

Polygala cruciata — **Cross-leaved milkwort, marsh milkwort.** June–Oct.; native; bogs, wet sandy soils; Coastal Plain; rare.

Polygala paucifolia — **Fringed polygala, gaywings.** May–July; native; cool moist woods, moist meadows; mountains; uncommon.

Polygala polygama — **Racemed milkwort.** June–July; native; dry open woods, rock outcrops, dry clearings; Piedmont and mountains; rare to uncommon.

Polygala sanguinea — **Purple milkwort, field milkwort.** May–Oct.; native; dry to moist fields, clearings; throughout; uncommon.

POLYGONACEAE (BUCKWHEAT FAMILY)

Eriogonum allenii — **Shale-barren wild buckwheat.** July–Sept.; native; shale barrens; mountains; rare.

Polygonum amphibium (including *P. coccineum* by Gleason and Cronquist) — **Water smartweed.** June–Sept.; native and/or introduced; freshwater marshes, streambanks, ditches; throughout; common.

Polygonum arifolium — **Halberd-leaved tearthumb.** July–Oct.; native; freshwater marshes, wet soils; throughout; common.

Polygonum cespitosum — **Long-bristled smartweed.** June–Nov.; introduced; borders of moist woods, disturbed sites; throughout; abundant.

Polygonum coccineum — see *P. amphibium.*

Polygonum hydropiper — **Water-pepper, common smartweed.** June–Nov.; introduced; moist fields, swales; throughout; common.

Polygonum hydropiperoides — **Mild water-pepper.** June–Nov.; native; streambanks, freshwater marshes, swales; throughout; common.

Polygonum lapathifolium — **Pale smartweed.** July–Nov.; native; moist fields, streambanks, disturbed sites; throughout; common.

Polygonum pensylvanicum — **Pennsylvania smartweed, pinkweed.** May–Oct.; native; moist fields, freshwater marshes; throughout; common.

Polygonum persicaria — **Lady's thumb.** June–Oct.; introduced; lawns, disturbed sites; throughout; common.

Polygonum punctatum — **Water smartweed.** July–Oct.; native; wet meadows, freshwater marshes, swamps, wet clearings; throughout; common.

Polygonum sagittatum — **Arrow-leaved tearthumb.** June–Oct.; native; wet meadows, freshwater marshes, wet ditches; throughout; common.

Polygonum scandens — **Climbing false buckwheat.** Aug.–Nov.; native; bottomland woods, freshwater marshes, thickets; throughout; common.

Polygonum tenue — **Slender knotweed.** June–Oct.; native; dry fields, serpentine barrens, disturbed sites; throughout; uncommon.

Polygonum virginianum — see *Tovara virginiana.*

Rumex acetosella — **Sheep sorrel.** May–Sept.; introduced; fields, roadsides, disturbed sites; throughout; abundant.

Rumex verticillatus — **Water dock.** June–Sept.; native; swamps, ponds; Coastal Plain; common.

Tovara virginiana (*Polygonum virginianum*) — **Jumpseed, Virginia knotweed.** July–Nov.; native; moist woods, roadsides, thickets; throughout; common.

PORTULACACEAE (**PURSLANE FAMILY**)

Claytonia virginica — **Spring beauty.** Mar.–May; native; moist woods, bottomland woods; throughout; abundant.

Talinum teretifolium — **Fameflower.** June–Sept.; native; rock outcrops, serpentine barrens; Piedmont and mountains; rare.

PRIMULACEAE (**PRIMROSE FAMILY**)

Anagallis arvensis — **Scarlet pimpernel, poor man's weatherglass.** June–Aug.; introduced; sandy fields, lawns, disturbed sites; throughout; common.

Dodecatheon meadia — **Shooting star.** Apr.–May; native; open upland woods (mainly calcareous soils), bluffs, seeps; Piedmont and mountains; uncommon.

Lysimachia ciliata — **Fringed loosestrife.** June–Aug.; native; bottomland woods, moist meadows, freshwater marshes, streambanks; throughout; common.

Lysimachia nummularia — **Moneywort.** June–Aug.; introduced; shallow streams and pools; throughout; common.

Lysimachia quadrifolia — **Whorled loosestrife.** June–Aug.; native; dry to moist open woods, thickets; throughout; common.

Lysimachia terrestris — **Swamp candles.** June–Aug.; native; freshwater marshes, ditches; throughout; uncommon.

Samolus floribundus (*S. parviflorus*) — **Water pimpernel.** June–Aug.; native; shallow waters and muddy edges of streams, ponds, freshwater marshes; throughout (mainly Coastal Plain); uncommon.

Samolus parviflorus — see *S. floribundus.*

Trientalis borealis — **Starflower.** May–June; native; cool moist woods; mountains; rare.

PYROLACEAE (**PYROLA/WINTERGREEN FAMILY**)

Chimaphila maculata — **Spotted wintergreen.** June–July; native; dry acidic woods; throughout; common.

Chimaphila umbellata — **Pipsissewa.** June–July; native; dry acidic woods; throughout; common.

Monotropa hypopithys — **Pinesap.** June–Sept.; native; dry to moist woods; throughout; uncommon.

Monotropa uniflora — **Indian pipe.** June–Sept.; native; moist woods; throughout; common.

Pyrola elliptica — **Shinleaf.** June–Aug.; native; dry woods; Piedmont and mountains; rare to uncommon.

Pyrola rotundifolia — **Round-leaved pyrola.** June–Sept.; native; moist woods; throughout; uncommon.

RANUNCULACEAE (**BUTTERCUP FAMILY**)

Aconitum reclinatum — **White monkshood.** Aug.–Sept.; native; cool moist woods, seeps, streambanks; mountains; rare.

Actaea alba (*A. pachypoda*) — **White baneberry, doll's eyes.** May–June; native; cool moist woods; mountains; uncommon.

Actaea pachypoda — see *A. alba.*

Anemone quinquefolia — **Wood anemone.** Apr.–July; native; moist woods, seeps; throughout; uncommon.

Anemone virginiana — **Thimbleweed.** June–Aug.; native; dry open woods, thickets; throughout; common.

Anemonella thalictroides — **Rue-anemone.** Mar.–May; native; dry to moist woods; throughout; common.

Aquilegia canadensis — **Wild columbine.** Apr.–July; native; rocky woods, moist rock ledges, cliffs, rocky clearings; throughout; common.

Caltha palustris — **Marsh marigold.** Apr.–May; native; cool slow-moving streams, seeps, seepage swamps; Piedmont and mountains; uncommon.

Cimicifuga racemosa — **Black cohosh, bugbane.** June–Aug.; native; moist woods, roadsides; throughout; common.

Clematis dioscoreifolia — see *C. terniflora.*

Clematis ochroleuca — **Curlyheads.** Apr.–June; native; dry rocky woods; Piedmont and mountains; uncommon.

Clematis terniflora (including *C. dioscoreifolia* by Gleason and Cronquist) — **Japanese clematis.** July–Oct.; introduced; thickets, roadsides, disturbed sites; throughout; common.

Clematis viorna — **Leatherflower.** May–Aug.; native; moist rocky woods, thickets; Piedmont and mountains; uncommon.

Clematis virginiana — **Virgin's bower.** July–Sept.; native; wet meadows, edges of woods, thickets; throughout; common.

Coptis groenlandica (included in *C. trifolia* by Gleason and Cronquist) — **Goldthread.** May–July; native; cool moist woods; mountains; rare.

Coptis trifolia — see *C. groenlandica.*

Delphinium tricorne — **Dwarf larkspur.** Apr.–May; native; moist woods, bluffs (usually calcareous soils); mountains; uncommon.

Hepatica acutiloba — **Sharp-lobed hepatica.** Mar.–Apr.; native to southern Appalachians (mainly planted in our area).

Hepatica americana — **Round-lobed hepatica.** Mar.–Apr.; native; dry woods, rocky woods; throughout; common.

Hydrastis canadensis — **Goldenseal.** May; native; cool moist woods; Piedmont and mountains; rare (due to overcollecting for medicinal uses).

Isopyrum biternatum — **False rue-anemone.** Apr.–May; native; moist woods; Piedmont; very rare.

Ranunculus abortivus — **Aborted buttercup, kidney-leaf buttercup, small-flowered crowfoot.** Mar.–June; native; dry to moist woods; throughout; abundant.

Ranunculus acris — **Tall buttercup.** May–Aug.; introduced; fields, disturbed sites; throughout; common.

Ranunculus bulbosus — **Bulbous buttercup.** Apr.–June; introduced; fields, roadsides, lawns; throughout; common.

Ranunculus ficaria — **Lesser celandine.** Apr.–May; introduced; bottomland woods, moist woods; Coastal Plain and Piedmont; common (locally abundant).

Ranunculus hispidus (see also *R. septentrionalis*) — **Hispid buttercup.** Apr.–May; native; dry upland woods; throughout; common.

Ranunculus recurvatus — **Hooked crowfoot.** Apr.–July; native; moist woods, streambanks; throughout; common.

Ranunculus sceleratus — **Cursed crowfoot.** May–Aug.; native; shallow pools, wet meadows, freshwater marshes; throughout; uncommon.

Ranunculus septentrionalis (included in *R. hispidus* by Gleason and Cronquist) — **Swamp buttercup.** Apr.–July; native; floodplains, seeps, slow-moving streams; throughout; common.

Thalictrum coriaceum — **Leatherleaf meadowrue.** May–June; native; upland woods, bottomlands; Piedmont and mountains; uncommon to common.

Thalictrum dioicum — **Early meadowrue.** Apr.–May; native; moist woods; throughout; common.

Thalictrum polygamum — see *T. pubescens.*

Thalictrum pubescens (*T. polygamum*) — **Tall meadowrue.** June–July; native; wet meadows, streambanks; throughout; common.

Thalictrum revolutum — **Waxy meadowrue.** May–July; native; dry open fields, sterile soils; throughout; uncommon.

Trautvetteria caroliniensis — **Tasselrue.** June–July; native; seeps, moist woods, streambanks; Piedmont and mountains; uncommon.

ROSACEAE (ROSE FAMILY)

Agrimonia gryposepala — **Tall agrimony.** June–Aug.; native; moist woods, moist meadows, clearings; throughout; common.

Agrimonia parviflora — **Small-flowered agrimony.** Aug.–Sept.; native; dry to moist woods, wet meadows, clearings; throughout; common.

Amelanchier arborea — **Common shadbush, serviceberry.** Mar.–Apr.; native; dry upland woods; throughout; common.

Aruncus dioicus — **Goatsbeard.** May–July; native; moist woods, clearings; throughout; uncommon to common.

Duchesnea indica — **Indian strawberry.** Apr.–Oct.; introduced; roadsides, lawns, disturbed sites; throughout; abundant.

Fragaria virginiana — **Wild strawberry.** Apr.–June; native; fields, borders of woods; throughout; common.

Geum canadense — **White avens.** Aug.–Sept.; native; moist woods; throughout; common.

Geum vernum — **Spring avens.** Apr.; native; moist woods; Piedmont and mountains; uncommon.

Geum virginianum — **Rough avens.** June–July; native; dry to moist woods, thickets; throughout; uncommon.

Gillenia trifoliata — see *Porteranthus trifoliatus.*

Physocarpus opulifolius — **Ninebark.** May–July; native; rock outcrops, rocky streambanks; mainly Piedmont and mountains; uncommon to common.

Porteranthus trifoliatus (*Gillenia trifoliata*) — **Bowman's-root, Indian physic.** May–July; native; open woods, clearings; Piedmont and mountains; uncommon.

Potentilla canadensis — **Dwarf cinquefoil.** May–June; native; dry open woods, clearings, lawns; throughout; abundant.

Potentilla norvegica — **Rough cinquefoil.** June–Oct.; native; borders of wood, fields; throughout; common.

Potentilla recta — **Rough-fruited cinquefoil.** May–Aug.; introduced; dry fields, roadsides, disturbed sites; throughout; common.

Potentilla simplex — **Common cinquefoil.** Apr.–July; native; borders of woods, moist fields, meadows, lawns, disturbed sites; throughout; common.

Potentilla tridentata — **Three-toothed cinquefoil.** May–Oct.; native; cliffs, rock ledges, mountaintops; mountains; rare.

Rosa acicularis — **Prickly wild rose.** June–July; native; cool rock outcrops; very rare (see Ice Mountain).

Rosa carolina — **Pasture rose.** May–July; native; open woods, fields, roadsides; throughout; common.

Rosa multiflora — **Multiflora rose.** May–July; introduced; fields, thickets, disturbed sites; throughout; abundant.

Rosa palustris — **Swamp rose.** June–July; native; wet meadows, freshwater marshes, swamps; throughout (mainly Coastal Plain and Piedmont); common.

Rubus hispidus — **Swamp dewberry.** June–Sept.; native; bogs, moist acidic woods, swamps; throughout; common.

Rubus odoratus — **Purple-flowering raspberry.** June–Aug.; native; moist edges of woods; Piedmont and mountains (mainly mountains); common.

Sanguisorba canadensis — **Canadian burnet.** June–Oct.; native; wet meadows, seeps, seepage swamps; Piedmont and mountains; rare.

Spiraea alba var. *latifolia* — see *S. latifolia*.

Spiraea latifolia (*S. alba* var. *latifolia*) — **Meadowsweet.** June–Sept.; native; moist fields, meadows; Piedmont and mountains; uncommon to common.

RUBIACEAE (**MADDER FAMILY**)

Cephalanthus occidentalis — **Buttonbush.** June–Ang.; native; freshwater marshes, swamps, streambanks; throughout; common.

Diodia teres — **Buttonweed.** July–Oct.; native; dry fields, roadsides, disturbed sites; throughout; common.

Galium aparine — **Cleavers.** May–July; native; moist woods, thickets, disturbed sites; throughout; abundant.

Galium boreale — **Northern bedstraw.** May–Aug.; native; cool rocky woods; mountains; rare.

Galium circaezans — **Wild licorice.** May–June; native; dry woods; throughout; common.

Galium lanceolatum — **Lance-leaved wild licorice.** June–July; native; dry woods; throughout (mainly mountains); uncommon.

Galium tinctorium — **Clayton's bedstraw.** May–Aug.; native; moist meadows, freshwater marshes; throughout; common.

Galium triflorum — **Sweet-scented bedstraw.** June–Sept.; native; moist woods; throughout; common.

Galium verum — **Yellow bedstraw.** June–Sept.; introduced; fields, road-sides; mountains; uncommon (locally abundant).

Hedyotis caerula — see *Houstonia caerulea*.

Hedyotis longifolia — see *Houstonia longifolia*.

Hedyotis purpurea — see *Houstonia purpurea*.

Houstonia caerulea (*Hedyotis caerulea*) — **Bluets.** Apr.–Sept.; native; dry woods, fields, clearings, lawns; throughout; common.

Houstonia longifolia (*Hedyotis longifolia*) — **Long-leaved houstonia.** June–Sept.; native; rocky woods, rock outcrops; throughout (mainly Piedmont and mountains); common.

Houstonia purpurea (*Hedyotis purpurea*) — **Large-leaved houstonia, large houstonia.** May–July; native; rocky woods, dry clearings; throughout (mainly Coastal Plain and Piedmont); common.

Mitchella repens — **Partridgeberry.** May–July; native; dry acidic woods; throughout; common.

SANTALACEAE (**SANDALWOOD FAMILY**)

Comandra umbellata — **Bastard toadflax.** Apr.–July; native; dry nutrient-poor soils, upland woods, upland clearings; throughout; common.

SARRACENIACEAE (**PITCHER-PLANT FAMILY**)

Sarracenia purpurea — **Northern pitcher-plant.** May–Aug.; native; bogs; Coastal Plain and mountains; rare.

SAURURACEAE (**LIZARD'S-TAIL FAMILY**)

Saururus cernuus — **Lizard's-tail.** June–Aug.; native; swamps, shallow water; throughout; common.

SAXIFRAGACEAE (**SAXIFRAGE FAMILY**)

Chrysosplenium americanum — **Golden saxifrage.** Apr.–May; native; seeps, seepage swamps; throughout (mainly Piedmont and mountains); uncommon.

Heuchera americana — **Alumroot.** Apr.–June; native; rock outcrops, rocky slopes; throughout; common.

Mitella diphylla — **Miterwort, Bishop's-cap.** Apr.–June; native; cool moist woods, seeps, seepage swamps; Piedmont and mountains; uncommon.

Penthorum sedoides — **Ditch stonecrop.** July–Sept.; native; wet woods, freshwater marshes, muddy riverbanks; throughout; uncommon.

Saxifraga michauxii — **Michaux's saxifrage.** June–Sept.; native; moist cliffs, rock ledges; mountains; rare.

Saxifraga micranthidifolia—**Lettuce saxifrage.** May–June; native; rocky streams, seeps, seepage swamps; mountains; uncommon to common.

Saxifraga pensylvanica — **Swamp saxifrage.** May–June; native; rocky streams, seeps, seepage swamps; Piedmont and mountains; uncommon.

Saxifraga virginiensis — **Early saxifrage.** Mar.–May; native; rocky woods, rock outcrops; throughout; common.

Tiarella cordifolia — **Foamflower.** Apr.–June; native; moist woods; Piedmont and mountains; uncommon.

SCROPHULARIACEAE (**SNAPDRAGON FAMILY**)

Agalinis purpurea (*Gerardia purpurea*) — **Purple gerardia.** July–Oct.; native; streambanks, wet meadows, clearings, roadsides; throughout; common.

Agalinis tenuifolia (*Gerardia tenuifolia*) — **Slender gerardia.** Aug.–Oct.; native; dry meadows, clearings; throughout; common.

Aureolaria flava (*Gerardia flava*) — **Smooth false-foxglove.** July–Sept.; native; dry woods; Piedmont and mountains; uncommon.

Aureolaria pedicularia (*Gerardia pedicularia*) — **Fern-leaved false-foxglove.** Sept.–Oct.; native; sandy woods, dry fields; throughout; uncommon.

Aureolaria virginica (*Gerardia virginica*) — **Downy false-foxglove.** June–Aug.; native; borders of dry woods; throughout; common.

Chelone glabra — **White turtlehead.** Aug.–Oct.; native; wet woods, wet meadows, streambanks, marshes, seepage swamps; throughout; common.

Chelone obliqua — **Red turtlehead.** Aug.–Oct.; native; wet woods, swamps; Coastal Plain; rare.

Cymbalaria muralis — **Kenilworth ivy.** May–Oct.; introduced; rock walls; throughout; uncommon.

Gerardia flava — see *Aureolaria flava.*

Gerardia pedicularia — see *Aureolaria pedicularia.*

Gerardia purpurea — see *Agalinis purpurea.*

Gerardia tenuifolia — see *Agalinis tenuifolia.*

Gerardia virginica — see *Aureolaria virginica.*

Linaria canadensis — **Blue toadflax.** Apr.–Sept.; native; dry sterile sandy soils, fields, roadsides; Coastal Plain and Piedmont; common.

Linaria vulgaris — **Butter-and-eggs.** June–Oct.; introduced; dry fields, roadsides; throughout; common.

Lindernia dubia — **False pimpernel.** June–Sept.; native; muddy riverbanks, streambanks; throughout; uncommon.

Melampyrum lineare — **Cow-wheat.** June–Sept.; native; dry woods, clearings, roadsides; Coastal Plain and mountains; common.

Mimulus alatus — **Winged monkey-flower.** June–Aug.; native; wet meadows, riverbanks, streambanks, freshwater marshes, wet soils; throughout; common.

Mimulus ringens — **Square-stemmed monkey-flower.** June–Sept.; native; wet meadows, freshwater marshes, streambanks, pond edges, wet soils; throughout; common.

Pedicularis canadensis — **Lousewort, wood betony.** Apr.–May; native; dry to moist woods, clearings; throughout (mainly mountains); common.

Penstemon canescens — **Gray beardtongue.** May–July; native; dry upland woods, fields; throughout (mainly mountains); common.

Penstemon digitalis — **White beardtongue, foxglove beardtongue.** May–July; native; fields, roadsides; Piedmont and mountains; uncommon to common.

Penstemon hirsutus — **Hairy beardtongue.** May–July; native; dry rocky soils, clearings; Piedmont and mountains; rare to uncommon.

Penstemon laevigatus — **Smooth beardtongue.** May–June; native; moist woods, moist meadows; throughout; uncommon.

Scrophularia lanceolata — **Hare figwort.** May–June; native; open woods, fields; throughout (mainly mountains); uncommon.

Scrophularia marilandica — **Maryland figwort.** June–July; native; open woods; throughout; uncommon.

Verbascum blattaria — **Moth mullein.** June–Sept.; introduced; fields, roadsides, disturbed sites; throughout; common.

Verbascum thapsus — **Common mullein.** June–Sept.; introduced; fields, roadsides, disturbed sites; throughout; abundant.

Veronica americana — **American brookline.** May–July; native; streambanks, seeps, springs; Piedmont and mountains; uncommon.

Veronica hederaefolia — **Ivy-leaved speedwell.** Mar.–June; introduced; woods, lawns, disturbed sites; throughout; abundant.

Veronica officinalis — **Common speedwell.** May–July; native; dry fields; throughout; common.

Veronica persica — **Bird's-eye speedwell.** Mar.–Aug.; introduced; lawns, roadsides, disturbed sites; throughout; common.

Veronica serpyllifolia — **Thyme-leaved speedwell.** Apr.–July; introduced; lawns, fields; throughout; common.

Veronicastrum virginicum — **Culver's-root.** June–Sept.; native; floodplains, rocky riverbanks; Piedmont and mountains; uncommon.

SOLANACEAE (TOMATO/NIGHTSHADE FAMILY)

Datura stramonium — **Jimsonweed.** July–Oct.; introduced; dry fields, disturbed sites; throughout; common.

Physalis heterophylla — **Clammy ground-cherry.** June–Sept.; native; dry to moist fields, woodlots, disturbed sites; throughout; common.

Physalis virginiana — **Virginia ground-cherry.** June–Aug.; native; dry fields, clearings; throughout; common.

Solanum carolinense — **Horse nettle.** May–Oct.; native; dry fields, disturbed sites; throughout; common.

Solanum dulcamara — **Bittersweet nightshade.** June–Sept.; introduced; moist open woods, thickets, disturbed sites; throughout (mainly Piedmont and mountains); common.

UMBELLIFERAE — see APIACEAE.

VALERIANACEAE (**VALERIAN FAMILY**)

Valeriana pauciflora — **Few-flowered valerian.** May–June; native; moist woods, floodplains, bottomland woods; Piedmont; rare.

Valerianella locusta (*V. olitoria*) — **Corn salad.** Apr.–June; introduced; fields, disturbed sites; throughout; uncommon.

Valerianella olitoria — see *V. locusta.*

VERBENACEAE (**VERVAIN FAMILY**)

Lippia lanceolata (*Phyla lanceolata*) — **Fog-fruit, frog-fruit.** May–Oct.; native; muddy stream banks, wet meadows, swales; throughout; uncommon.

Phyla lanceolata — see *Lippia lanceolata.*

Verbena hastata — **Blue vervain.** June–Oct.; native; moist meadows, freshwater marshes, riverbanks, streambanks; throughout; uncommon.

Verbena simplex — **Narrow-leaved vervain.** June–Sept.; introduced; dry sandy fields, clearings; throughout; common.

Verbena urticifolia — **White vervain.** June–Oct.; native; moist open woods, fields, thickets; throughout; common.

VIOLACEAE (**VIOLET FAMILY**)

Hybanthus concolor — **Green violet.** May–June; native; rock outcrops, rocky upland woods (usually calcareous soils); Piedmont and mountains; uncommon.

Viola blanda — **Sweet white violet.** Apr.–May; native; moist woods; throughout; uncommon.

Viola canadensis — **Canada violet.** Apr.–May; native; cool moist woods; Piedmont and mountains; uncommon.

Viola conspersa — **Dog violet.** Apr.–May; native; moist woods; Piedmont and mountains; uncommon.

Viola cucullata — **Marsh blue violet.** Apr.–May; native; cool rocky streams, seepage swamps; throughout; common.

Viola fimbriatula (included in *V. sagittata* by Gleason and Cronquist) — **Ovate-leaved violet, Northern downy violet.** Apr.–May; native; dry woods, clearings; Piedmont and mountains; uncommon.

Viola hastata — **Halberd-leaved violet.** Apr.–May; native; cool dry upland wood; mountains; uncommon.

Viola hirsutula (included in *V. villosa* by Gleason and Cronquist) — **Southern wood violet.** Apr.–May; native; dry upland woods; throughout (mainly Piedmont and mountains); uncommon.

Viola kitaibeliana — see *V. rafinesquii.*

Viola macloskeyi — see *V. pallens.*

Viola pallens (included in *V. macloskeyi* by Gleason and Cronquist) — **Northern white violet.** Apr.–May; native; streambanks, seeps, cool moist woods; mountains; uncommon.

Viola palmata (see also *V. triloba*) — **Palmate-leaved violet, wood violet, early blue violet.** Apr.–May; native; dry woods, clearings; Piedmont and mountains; common.

Viola papilionacea (included in *V. sororia* by Gleason and Cronquist) — **Common blue violet.** Apr.–May; native; moist woods, lawns, disturbed sites; throughout; abundant.

Viola pedata — **Birdfoot violet.** Apr.–May; native; dry rocky or sandy clearings, rock outcrops, shale barrens; throughout; uncommon to common.

Viola pensylvanica (included in *V. pubescens* by Gleason and Cronquist) — **Smooth yellow violet.** Apr.–May; native; moist woods, bottomlands; throughout (mainly Piedmont and mountains); common.

Viola primulifolia — **Primrose-leaved violet.** Apr.–May; native; wet woods, streambanks, clearings; throughout (mainly Coastal Plain); uncommon.

Viola pubescens (see also *V. pensylvanica*) — **Downy yellow violet.** Apr.–May; native; dry upland woods; throughout (mainly Piedmont and mountains); uncommon.

Viola rafinesquii (included in *V. kitaibeliana* in *Gray's Manual*) — **Field pansy.** Apr.–May; native; fields, roadsides, lawns; throughout; common.

Viola sagittata (see also *V. fimbriatula*) — **Arrow-leaved violet.** Apr.–May; native; dry fields, clearings; throughout; uncommon.

Viola septentrionalis (included in *V. sororia* by Gleason and Cronquist) — **Northern blue violet.** Apr.–May; native; cool moist woods; mountains; uncommon.

Viola sororia (see also *V. papilionacea* and *V. septentrionalis*) — **Woolly blue violet.** Apr.–May; native; wet to moist woods, clearings; throughout; uncommon.

Viola striata — **Pale violet, cream violet.** Apr.–May; native; moist woods, bottomlands; throughout; common.

Viola triloba (included in *V. palmata* by Gleason and Cronquist) — **Three-lobed violet.** Apr.–May; native; dry upland woods, clearings; throughout (mainly Piedmont and mountains); common.

Viola villosa — see *V. hirsutula.*

Appendix A
New Scientific Names Used in This Book

Actaea alba (*A. pachypoda*)

Agalinis purpurea (*Gerardia purpurea*)

Agalinis tenuifolia (*Gerardia tenuifolia*)

Alliaria petiolata (*A. officinalis*)

Aster lanceolatus (*A. simplex*)

Aureolaria flava (*Gerardia flava*)

Aureolaria pedicularia (*Gerardia pedicularia*)

Aureolaria virginica (*Gerardia virginica*)

Cardamine rhomboidea (*C. bulbosa*)

Circaea lutetiana (*C. quadrisulcata*)

Cuphea viscosissima (*C. petiolata*)

Eupatorium rotundifolium (*E. pubescens*)

Helenium flexuosum (*H. nudiflorum*)

Hibiscus laevis (*H. militaris*)

Hieracium caespitosum (*H. pratense*)

Hypericum prolificum (*H. spathulatum*)

Matelea carolinensis (*Gonolobus carolinensis*)

Murdannia keisak (*Aneilema keisak*)

Nemophila triloba (*N. microcalyx*)

Phragmites australis (*P. communis*)

Pluchea odorata (*P. purpurascens*)

Porteranthus trifoliatus (*Gillenia trifoliata*)

Rhododendron periclymenoides (*R. nudiflorum*)

Rhododendron prinophyllum (*R. roseum*)

Sagittaria lancifolia (*S. falcata*)

Samolus floribundus (*S. parviflorus*)

Scutellaria galericulata (*S. epilobiifolia*)

Taenidia montana (*Pseudotaenidia montana*)

Thalictrum pubescens (*T. polygamum*)

Triodanis perfoliata (*Specularia perfoliata*)

Valerianella locusta (*V. olitoria*)

Verbesina alternifolia (*Actinomeris alternifolia*)

Viola rafinesquii (*V. kitaibeliana*)

Appendix B

Blooming Date Calendar

Feb Mar Apr May Jun Jul Aug Sep Oct

Skunk cabbage (*Symplocarpus foetidus*)
Harbinger-of-spring (*Erigenia bulbosa*)
Dead-nettle, purple (*Lamium purpureum*)
Hepatica, round-lobed (*Hepatica americana*)
Phlox, moss (*Phlox subulata*)
Spring beauty (*Claytonia virginica*)
Bloodroot (*Sanguinaria canadensis*)
Speedwell, ivy-leaved (*Veronica hederaefolia*)
Twinleaf (*Jeffersonia diphylla*)
Arbutus, trailing (*Epigaea repens*)
Buttercup, aborted (*Ranunculus abortivus*)
Ragwort, golden (*Senecio aureus*)
Rue-anemone (*Anemonella thalictroides*)
Saxifrage, early (*Saxifraga virginiensis*)
Trout-lily (*Erythronium americanum*)
Toothwort, cut-leaved (*Dentaria laciniata*)
Bluets (*Houstonia caerulea*)
Bluebells, Virginia (*Mertensia virginica*)
Cress, spring (*Cardamine rhomboidea*)
Dutchman's breeches (*Dicentra cucullaria*)
Violet, common blue (*Viola papilionacea*)
Alexanders, golden (*Zizia aurea*)
Buttercup, bulbous (*Ranunculus bulbosus*)
Chickweed, star (*Stellaria pubera*)
Phlox, wild blue (*Phlox divaricata*)
Pussytoes, plantain-leaved (*Antennaria plantaginifolia*)
Toothwort, slender (*Dentaria heterophylla*)
Trillium, sessile (*Trillium sessile*)
Ginger, wild (*Asarum canadense*)
Strawberry, Indian (*Duchesnea indica*)
Violet, birdfoot (*Viola pedata*)
Violet, smooth yellow (*Viola pensylvanica*)
Chickweed, field (*Cerastium arvense*)
Cinquefoil, common (*Potentilla simplex*)
Columbine, wild (*Aquilegia canadensis*)
Dogwood, flowering (*Cornus florida*)
Fleabane, common (*Erigeron philadelphicus*)
Geranium, wild (*Geranium maculatum*)
Iris, vernal (*Iris verna*)
Redbud (*Cercis canadensis*)
Squirrel corn (*Dicentra canadensis*)
Stonecrop, wild (*Sedum ternatum*)
Wood-sorrel, violet (*Oxalis violacea*)
Chrysogonum (*Chrysogonum virginianum*)
Jack-in-the-pulpit (*Arisaema triphyllum*)

	Feb	Mar	Apr	May	Jun	Jul	Aug	Sep	Oct

Meadowrue, early (*Thalictrum dioicum*)
Pink, wild (*Silene caroliniana*)
Sage, lyre-leaved (*Salvia lyrata*)
Stargrass, yellow (*Hypoxis hirsuta*)
Strawberry, wild (*Fragaria virginiana*)
Sweet Cicely (*Osmorhiza claytoni*)
Alumroot (*Heuchera americana*)
Bellwort, perfoliate (*Uvularia perfoliata*)
Fleabane, common (*Erigeron philadelphicus*)
Mayapple (*Podophyllum peltatum*)
Pinxter flower (*Rhododendron periclymenoides*)
Trillium, large-flowered (*Trillium grandiflorum*)
Azalea, rose (*Rhododendron prinophyllum*)
Buttercup, tall (*Ranunculus acris*)
Heal-all (*Prunella vulgaris*)
Orchis, showy (*Orchis spectabilis*)
Partridgeberry (*Mitchella repens*)
Pink, Deptford (*Dianthus armeria*)
Solomon's-seal, smooth (*Polygonatum biflorum*)
Spiderwort (*Tradescantia virginiana*)
Beardtongue, gray (*Penstemon canescens*)
Blue-eyed grass, stout (*Sisyrinchium angustifolium*)
Lady's-slipper, pink (*Cypripedium acaule*)
Lady's-slipper, yellow (*Cypripedium calceolus*)
Mountain laurel (*Kalmia latifolia*)
Rattlesnake-weed (*Hieracium venosum*)
Solomon's-seal, false (*Smilacina racemosa*)
Waterleaf, Virginia (*Hydrophyllum virginianum*)
Campion, bladder (*Silene vulgaris*)
Clover, white (*Trifolium repens*)
Daisy, ox-eye (*Chrysanthemum leucanthemum*)
Dame's rocket (*Hesperis matronalis*)
Flag, larger blue (*Iris versicolor*)
Iris, yellow (*Iris pseudacorus*)
Leatherflower (*Clematis viorna*)
Puttyroot (*Aplectrum hyemale*)
Rosebay (*Rhododendron maximum*)
Skullcap, hyssop (*Scutellaria integrifolia*)
Smartweed, Pennsylvania (*Polygonum pensylvanicum*)
Snakeroot, clustered (*Sanicula gregaria*)
Sweet clover, yellow (*Melilotus officinalis*)
Venus's looking-glass (*Triodanis perfoliata*)
Vetch, narrow-leaved (*Vicia angustifolia*)
Vetch, spring (*Vicia sativa*)
Chicory (*Cichorium intybus*)

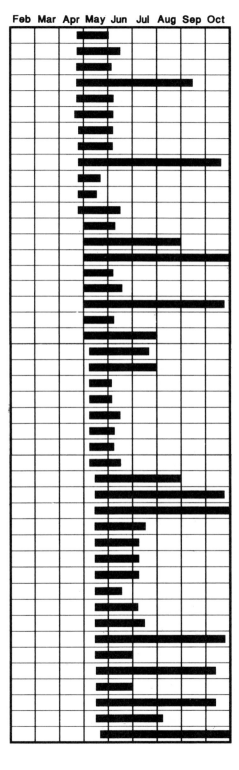

Evening-primrose, cut-leaved (*Oenothera laciniata*)
Hawkweed, field (*Hieracium caespitosum*)
Rose, pasture (*Rosa carolina*)
Skullcap, hairy (*Scutellaria elliptica*)
Sundrops (*Oenothera fruticosa*)
Yarrow (*Achillea millefolium*)
Bindweed, field (*Convolvulus arvensis*)
Black-eyed Susan (*Rudbeckia hirta*)
Dayflower, Virginia (*Commelina virginica*)
Evening-primrose, common (*Oenothera biennis*)
Ground-cherry, Virginia (*Physalis virginiana*)
Queen Anne's lace (*Daucus carota*)
Pimpernel, scarlet (*Anagallis arvensis*)
Ruellia, hairy (*Ruellia caroliniensis*)
Tearthumb, arrow-leaved (*Polygonum sagittatum*)
Thimbleweed (*Anemone virginiana*)
Viper's bugloss (*Echium vulgare*)
Wintergreen, spotted (*Chimaphila maculata*)
Butterflyweed (*Asclepias tuberosa*)
Milkweed, common (*Asclepias syriaca*)
Prickly pear (*Opuntia humifusa*)
Rose, swamp (*Rosa palustris*)
Twayblade, lily-leaved (*Liparis lilifolia*)
Buttonbush (*Cephalanthus occidentalis*)
Loosestrife, fringed (*Lysimachia ciliata*)
Basil balm (*Monarda clinopodia*)
Butterfly pea (*Clitoria mariana*)
Knapweed, spotted (*Centaurea maculosa*)
Cohosh, black (*Cimicifuga racemosa*)
Jewelweed, spotted (*Impatiens capensis*)
Loosestrife, whorled (*Lysimachia quadrifolia*)
Meadowrue, tall (*Thalictrum pubescens*)
Milkweed, swamp (*Asclepias incarnata*)
Monkey-flower, square-stemmed (*Mimulus ringens*)
Mullein, common (*Verbascum thapsus*)
Pokeweed (*Phytolacca americana*)
St. Johnswort, spotted (*Hypericum punctatum*)
Sunflower, thin-leaved (*Helianthus decapetalus*)
Thistle, nodding (*Carduus nutans*)
Thistle, pasture (*Cirsium pumilum*)
Vervain, blue (*Verbena hastata*)
Vervain, white (*Verbena urticifolia*)
Bergamot, wild (*Monarda fistulosa*)
Bouncing Bet (*Saponaria officinalis*)
Campion, starry (*Silene stellata*)

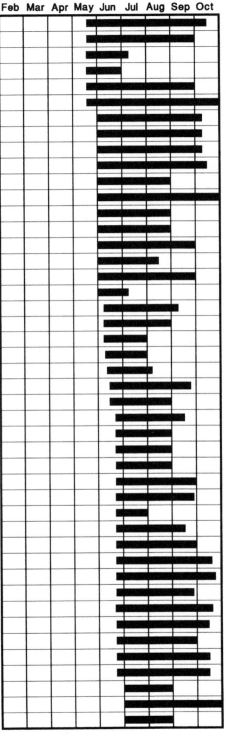

Feb Mar Apr May Jun Jul Aug Sep Oct

Species	Feb	Mar	Apr	May	Jun	Jul	Aug	Sep	Oct
Indian tobacco (*Lobelia inflata*)						■	■	■	■
Mint, wild (*Mentha arvensis*)						■	■	■	■
Rattlesnake-plantain, downy (*Goodyera pubescens*)						■	■		
Rose mallow, swamp (*Hibiscus moscheutos*)						■	■	■	
Sunflower, woodland (*Helianthus divaricatus*)						■	■	■	■
Bushclover, slender (*Lespedeza virginica*)							■	■	
Cardinal flower (*Lobelia cardinalis*)						■	■	■	
False-foxglove, smooth (*Aureolaria flava*)						■	■	■	
Goldenrod, early (*Solidago juncea*)						■	■	■	
Hawkweed, panicled (*Hieracium paniculatum*)						■	■	■	
Lily, Turk's-cap (*Lilium superbum*)						■	■		
Rose mallow, halberd-leaved (*Hibiscus laevis*)							■	■	
Teasel (*Dipsacus laciniatus*)						■	■	■	
Aster, white wood (*Aster divaricatus*)						■	■	■	■
Blazing-star, spiked (*Liatris spicata*)						■	■	■	
Boneset (*Eupatorium perfoliatum*)							■	■	■
Bur-marigold, larger (*Bidens laevis*)							■	■	
Elephant's-foot (*Elephantopus carolinianus*)							■	■	
Gerardia, purple (*Agalinis purpurea*)							■	■	
Joe-Pye-weed, hollow (*Eupatorium fistulosum*)							■	■	
Mistflower (*Eupatorium coelestinum*)						■	■	■	
Mountain-mint, narrow-leaved (*Pycnanthemum tenuifolium*)						■	■		
Orchid, cranefly (*Tipularia discolor*)						■	■		
Rosinweed, whorled (*Silphium trifoliatum*)						■	■	■	
Tick-trefoil, hoary (*Desmodium canescens*)						■	■	■	
Wingstem (*Verbesina alternifolia*)							■	■	
Goldenrod, blue-stemmed (*Solidago caesia*)							■	■	■
Aster, bushy (*Aster dumosus*)							■	■	■
Aster, heart-leaved (*Aster cordifolius*)							■	■	■
Aster, New England (*Aster novae-angliae*)							■	■	■
Avens, white (*Geum canadense*)							■	■	
Goldenrod, elm-leaved (*Solidago ulmifolia*)							■	■	■
Goldenrod, zigzag (*Solidago flexicaulis*)							■	■	■
Jerusalem artichoke (*Helianthus tuberosus*)							■	■	■
Ironweed, New York (*Vernonia noveboracensis*)							■	■	
Silverrod (*Solidago bicolor*)							■	■	■
Snakeroot, white (*Eupatorium rugosum*)							■	■	■
Sneezeweed, yellow (*Helenium autumnale*)							■	■	■
Tickseed-sunflower (*Bidens polylepis*)							■	■	■
Turtlehead, white (*Chelone glabra*)							■	■	■
Aster, late purple (*Aster patens*)								■	■
Goldenrod, late (*Solidago gigantea*)								■	■
Lobelia, great (*Lobelia siphilitica*)								■	
Gentian, fringed (*Gentiana crinita*)								■	■
Gentian, closed (*Gentiana clausa*)									■

Appendix C

Regional Organizations and Park Administrative Offices in the Washington-Baltimore Area

Selected Regional Organizations

Audubon Naturalist Society, 8940 Jones Mill Rd., Chevy Chase, MD 20815. (301) 652-9188.

Blandy Experimental Farm (State Arboretum of Virginia), P.O. Box 175, Boyce, VA 22620. (703) 837-1758.

Botanical Society of Washington, Department of Botany, National Museum of Natural History, Smithsonian Institution. Constitution Ave. at 10th St., NW, Washington, DC 20560. (202) 357-1300.

Cylburn Arboretum (Department of Recreation and Parks, City of Baltimore), 4915 Greenspring Ave., Baltimore, MD 21209. (401) 367-2217.

Green Spring Gardens Park (Fairfax County Park Authority), 4603 Green Spring Rd., Alexandria, VA 22312. (703) 642-5173.

Maryland Native Plant Society, P.O. Box 4877, Silver Spring, MD 20914.

Mount Cuba Center for the Study of Piedmont Flora, Box 3570, Greenville, DE 19807. (302) 239-4244.

National Arboretum (U.S. Department of Agriculture), 3501 New York Ave., NE, Washington, DC 20002. (202) 475-4815.

National Wildlife Federation, 8925 Leesburg Pike, Vienna, VA 22180. (703) 790-4000.

Natural Heritage Programs

Division of Natural Heritage, Virginia Dept. of Conservation and Recreation, 1500 E. Main St., Suite 312, Richmond, VA 23219. (804) 786-7951.

Natural Heritage Program, Maryland Department of Natural Resources, Tawes State Office Bldg., 580 Taylor Ave., Annapolis, MD. 21401 (410) 974-2870.

Pennsylvania Natural Diversity Inventory, PNDI–East, The Nature Conservancy, 34 Airport Dr., Middleton, PA 17057. (717) 948-3962.

West Virginia Natural Heritage Program, P.O. Box 67, Elkins, WV 26241. (304) 637-0245.

Natural History Society of Maryland, 2643 N. Charles St., Baltimore, MD 21218. (410) 235-6116.

Nature Conservancy, The
  Maryland: 2 Wisconsin Circle, Suite 600, Chevy Chase, MD 20815. (301) 656-8673.
  Pennsylvania: 1211 Chestnut St., Philadelphia, PA 19107. (215) 963-1400.
  Virginia: 1110 Rose Hill Dr., Charlottesville, VA 22901. (804) 295-6106.
  West Virginia: P.O. Box 3754, Charleston, WV 25337. (304) 345-4350.

Virginia Native Plant Society, P.O. Box 844, Annandale, VA 22003.

West Virginia Native Plant Society, Corresponding Secretary, P.O. Box 2755, Elkins, WV 26241.

Selected Park Administrative Offices in the Washington-Baltimore Area

Calvert County, Natural Resources Division, Calvert County Courthouse, Prince Frederick, MD 20678. (410) 535-5327.

Carroll County, Department of Recreation and Parks, 125 N. Court St., Suite 205, Westminster, MD 21157. (410) 857-2103.

City of Baltimore, Department of Recreation and Parks, 3001 East Drive, Baltimore, MD 21217. (410) 396-7900.

Fairfax County Park Authority, 3701 Pender Drive, Fairfax, VA 22030. (703) 246-5700.

Howard County, Department of Recreation and Parks, Executive Center, Suite 170, 3300 N. Ridge Rd., Ellicott City, MD 21043.

Maryland Department of Natural Resources, Tawes State Office Bldg., 580 Taylor Ave., Annapolis, MD 21401. (410) 974-3195.

Maryland National Capital Park and Planning Commission, Montgomery County Department of Parks, 9500 Brunett Ave., Silver Spring, MD 20901. (301) 495-2525.

Prince George's County Department of Recreation and Parks, 6600 Kenilworth Ave., Riverdale, MD 20740. (301) 918-8111.

National Park Service, U.S. Department of Interior
  C&O Canal National Historical Park, Box 158, Sharpsburg, MD 21782. (301) 432-5124.
  George Washington Memorial Parkway, c/o Turkey Run Park, McLean, VA 22201. (703) 285-2598.
  National Capital Parks East, 1099 Anacostia Dr., SE, Washington, DC 20020. (202) 433-1190.
  Shenandoah Office, Luray, VA 22835. (703) 999-2266.

Northern Virginia Regional Park Authority, 5400 Ox Rd., Fairfax Station, VA 22039. (703) 352-5900.

Prince William County Park Authority, 12249 Bristow Rd., Bristow, VA 22013. (703) 361-7871.

Virginia Department of Conservation and Recreation, Division of Parks and
    Recreation, 1500 E. Main St., Richmond, VA 23219. (804) 786-1712.
West Virginia Department of Natural Resources, Bldg. 3, Rm. 669, 1900 Ka-
    nawha Blvd. E., Charleston, WV 25305-0660. (304) 558-2754.

Bibliography

Berman, Richard L., and Deborah Gerhard. 1991. *Natural Washington.* McLean, Va.: EPM Publications.

Briggs, Shirley A. ed. 1954. Washington—*City in the Woods.* Washington, D.C.: Audubon Society of the District of Columbia.

Britton, Nathaniel Lord, and Hon. Addison Brown. 1970. *An Illustrated Flora of the Northern United States and Canada.* Vols. 1–3. New York: Dover Publications.

Brooks, Maurice. 1975. *The Appalachians.* Grantsville, W. Va.: Seneca Books.

Brown, Melvin L., and Russell G. Brown. 1984. *Herbaceous Plants of Maryland.* Baltimore: Port City Press.

Brown, Russell G., and Melvin L. Brown. 1972. *Woody Plants of Maryland.* Baltimore: Port City Press.

Carr, Martha S. 1950. *The District of Columbia: Its Rocks and Their Geologic History.* U.S. Geological Survey Bulletin 967. Washington, D.C.: U.S. Government Printing Office.

Choukas-Bradley, Melanie, and Polly Alexander. 1987. *City of Trees: The Complete Field Guide to the Trees of Washington, D.C.* Baltimore: Johns Hopkins University Press.

Conners, John A. 1988. *Shenandoah National Park; an Interpretive Guide.* Blacksburg, VA.: McDonald & Woodward Publishing.

Core, Earl L. 1966. *Vegetation of West Virginia.* Parsons, W. Va.: McClain Printing.

Courtenay, Booth, and James Hall Zimmerman. 1972. *Wildflowers and Weeds.* New York: Van Nostrand Reinhold.

Denton, Molly Taber. 1979. *Wildflowers of the Potomac Appalachians.* Washington, D.C.: Potomac Appalachian Trail Club.

Dietrich, Richard V. 1970. *Geology and Virginia.* Charlottesville: University Press of Virginia.

Fernald, Merritt Lyndon. 1970. *Gray's Manual of Botany.* 8th edition. New York: D. Van Nostrand.

Fisher, George W., F. J. Pettijohn, J. C. Reed, Jr., and Kenneth Weaver, eds. 1970. *Studies of Appalachian Geology: Central and Southern.* New York: John Wiley & Sons.

Frye, Keith. 1986. *Roadside Geology of Virginia.* Missoula, Mont.: Mountain Press Publishing.

Gleason, Henry A., and Arthur Cronquist. 1991. *Manual of Vascular Plants of Northeastern United States and Adjacent Canada.* 2nd edition. Bronx: New York Botanical Garden.

Godfrey, Michael A. 1980. *A Sierra Club Naturalist's Guide: The Piedmont.* San Francisco: Sierra Club Books.

Harvill, Jr., A.M., Ted R. Bradley, Charles E. Stevens, Thomas F. Wieboldt, Donna M. E. Ware, Douglas W. Ogle, Gwynn W. Ramsey, Gary P. Fleming. 1992. *Atlas of the Virginia Flora.* 3rd edition. Burkeville, Va.: Virginia Botanical Associates.

Haug, Elaine. 1984. *The Flora of Prince William County.* Manassas, Va.: Prince William Wildflower Society.

Hermann, Frederick J. 1946. *A Checklist of Plants in the Washington-Baltimore Area.* 2nd edition. Conference on District Flora. Washington, D.C.: Smithsonian Institution Press.

Hitchcock, A. S., and Paul C. Standley. 1919. *Flora of the District of Columbia and Vicinity.* Washington, D.C.: U.S. Government Printing Office.

House, Millie B. 1986. *The Joy of Wildflowers; A Fieldbook of Familiar Flowers of Rural and Urban Habitats in the Eastern United States.* New York: Prentice Hall Press.

Johnson, Charles W. with the advice and assistance of Ian A. Worley. 1985. *Bogs of the Northeast.* Hanover, N.H.: University Press of New England.

Kartesz, John T. and Rosemarie Kartesz. 1980. *A Synonymized Checklist of the Vascular Flora of the United States, Canada, and Greenland.* Vol. 2. *The Biota of North America.* Chapel Hill: University of North Carolina Press.

Lawrence, Susannah. 1984. *The Audubon Society Field Guide to the Natural Places of the Mid-Atlantic States: Coastal.* New York: Pantheon Books.

Lawrence, Susannah, and Barbara Gross. 1984. *The Audubon Society Field Guide to the Natural Places of the Mid-Atlantic States: Inland.* New York: Pantheon Books.

Lobstein, Marion Blois. 1988. *Spring Wildflowers of Northern Virginia: A Checklist.* Manassas, Va.: Prince William Wildflower Society, Virginia Native Plant Society.

Lobstein, Marion Blois. 1990. *Summer and Fall Wildflowers of Northern Virginia: A Checklist.* Manassas, Va.: Prince William Wildflower Society, Virginia Native Plant Society.

Lobstein, Marion Blois. 1990. *Trees, Shrubs, and Woody Vines of Northern Virginia: A Checklist.* Manassas, Va.: Prince William Wildflower Society, Virginia Native Plant Society.

Ludwig, J. Christopher, compiler. *Natural Heritage Resources of Virginia. Rare Vascular Plant Taxa and Virginia Plant Watch List.* 1993. Richmond: Division of Natural Heritage, Virginia Department of Conservation and Recreation.

Magyar, Irene, et. al. *Geology of the Washington Area* (not published).

Martin, Edwin M. 1984. *A Beginner's Guide to Wildflowers of the C&O Towpath.* Washington, D.C.: Smithsonian Institution Press.

Maryland Natural Heritage Program. 1988. *Rare, Threatened, and Endangered Plants of Maryland.* Annapolis: Maryland Department of Natural Resources.

Maryland Natural Heritage Program. 1990. *Serpentine Grasslands.* Annapolis: Maryland Department of Natural Resources.

Nature Conservancy, The. Maryland Chapter. 1986–1991. *Maryland Chapter Newsletter.* Chevy Chase.

Nature Conservancy, The. Maryland Chapter. 1991. *Mountains to Marshes: The Nature Conservancy Preserves in Maryland.* Ann Arbor, Mich.: McNaughton & Gunn.

Nature Conservancy, The. Virginia Chapter. Spring and summer issues, 1988. *Virginia Conservancy News.* Charlottesville.

Newcomb, Lawrence. 1977. *Newcomb's Wildflower Guide.* Boston: Little, Brown.

Niering, W. 1924. *Wetlands.* The Audubon Society Nature Guides. New York: Alfred A. Knopf.

Norden, Arnold W., Donald C. Forester, George H. Fenwick, editors. 1984. *Threatened and Endangered Plants and Animals of Maryland.* Annapolis: Maryland Natural Heritage Program, Department of Natural Resources.

Peterson, Roger Tory, and Margaret McKenny. 1968. *A Field Guide to Wildflowers of Northeastern and North-central North America.* Boston: Houghton Mifflin.

Phillips, Claude E. *Wildflowers of Delaware and the Eastern Shore.* 1978. Hockessin: Delaware Nature Education Society.

Radford, Albert E., Harry E. Ahles, and C. Ritchie Bell. 1983. *Manual of the Vascular Flora of the Carolinas.* Chapel Hill: University of North Carolina Press.

Reed, John C., Jr., Robert S. Sigafoos, and George W. Fisher. 1980. *The River and the Rocks: The Geological Story of Great Falls and the Potomac River Gorge.* U.S. Geological Survey Bulletin 1471. Washington, D.C.: U.S. Government Printing Office.

Scott, Jane. 1984. *Botany in the Field. An Introduction to Plant Communities for the Amateur Naturalist.* New York: Prentice Hall Press.

Shetler, Stanwyn G., and Susan K. Wiser. 1987. *First Flowering Dates for Spring-blooming Plants of the Washington, D.C. Area for the Years 1970 to 1983*. Proceedings of the Biological Society of Washington 100 (4): pp. 993–1017.

Smith, Richard M. 1989. *Wild Plants of America*. New York: John Wiley & Sons.

Solem, Robert P., Delos C. Dupree, and Joanne K. Solem. 1982. *Howard County Spring Wildflower List*. Howard County: Maryland Ornithological Society.

Strausbaugh, P. D., and Earl L. Core. 1977. *Flora of West Virginia*. Grantsville, W. Va.: Seneca Books.

Stupka, Arthur, with the assistance of Donald H. Robinson. 1965. *Wildflowers in Color*. New York: Harper & Row.

Terwilliger, Karen, coordinator. 1991. *Virginia's Endangered Species: Proceedings of a Symposium*. Blacksburg, Va.: McDonald & Woodward Publishing.

Thomas, Bill, and Phyllis Thomas. 1980. *Natural Washington*. New York: Holt, Rinehart & Winston.

Tiner, Ralph W., Jr. 1987. *A Field Guide to Coastal Wetland Plants of the Northeastern United States*. Amherst: University of Massachusetts Press.

Tiner, Ralph W., Jr. 1988. *Field Guide to Nontidal Wetland Identification*. Annapolis: Maryland Department of Natural Resources, and Newton Corner, Mass.: U.S. Fish & Wildlife Service. Cooperative publication.

Vokes, H. E., and J. Edwards, Jr. Rev. 1974. *Geography and Geology of Maryland*. Maryland Geological Survey, Bulletin 19. Annapolis: Maryland Department of Natural Resources.

Wilds, Claudia. 1983. *Finding Birds in the National Capital Area*. A Smithsonian Nature Guide. Washington, D.C.: Smithsonian Institution Press.

Williams, Garrett. *Washington D.C.'s Vanishing Springs and Waterways*. Circular 752. 1977. U.S. Geological Survey. Washington, D.C.: U.S. Government Printing Office.

Wofford, B. Eugene. 1989. *Guide to the Vascular Plants of the Blue Ridge*. Athens: University of Georgia Press.

Index

Wildflower species discussed in Chapters 2–10 are included here; additional wildflower species, covered only in Chapters 11–12, are listed under family headings in those chapters. All places discussed in Chapters 2–10 are in boldface.

Accotink Bay Wildlife Refuge, 197
Achillea millefolium, 58, 226, 241
Aconitum reclinatum, 213, 219, 271
Acorus calamus, 2, 36, 109, 125, 199, 200, 220, 231
Actaea alba, 39, 217, 271; *pachypoda,* 271
Actinomeris alternifolia, 241
Aegopodium podagraria, 90, 238
Agalinis purpurea, 81, 118, 167, 276; *tenuifolia,* 56, 81, 177, 276
Alexanders: golden, 41, 44, 46, 48, 70, 120, 165, 167, 184, 240; heart-leaved, 134, 140, 143, 209, 213, 215, 219, 240
Alisma subcordatum, 51, 100, 231
Alliaria officinalis, 251; *petiolata,* 144, 181, 251
Allium cernuum, 167, 233; *tricoccum,* 161, 168, 233
Altona-Piedmont Marsh, 221
Alumroot, 30, 37, 46, 48, 140, 142, 173, 193, 201, 276
Amelanchier arborea, 25, 273
Amianthium muscaetoxicum, 215, 217, 219, 233
Ampelamus albidus, 26, 240
Anagallis arvensis, 185, 270
Andropogon gerardi, 30, 81, 92, 236; *scoparius,* 81, 92, 183, 236

Aneilema keisak, 232
Anemone quinquefolia, 46, 55, 70, 82, 84, 85, 87, 99, 134, 165, 181, 201, 209, 271; *virginiana,* 108, 145, 148, 211, 271
Anemone, wood, 46, 55, 70, 82, 84, 85, 87, 99, 134, 165, 181, 201, 209, 271
Anemonella thalictroides. See Rue-anemone
Angle-pod, 112, 114, 241
Antennaria neglecta, 25, 241; *plantaginifolia,* 23, 43, 46, 76, 77, 99, 133, 137, 181, 188, 220, 241; *virginica,* 147, 223, 241
Anthemis arvensis, 36, 241; *cotula,* 70, 102, 108, 241
Antietam National Battlefield, 144
Apios americana, 64, 194, 197, 203, 257
Aplectrum hyemale, 62, 105, 108, 122, 162, 165, 169, 187, 207, 235
Apocynum androsaemifolium, 216, 240
Aquilegia canadensis. See Columbine, wild
Arabidopsis thaliana, 99, 113, 251
Arabis laevigata, 42, 70, 140, 141, 143, 162, 188, 190, 251; *lyrata,* 29, 43, 46, 48, 52, 73, 79, 94, 113, 140, 143, 148, 166, 188, 190, 251; *patens,* 46, 137, 140, 141, 143, 251
Aralia nudicaulis, 70, 75, 79, 89, 90, 131, 165, 210, 215, 216, 240
Arbutus, trailing, 19, 48, 59, 72, 75, 76, 77, 83, 90, 100, 104, 108, 122, 129, 134, 135, 163, 167, 198, 223, 226, 256
Arctium minus, 117, 242
Arenaria serpyllifolia, 52, 102, 108, 113, 254
Arisaema dracontium, 26, 44, 48, 52, 231; *triphyllum (see* Jack-in-the-pulpit)

Library of Congress Cataloging-in-Publication Data

Fleming, Cristol.
    Finding wildflowers in the Washington-Baltimore area / by Cristol Fleming, Marion Blois
Lobstein, and Barbara Tufty ; with a foreword by Stanwyn G. Shetler.
        p.   cm.
    Includes bibliographical references (p.   ) and index.
    ISBN 0-8018-4994-2 (hc : alk. paper). — ISBN 0-8018-4995-0 (pbk. : alk. paper)
    1. Wild flowers—Maryland—Identification.   2. Wild flowers—Virginia—Identification.
3. Wild flowers—Washington (D.C.)—Identification.   4. Wild flowers—West Virginia—
Identification.   I. Lobstein, Marion Blois.   II. Tufty, Barbara.   III. Title.
OQ165.F58   1995
582.13'09752—dc20   94-33332